Performing Artists

Performing Artists

Volume 1 ★ A–F

Molly Severson

An imprint of Gale Research Inc.,
an International Thomson Publishing Company

I(T)P

NEW YORK • LONDON • BONN • BOSTON • DETROIT • MADRID
MELBOURNE • MEXICO CITY • PARIS • SINGAPORE • TOKYO
TORONTO • WASHINGTON • ALBANY NY • BELMONT CA • CINCINNATI OH

Performing Artists: From Alvin Ailey to Julia Roberts

Molly Severson, *Editor*

Staff

Carol DeKane Nagel, *U·X·L Developmental Editor*
Thomas L. Romig, *U·X·L Publisher*

Mary Kelley, *Production Associate*
Evi Seoud, *Assistant Production Manager*
Mary Beth Trimper, *Production Director*

Cynthia Baldwin, *Art Director*

H. Diane Cooper, *Permissions Associate (Pictures)*
Margaret A. Chamberlain, *Permissions Supervisor (Pictures)*

Marty Somberg/Somberg Design, Ann Arbor, MI *Cover Design*
The Graphix Group, Fenton, MI *Typesetting*

∞™ This book is printed on acid-free paper that meets the minimum requirements of American National Standard for Information Sciences—Permanence Paper for Printed Library Materials, ANSI Z39.48-1984.

ISBN 0-8103-9868-0 (Set)
ISBN 0-8103-9869-9 (Volume 1)
ISBN 0-8103-9870-2 (Volume 2)
ISBN 0-8103-9871-0 (Volume 3)

Printed in the United States of America

I(T)P™ U·X·L is an imprint of Gale Research Inc.,
an International Thomson Publishing Company.
ITP logo is a trademark under license.

Contents

Volume 2: G-M

Performing Artists by Field of Endeavor

Comedy:

Dance:

Film and Television:

Music:

Reader's Guide

Performing Artists: From Alvin Ailey to Julia Roberts features biographies of 120 popular singers, actors, dancers, comedians, musicians, and television personalities who have made an impact on the performing arts. Selected and written especially with students in mind, the entries focus on the early lives and motivations of the performers as well as highlights (and lowlights) of their careers.

Arranged alphabetically over three volumes, the biographies open with the birth dates and places of the individuals and, where necessary, with death dates and places. Each entry features a portrait of the biographee, a three- to nine-page essay on the performer's life and career, and a list of sources for further reading. Additionally, sidebars containing interesting details about the performers are sprinkled thoughout the text, as are 25 movie stills and other action shots. A cumulative index providing easy access to the people and works mentioned in *Performing Artists* concludes each volume.

Comments and Suggestions

We welcome your comments on this work as well as your suggestions for individuals to be featured in future editions of *Performing Artists: From Alvin Ailey to Julia Roberts*. Please write: Editor, *Performing Artists,* U·X·L, 835 Penobscot Bldg., Detroit, Michigan 48226-4094; call toll-free: 1-800-877-4253; or fax 1-313-961-6348.

Paula Abdul

Born June 19, 1963
Los Angeles, California

SINGER, DANCER, AND
CHOREOGRAPHER

A multifaceted performer, Paula Abdul has made a name for herself as a dancer, choreographer, and vocalist. She is one of the most sought-after choreographers in Hollywood and her 1988 debut album, *Forever Your Girl,* launched her career as a popular singer.

Born on June 19, 1963, Abdul is the second daughter of Harry and Lorraine Abdul. Her father, of Syrian and Brazilian extraction, was a livestock dealer, and her mother, a Jewish French-Canadian, worked at the Hollywood film studios and was for many years an assistant to famed director Billy Wilder. Abdul and her sister Wendy, seven years her senior, grew

"Paula is a fighter. She gets what she wants, but somehow, she's managed to stay one of the world's sweetest people."—Jackie Jackson

up in North Hollywood in a middle-class area known as the Condos. Abdul started dancing at age seven, about the same time that her parents divorced. Soon she was spending her summers performing with Young Americans, a traveling theatrical musical group. At age ten she studied tap and jazz dancing and won a scholarship to study with Joe Tremaine and the Bella Lewitzky Company.

Abdul was influenced by the musical tastes of her sister, who introduced her to the music of Joni Mitchell, Stevie Wonder, Carole King, and the band Iron Butterfly. Abdul started singing while in her teens and participated in many activities during her years at Van Nuys High School, which had been attended by such celebrities as Marilyn Monroe and Robert Redford. Abdul was head cheerleader, class president, a flutist in the orchestra, and a member of the science team.

Gets job as "Laker Girl"

In 1980 Abdul beat out hundreds of others for a job with the Laker Girls, the Los Angeles Lakers' professional cheerleading squad. In the early 1980s, Abdul was also a student at Cal State Northridge, where she studied radio and television sportscasting. But what had started as just fun became a job that lasted six years. After her first year with the Laker Girls, Abdul was choreographing the routines, in which she emphasized dancing and de-emphasized the gymnastics of cheerleading. Abdul maintains that she did some of her best choreography while with the Laker Girls.

Because there are many people from the entertainment business in the stands at Lakers games, Abdul's work with the Laker Girls was an advertisement for her choreographic skills. In 1984, after seeing her at a Lakers game, the Jacksons asked Abdul to choreograph a routine for the cut "Torture" from their *Victory* album. Scared and unsure of herself, Abdul nevertheless jumped at the opportunity. "My only problem was how to tell the Jacksons how to dance," she told Dennis Hunt of the *Los Angeles Times*. "Imagine me telling them what routines to do." She then worked as a private dance trainer for Janet Jackson, with whom she became a close friend. "Janet's my prize student," Abdul told *People*. "She worked her butt off for me. The end result is that we make each other look extremely good." Abdul staged Jackson's hit "What Have You Done for Me Lately?" and several follow-up videos.

Following her work with the Jacksons, Abdul was flooded with job offers, becoming so busy that she was forced to quit the Laker Girls. Abdul has choreographed a number of commercials and videos for such groups as ZZ Top, Duran Duran, and the Pointer Sisters. On the motion picture scene, she has coached the movements of Eddie Murphy and Arsenio Hall in *Coming to America,* and Arnold Schwarzenegger in *The Running Man,* among others. Abdul remembered Murphy as a reluctant student in *People*: "Eddie was too scared to learn to dance from me."

In 1989 Abdul surprised the music industry with her funky and personable debut album, *Forever Your Girl,* which rose to multi-platinum status with the top hits "Straight Up," "Cold Hearted," and the title song. Abdul followed the album with a series of eye-catching videos that showcase her choreography and helped fuel the album's huge sales.

Despite the record's apparent success, Abdul realized her technical limitations as a singer. In an effort to improve her voice she worked with a vocal coach in a rigorous training program before releasing the 1991 album *Spellbound*. Reviews were mixed, but the album produced the number one hit "The Promise of a New Day," while the ballad "Rush, Rush" spent four weeks at the top of the pop charts. Abdul's goal with this album was to stretch beyond the processed dance numbers of *Forever Your Girl*, and create a funkier, more authentic sound. Arion Berger of *Rolling Stone* credits her with some success: "While *Spellbound* isn't going to alienate any party people, it is an edgier and slightly more experimental product than the cream-puffery of *Forever Your Girl*."

Among her recent accomplishments, Abdul created dance sequences for the 1990 and 1991 Academy Awards ceremonies and worked with Oliver Stone on choreography for the movie *The Doors*. She is known in the entertainment industry as a hard-working and likable performer. In 1992 Abdul married the actor Emilio Estevez, but the marriage had some troubles and in 1994 the couple was divorced.

Awards

Abdul won numerous awards, including a *Soul Train* Award; National Academy of Video Arts and Sciences Choreographer of the Year Award, 1987; an Emmy for her choreography on *The Tracey Ullman Show*, 1988-89; and MTV awards for best female video, best choreography in a video, best dance video, and best editing in a video, all for "Straight Up," all 1989.

Sources

Dance Magazine, April 1988.

Los Angeles Times, February 12, 1989.

People, March 12, 1990; June 16, 1991.

Providence Journal Bulletin, July 30, 1989; September 1989.

Rolling Stone, November 30, 1989; June 27, 1991.

Time, May 11, 1992.

Us, December 11, 1989.

Alvin Ailey

Born January 5, 1931, Rogers, Texas
Died December 1, 1989, New York, New York

"Ailey's own best works are charged with a dazzling and uninhibited movement and life."—John Gruen

CHOREOGRAPHER AND DANCER

One of the most significant forces in modern dance, Alvin Ailey drew together elements of classical ballet, folk dance, modern dance, and the Broadway chorus line into a style that has been widely imitated, yet remains distinctly his own. Ailey is justly celebrated as a choreographer, for it was as a mentor to his own troupe of dancers that he introduced modern dance to mass audiences across the world.

The Alvin Ailey American Dance Theatre, which survived Ailey's death in 1989, has expanded enormously since it began with eight dancers dedicated to the black folk arts. Today it consists of a main company with 30 dancers, a repertory of over 150 works, a junior troupe spotlighting young dancers, and a school training over 1,000 students. Having toured the world many times over, the Ailey company provided Ailey with the vehicle to introduce hundreds of new pieces, many of which have become repertory standards. The choreographer was given a raft of honorary degrees and has garnered dozens of citations, ranging from the Capezio Award (1979) to the Kennedy Center Honor for Life-time Achievement in the Arts (1988).

An athletic teenager, Ailey approached modern dance as a kind of gymnastics. He doubted he had talent for it and several times during his youth abandoned dance altogether, only to return with enthusiasm renewed. As a black dancer he found limited opportunities, at times supporting himself in supper clubs and theatrical venues. He did not disdain such work as "commercial," as some dancers do, but instead enjoyed the experience.

Ailey's work is rooted in the black experience. His signature piece, *Revelations,* was performed to a jazz score by Duke Ellington and took the dance world by storm in 1959. "The black pieces that come from blues, spirituals and gospels are part of what I am," he told Ellen Cohen in the *New York Times Magazine* in 1973. "They are as honest and truthful as we can make them. I'm interested in putting something on stage that would have a very wide appeal without being condescending; that will reach an audience and make it part of the dance; that will get everyone into the theatre. What do they mean when they say it's Broadway? If it's art and entertainment—thank God, that's what we want it to be."

Happily, *Revelations* was not "written in the air," as is so much modern choreography, but has been entrenched in the Ailey repertory and is often interpreted by other companies as well. After *Revelations* came major works performed to jazz, blues, gospel, and field songs. By the early 1960s the Ailey company was a fixture on the highly competitive New York dance scene. In *The Private World of Ballet,* John Gruen observed that Ailey's work "is marked by the free use of disparate elements of the dance vocabulary. At its best, the Ailey group generates an uncommon exhilaration, achieved by a tumultuous and almost tactile rhythmic pulse."

Ailey changed the dance world as much by his leadership as by his choreography. He performed some four dozen works every year and was generous in the opportunities he gave to other choreographers. Audiences at Ailey programs can expect to see several Ailey works in revival; pieces created by the troupe's own dancers, past and present; dances created by Ailey students; and works by other modern choreographers. In the self-promoting world of modern dance this generosity is rare. By commissioning hundreds of new works over the years, the Alvin Ailey Dance Theatre has provided the financial backing and exposure necessary for young dance makers to survive.

Influenced by his church

Alvin Ailey was born in Rogers, Texas, a small town 50 miles south of Waco, on January 5, 1931. His father left the family when Ailey was three. He told Cohn: "I have deep memories of the situation.... Sharecropping, picking cotton, people being lynched, all the black men having been to prison, segregated schools, movie theatres where I had to sit in the balcony. I don't remember my people being bitter or it being discussed at home. It was simply the way it was." The church played a dominant role. Ailey attended Sunday school, belonged to the Baptist Young People's Union, and went to Holy Roller meetings at night. He recalls throwing rocks at cottonmouth snakes and Saturday night barbeques at the local roadhouse.

"What I remember of my childhood is that we lived around with relatives," he told Gruen. "There was poverty. Those were the Depression years. I went to elementary school in Navasota, Texas, a tacky little town. The school was across the railroad tracks. One of my earliest memories is climbing under the trains to get to school, and of course, it was a black school.

"There were certain parts of town one didn't go to—certain things one didn't do. The first dance I ever choreographed came out of these early experiences. I call them Blood Memories. I remember the Saturday night place where everybody went, doing the country dances. There were folk singers and guitar players and it all turned me on terribly. And there was the whole experience with the Baptist Church—the Baptisms and the gospel shouts—the itinerant folk singers, like Sonnyboy Williamson. So that early black experience colored everything that I did." When Ailey was 12, he and his mother moved to Los Angeles, where she worked for the Lockheed aircraft company. She also cleaned homes but kept this fact from her son. In Los Angeles, he was exposed to the sophistication of 1940s Hollywood: the dancers Gene Kelly and Fred Astaire were an inspiration. Playing football and joining the gymnastics team in high school, the boy discovered a different sort of athleticism: tap dancing as taught by a neighbor, Loretta Butler, on her shellacked living room floor dance studio.

Meets Lester Horton

A high school friend who was studying classical ballet introduced Ailey to the black dance world of Los Angeles, the most vibrant such community in the country after New York City's Harlem. The dominant figure on the Los Angeles scene was Lester Horton. Horton, who found inspiration in Japanese, Native American, and other dance forms, ran a school in Hollywood where black artists, intellectuals, and entertainers congregated. Ailey was enthralled and signed up as a student.

But doubt soon eroded his enthusiasm, and after one month he dropped out, then went to the University of California at Los Angeles to study romance languages. He explained to Gruen, "I didn't really see myself as a dancer. I mean, what would I dance? It was 1949. A man didn't just become a dancer. Especially a black man. I mean, you could be a [Katherine] Dunham dancer, or you could be a tap dancer—you know, show business, big swing." Horton, though, reached out to the young man, offered him a scholarship, and brought him back to the fold.

Horton, himself a former set designer and stage manager, believed dancers should master every function associated with a production. Ailey, accordingly, found himself mopping the stage, changing the lighting gels, working in the costume shop, and painting scenery. Now living on his own, he took work as a waiter to pay the rent. "I was happy," he reminisced to Gruen. "Lester let us know that we were all beautiful. There were Japanese and Mexicans and blacks, whites, greens and pinks. And it was great. I was very happy being in the milieu of the dancers. I was 18."

But a year later he again dropped out and moved up north to attend college in San Francisco. He supported himself loading baggage for Greyhound. Eventually he began dancing in a nightclub, a "marvelous experience" he would call it years later. The show toured Los Angeles, and Ailey met up with Horton once again. Horton was delving even further from the mainstream, choreographing works inspired by the painter Paul Klee, the novelist Federico García Lorca, and composers, including Duke Ellington and Igor Stravinsky.

In 1953 Ailey once again dropped his college studies and declared himself a dance student, teaching dance to children when not dancing himself. That winter Horton suffered a fatal heart attack, and Ailey tried to assume his mantle. Facing a season at the prestigious Jacob's Pillow festival the next summer, Ailey choreographed two pieces in the only style he knew: Horton's. One work was a tribute to his master, *According to St. Francis,* and the other was based on themes by playwright Tennessee Williams, *Mourning Morning.* The works went over badly; the festival manager wrote a scathing letter denouncing the pieces as "kitchen sink ballets" without form.

The dismal showing discouraged the faltering troupe, which dissolved a few months later. The next call Ailey got was from Broadway producer Herbert Ross, and the dancer hurried to New York to join the cast of *House of Flowers,* the musical adaptation of Truman Capote's book.

It was a troubled endeavor: the legendary George Balanchine had just been dismissed as choreographer, the director and the performers were not speaking, and audiences were small. Nevertheless, the show lasted five months, providing Ailey with a foothold into New York. He took full advantage, broadening his education at every turn. He studied modern dance with Martha Graham, ballet with Karel Shook, composition with Doris Humphrey, and acting with Stella Adler.

Lands job in musical

In 1957 he worked the musical *Jamaica,* starring Lena Horne, and continued to dance in various small companies. In March 1958 he and a friend, Ernest Parham, gathered 35 dancers and gave eight concerts at the 92nd Street YMCA. Audiences were treated to the Premier of Blues Suite, some Latin dances, and a solo Ailey tribute to Lester Horton. The *New York Times* praised the performance, and Ailey began planning a second concert for 1959, again to be held at the Y.

In 1959 Ailey formed his own company, a troupe of eight black dancers dedicated to black music and culture. The company took residence at the Clark Center for the Performing Arts, at Eighth Avenue and 51st St. There they remained until 1969, when they moved to Brooklyn. The move was a mistake—Brooklyn lacked Manhattan's sophistication. Feeling out of place, Ailey stayed three uncomfortable years.

By that time Ailey had retired as a dancer—his chronic weight problem shortened his career—but his troupe was furthering its reputation as the country's most renowned modern dance group. In Judith Jamison, Ailey had the first full-fledged star soloist of modern dance. And, in several young white dancers, Ailey now had an integrated company. Ailey rejected the argument that black dance should be only for blacks. "Whites and Orientals in *Revelations* are historically inaccurate," he told Cohn. "But it works anyway. It's like saying only French people should do Racine or Moliere."

During the 1970s the company's popularity continued to grow, the result of a series of world tours sponsored by the U.S. State Department that saw performances in 44 countries on six continents. Other arts subsidies helped underwrite the enormous cost of running an ambitious dance company. Nevertheless, Ailey coped with a constant financial crunch. Often he would take a commission to choreograph a dance, then use the money to pay old phone bills.

In 1980 the choreographer suffered a serious personal setback: a mental breakdown that hospitalized him for several weeks. He attributed his problems to mid-life crisis, the death of close friend Joyce Trisler, and financial pressures. But Ailey returned to work with a new philosophy. He explained to *Newsday*'s Janice Berman: "Give up something. Do less. Concentrate on what's really important."

Throughout the 1980s Ailey's reputation grew as a leader of modern dance and the dance world was crushed when Ailey died of a rare blood disease in December 1989. His company continues to perform, however, with former star performer Judith Jamison at the helm. Many remember Ailey as Cohn described him: "Even slumped back in his chair, Ailey is imposing, an aristocratic figure, peering out at the world from narrow eyes in a massive proudly held head. Voluble, a gifted raconteur and mimic, his rich, musical voice slides in and out of accents with ease. He laughs often and with great gusto, delighting in show business anecdotes."

In 1992 the National Museum of Dance honored the memory of Ailey by inducting him into the Dance Hall of Fame.

Sources

Ballet News, November 1983.

Dance Magazine, October 1978; December 1983.

Earl Blackwell's Celebrity Register, Times Publishing Group, 1986.

Gruen, John, *The Private World of Ballet,* Viking, 1975.

Jet, July 20, 1992; December 18, 1989.

Newsday, December 4, 1988.

New York Times Magazine, February 12, 1973.

Rogosin, Elinor, *The Dance Makers: Conversations with American Choreographers,* Walker & Company, 1980.

Time, July 15, 1991.

Debbie Allen

Born January 16, 1950
Houston, Texas

"Being rooted in a really good family life situation allows me creative freedom.... I've found myself even more creative since I've had my children."

DANCER, SINGER, ACTRESS, TELEVISION PRODUCER, WRITER, AND DIRECTOR

Debbie Allen has arrived as one of American show business's brightest stars. She has spent a lifetime preparing for her current breaks. Her philosophy is that "luck is when opportunity meets preparation." Actress, singer, dancer, director, and producer Allen was born in Houston, Texas, on January 16, 1950, to a Pulitzer Prize nominee for poetry, Vivian (Ayers) Allen, and a dentist, Andrew Allen. She is the third of four children (one sister and two brothers) in a rather artistic family that includes Phylicia Rashad, who starred in *The Cosby Show*, and Andrew "Tex" Allen, a jazz musician.

At the age of three, Allen began her dance training. By age eight she had settled on a future in musical theater, inspired by a performance of *Revelations* by Alvin Ailey's dance troupe. Her mother, whom she considers her mentor, was an active participant in her training, so much so that when she attempted to enroll Allen in the Houston Foundation for Ballet and was denied due to what was perceived to be existing segregation practices, Vivian Allen contracted a former dancer with the Ballet Russe to give her daughter private lessons. Later she took her three older children and moved to Mexico City where Allen trained with the Ballet Nacional de Mexico. There Allen became fluent in Spanish and attended performances of the Ballet Folklorico de Mexico. Back in Houston, at age 14, she was finally admitted to the Houston Foundation for Ballet on full scholarship. Allen was the only black in the company.

The Houston Foundation for Ballet was not the final racial obstacle to Allen's training. As her senior year of high school approached she sought but was denied admission to the North Carolina School of the Arts in Winston-Salem. Though the director cited inappropriate body type as the reason for refusal, Allen credited this rejection to a racial quota system, since she had been asked to demonstrate technique to others auditioning at that time. This rejection proved to be difficult for the young dancer to accept, causing her to stop training for a year; instead, she studied Greek classics, speech, and theater arts at Howard University in Washington, D.C.

At Howard, choreographer Mike Malone reintroduced Allen to dance. After recruiting her for his dance troupe, he gave her a part in the Burn Brae Dinner Theater's production of *The Music Man*. Allen began to perform with student groups at the university while also studying at the National Ballet School. Additionally, the busy dancer became the head of the dance department at the Duke Ellington School of the Performing Arts. She received her bachelor of fine arts degree cum laude from Howard in 1971.

Hits Broadway stage

Although she loved teaching, Allen also yearned for the stage and decided to go to New York after her graduation. Her first Broadway performance was in the chorus of the musical adaptation of Ossie Davis's play *Purlie Victorious*, titled *Purlie*. After just six weeks in that show, Allen left to become a principal dancer in George Faison's modern dance troupe, the Universal Dance Experience.

In 1973 Allen returned to the Broadway stage in *Raisin*, a musical rendering of the Lorraine Hansberry classic *A Raisin in the Sun*. Adding a kick and a turn to her dance steps whenever possible, she was quickly elevated to the featured role of Beneatha. The theater critic for the *New York Post*, Richard Watts, took notice of "the attractively humorous and zestful Debbie Allen," while *Women's Wear Daily*'s Martin Gottfried found her "enchanting ... and [with] chance enough to show a special talent for dance and a delightful quality altogether."

After a nearly two-year run in *Raisin*, Allen began working in television in both commercials and series. Her first commercial, selling disposable diapers, gave her a chance to work with her sister. Though her next effort, a comedy-variety series titled *3 Girls 3*, was a critical success, it did poorly in the ratings and was quickly canceled. Subsequently, she took on television specials, working with Ben Vereen on his special *Stompin' at the Savoy* and with Jimmie Walker in the made-for-television movie *The Greatest Thing That Almost Happened*.

Back on stage in 1977, Allen starred with Leslie Uggams and Richard Roundtree as Miss Adelaide in the National Company's revival of *Guys and Dolls*. In 1978 she was selected for the lead in a disco version of *Alice in Wonderland*. The production was a disappointing failure and closed after only a short run. Allen described the *Alice* flop as devastating.

Displaying Texas-sized enthusiasm and energy, she returned to television in 1979 as Alex Haley's wife in the top-rated autobiographical miniseries *Roots: The Next Generation*. On stage, she joined the cast of *Ain't Misbehavin'*. That year also marked Allen's film debut in *The Fish That Saved Pittsburgh*. The hard working actress and dancer worked in two capacities on the film, behind the camera as choreographer, and in front of it as a cheerleader.

Nominated for Tony

In 1980 it was back to Broadway in a revival of *West Side Story*. Jerome Robbins's choreography provided the perfect vehicle to display Allen's talent. This role would finally be the one she had hoped for, one that would place her in that charmed circle of stars who could name their own projects. Indeed, she so overwhelmed the critics that Clive Barnes of the *New York Post* was led to believe that this role would catapult her to stardom. Walter Kerr of the *New York Times* concurred, commenting that "Debbie Allen is worth checking out on the double.... She whips across the stage floor dizzyingly." Her peers agreed with the public and critical assessment of her performance and nominated her for the Antoinette Perry ("Tony") Award and gave her the Drama Desk Award.

That year Allen also took a bit part in the hit movie *Fame*, playing the dance instructor Lydia Grant in the fictionalized look at New York City's High School for the Performing Arts. She only had two lines but was able to execute them in such a way as to make them her ticket to an enduring onscreen presence. The movie became a television spinoff with Allen reprising the part of the strong yet empathetic dance instructor. She also contracted to choreograph the show. *Fame* achieved critical acclaim but declined in the ratings due to its mid-season arrival and being scheduled against an established hit, *Magnum P.I. Current Biography Yearbook* commented that it may also have been impeded by "a national viewing public possibly nonplussed by the most ethnically diverse cast on television." Despite its ratings the show ran from 1982 to 1983 on NBC, winning five Emmy awards (two for Allen for choreography) and a Golden Globe Award for Allen for best actress in a series. The show was quickly picked up as an independent project and was distributed to 116 nonaffiliated stations. Seen in 30 states in syndication markets, the show gained a new level of popularity. It also became a number one show in syndication in Great Britain, continental Europe, and Australia. For the show's fourth season (1985-86), Allen was contracted to produce and direct the show in addition to the choreography.

In 1981 Allen had returned to film, taking a part in the movie *Ragtime.* Playing a distraught woman trying to cope with many hardships, Allen held her own in a cast of seasoned big-screen stars, including James Cagney, Moses Gunn, and Howard Rollins, Jr. Other film parts were scarce due to the lack of roles for blacks.

During her 1983 work on *Fame,* Allen took time off to make a television movie titled *Women of San Quentin,* in which she played a hard prison guard. In 1985 she again made time for a television production, choreographing, cowriting, and performing in the special *Dancin' in the Wings.*

Back on the big screen in 1986, Allen starred with Richard Pryor in his "semi-autobiography," *Jo Jo Dancer, Your Life is Calling.* Bob Fosse's choreography in the revival of *Sweet Charity* beckoned her back to the Broadway stage that same year. The show won Allen her second Tony nomination. She also filled out her busy year by directing episodes of *Family Ties* and *Bronx Zoo.*

Turns around A Different World

The 1987-88 season was a rocky one for *The Cosby Show* spinoff *A Different World.* The show consistently attained top ratings on the coattails of *The Cosby Show* but received critical jeers. Executive producer Bill Cosby challenged Allen to take over behind the camera. Accepting the challenge, she was able to revive the show through creative directing and meatier, more realistic plots.

Allen's natural talent and effervescence were most visible in choreographical achievements in *Polly* and *Polly—Coming Home*, a black adaptation of the Pollyanna stories, which aired on ABC in 1989 and 1990. For the 1990 *Motown 30 Special*, a chronology of the 30 years of the black-founded record company, Allen created a dance retrospective that traced the roots of break dancing. The 1990-91 television season saw her named producer, director, occasional writer, and guest star on *A Different World*.

This versatile performer recorded her first album, *Special Look,* in 1989. Her plans are to rival Paula Abdul and Janet Jackson with her own triple threat of singing, dancing, and exciting stage and visual presence. She also choreographed the 1992 TV movie musical *Stompin' at the Savoy,* as well as the 1991-93 Academy Awards show.

Allen's whirlwind career has not precluded a personal life. She has been married twice. Her first marriage, to CBS Records executive Winfred Wilford, was a bicoastal affair. She worked on her career in New York, and he on his in Los Angeles. The marriage did not survive and the couple divorced in 1983 after roughly eight years together. In 1984 she married Norman Nixon, a former basketball star with the Los Angeles Lakers and the Los Angeles Clippers. The two had been friends since 1978, though Nixon did not see her perform until 1982, and she did not see him play until later that year. The couple have two children. Allen credits Nixon with supporting her in a way that allows her to aggressively pursue her career. "Being rooted in a really good family life situation allows me creative freedom.... I've found myself even more creative since I've had my children," she remarked of her family in *Ebony*.

Sources

Cohen-Strayner, Barbara Naomi, *Biographical Dictionary of Dance,* Schirmer Books, 1982.

Current Biography Yearbook, H. W. Wilson, 1987.

Ebony, February 1988; November 1989.

Essence, May 1992.

Mapp, Edward, *Directory of Blacks in the Performing Arts,* Scarecrow Press, 1978.

New York Theatre Critics' Reviews, No. 26 (1973): pp. 218-21; No. 3 (1980): pp. 366-71.

TV Guide, April 11, 1992.

Variety, April 1, 1991.

Who's Who among Black Americans, 5th ed., Educational Communications, 1988.

Tim Allen

Born June 13, 1953
Denver, Colorado

ACTOR AND COMEDIAN

A shrewd negotiator as well as an exceptionally talented comic, Tim Allen parlayed a successful nightclub act into an even more successful television sitcom, *Home Improvement.* In making the transition to TV, Allen was on shaky ground, and he knew it. Several other stand-up comics had launched ill-conceived sitcom debuts, and had their careers stymied in the process. Allen made certain that his television show would showcase his unique "masculinist" brand of humor. With the help of a group of talented writers, he came up with *Home Improvement,* a program about the host of a do-it-yourself show. With Allen's likable character, the show zoomed to the number five position in the TV ratings, becoming a hit almost overnight.

"Feminism was never intended to be antimale, so masculinism is not antifemale. It's different than chauvinism—it's a celebration of what is male. And you don't have to be macho to be a masculinist."

Father killed by a drunk driver

Allen was born on June 13, 1953, in Denver, Colorado, into a family with four other boys and one girl. His father was an "automotive guy," Allen commented to Patty Lanoue Stearns in *Friends.* "He'd tinker with cars a lot. He'd always put dual exhaust, different manifolds on. He made the family wagon loud and fast—my kind of guy." Allen has fond memories of bonding with his father and brothers by attending such events as auto races. Unfortunately, when Allen was in his early teens, his father was killed in a car accident by a drunk driver.

After this tragedy, Allen's mother packed up her six kids and moved back to her family home in Birmingham, Michigan. There she became reacquainted with a man whom she had dated in high school. Coincidentally, he was also widowed. The two soon married, and two more brothers and a sister were added to the family.

Allen skated through high school, having fun and applying himself when he felt like it. The only prediction of what was to come for him was the fact that he liked shop class, but, he remarked in *Friends:* "I didn't want to make it my living. I had trouble with shop teachers, because they were always missing fingers. It's hard listening to people with no fingers." After graduating, Allen briefly attended Central Michigan University before transferring to Western Michigan University, where he graduated with a bachelor's degree in television production in 1976.

Jailed for dealing drugs

Allen's first post-college job was in a sporting goods store. His zaniness and creativity eventually earned him a position with the store's small advertising agency. Tim was then hit with another problem—a drug bust. He had been a small-time cocaine dealer to make money in college. He claimed that he never used drugs himself, but an undercover police ring infiltrated his customers, using Tim to get to the bigger dealers. In the process, Allen was arrested. "Basically, I pleaded guilty. I knew what I did was wrong. I did not drag it out in a trial. I knew I made a major mistake. I laid down. Punish me," Allen confided to Daniel Cerone in the *Los Angeles Times.*

It took eight months before Allen finally received sentencing. On a dare, and hoping it would impress the judge handling his case, Allen decided to make his stand-up debut at the Comedy Castle in Detroit. Allen thought he would get a lenient sentence because of his good record and character. But the judge had something else in mind and wanted to use Allen to set an example. Allen was sentenced to 28 months at the

Sandstone Federal Correctional Institution in Minnesota. While imprisoned, he continued to correspond with the owner of the Comedy Castle, as well as his girlfriend, Laura, whom he wed after his release.

Reflecting on his experience, Allen related to Andrew Abrahams in *Ladies' Home Journal*: "I'm glad I paid for it and got straightened out. [It] started this process of deciding what was important. It was like a close call with death." Yet part of him felt dissatisfied with society upon his reentry. "When I got out, I was angry because nothing had changed.... I thought if I was to be made a lesson, if I had come out and somehow magically the [nation's] cocaine problem would have disappeared ... but the problem was getting nothing but worse, and I felt guilty about being part of that problem," he commented in the *Los Angeles Times*.

Fine-tunes stand-up act

Yet Allen had learned something in prison that would ultimately help his career. He had experienced a sense of camaraderie and brotherly love that he combined with his early passions for fast cars and shop classes to form a uniquely masculinist brand of humor that he crafted into an exciting stand-up act. He discovered early on what was to be his signature sound—a grunting "AH, AH, AH" noise somewhere between that of a Neanderthal and a baboon. He picked up this trademark by listening to his audiences and remembering the sounds his brothers used to make around the dinner table.

While Allen's stand-up career was blossoming, he was also involved in writing, producing, and acting in commercials. True to form, he was even seen in several "Mr. Goodwrench" spots. He was a cable television darling, and his TV special *Men Are Pigs* was aired on Showtime in 1990.

Around this time, Walt Disney Company chairman Michael Eisner became interested in Allen's charisma and onstage persona and even went to see him perform. Upon learning of Eisner's curiosity, Allen was convinced he had the powerful executive hooked. "I'm not a business man," he told Michael E. Hill in the *Washington Post TV Week*. "There was no reason for them to want to see me"—unless, of course, the company was interested in making him an offer. When they finally met, Eisner offered Allen roles on already-written projects, including *Turner & Hooch* and *Dead Poets Society*. Allen didn't feel that he was suited to either of these parts and, much to everyone's surprise, he turned them down and suggested something else. "I showed them a specific idea. I wanted to do the show I had written. I hammered it out with another friend of mine and met with three producers. Matt [Williams] was reluctant," Allen admitted in the *Washington Post TV Week*.

Disney agreed to try Allen's idea and also contacted Williams, the man credited with creating the popular *Roseanne* series. Unfortunately, Williams and actress Roseanne Arnold had clashed about control of the show, and Williams was eventually forced out. Williams felt that crafting a sitcom out of a comedian's act was difficult; a show that adapted the comic's onstage persona too literally, for example, could be construed as unoriginal. In addition, Williams felt the odds of creating a successful show were pretty minimal. "At the risk of sounding arrogant," he commented in the *Los Angeles Times*, "when you think about all the people who tried it, the success rate really isn't that high."

When the two creative forces met, though, Williams was impressed. At Allen's Detroit-area home, Allen told Williams that he "wanted a home-improvement show from hell, more like a man improvement show," as quoted in the *Washington Post TV Week*. "Matt loved the idea," Allen continued, "but had just gotten out of working with a comic who, in his eyes, burned him." The two hammered out their differences, however, and Williams made it clear from the start that he would be the executive producer.

Series begins production

As the series was beginning production, rumors started to circulate about Allen's former jail sentence, which he had kept quiet for years. After consulting with his publicist, Allen reluctantly decided to come forward with the news. First he told Disney, then he went to *USA Today*, hoping that people would read his story there before it got into the tabloids. His tactics seemed to work, according to Disney management. "The audience reacted predictably," Disney's Richard Frank observed in *TV Guide*. "They said, 'OK, we buy the fact that someone can make a mistake, and that his life can change for the better.' "

Home Improvement turned out to be just too irresistible for fans to abandon it because of the star's one-time drug bust. Tim Taylor, the show's main character, is Allen's alter ego. He is an outwardly "normal" guy who lives in the Detroit area, has a wife and three boys, and goes to work every day. However, his profession happens to be hosting a cable television home-improvement-type show called *Tool Time*. Taylor's seeming expertise as the host of this show does not translate into his home life, where his solution to every situation is to add "more power." In doing this, he succeeds, among other things, in blowing up a dishwasher and disabling a lawnmower.

"Tim is Dagwood [a character from the comic strip Blondie] with an attitude, an aggressive goof-up whose masculine pride frequently gets him in trouble with the rest of the family," wrote Ken Tucker in *Entertainment Weekly.* At work, Taylor has a sidekick named Al Borland—played by Richard Karn—who is perfectly competent and apparently more popular with the audience yet bows to Taylor's lesser abilities and greater charm. Reminiscent of the relationship between Bob Vila and Norm Abram from the PBS show *This Old House,* the chemistry between the two creates hilarious situations. At home, Taylor's wife, Jill (Patricia Richardson), provides an ample foil to his masculine schemes and pranks. She proves that she can match wits with her very clever husband and often displays her upper hand. "*Improvement* is most fun when Jill is shooting holes in one of Tim's man-right/woman-wrong pronouncements," noted Tucker.

The wisdom of Wilson

Another intriguing element of the show is Wilson (Earl Hindman), the next-door neighbor. In developing the series, Allen envisioned him, according to the *Washington Post TV Week,* as "a neighbor who is a man's soul, whom I see only from the eyes up." Wilson is just that. Whenever Taylor finds himself in a difficult spot with his family, Wilson mysteriously offers him advice like "I'm afraid that reality as we know it is someone else's dream." His profile—or his eyes peeping over the privacy fence—is all the audience ever sees of the mystical philosopher.

Several of Wilson's views seem derived from poet/author Robert Bly's examination of masculine behavior, *Iron John.* Some critics, in fact, have speculated that Allen's comedy is merely Bly's wisdom in disguise. "This is a show with a male point of view," Allen told Mike Duffy of the *Detroit Free Press.* "It's done through my perspective. So sometimes it can seem like I'm a macho jerk." This perspective seems to have won over male television viewers. ABC-TV spokesman Jim Brochu told the *Detroit Free Press* that in this matter, the show is "very unique. Men are the hardest audience to get. And *Home Improvement* is doing a good job of attracting that male audience."

"In his sitcom debut, Tim Allen is a natural—not just funny, but an interesting TV presence: charming but a little edgy, a wise guy, but a wise guy with a lot on the ball," announced Tucker. Audiences seemed to agree. In addition to the remarkable male audience the show has won, it reached number five in the television ratings its first season. Since then the show has consistently been number two in the ratings—second only to *60 Minutes.* Both Allen and *Home Improvement* won top sitcom honors at the 1993 People's Choice Awards, and ABC has recently extended the show's contract for another three years.

Along with this success, Allen taped another cable television special of his stand-up work, *Tim Allen Rewires America.* In it, he got to indulge in more of his masculinist humor, which he described as his "rendition of feminism for men" in *MultiVision Cable TV.* He continued in *TV Time*: "Feminism was never intended to be antimale, so masculinism is not antifemale. It's different than chauvinism—it's a celebration of what is male. And you don't have to be macho to be a masculinist."

Despite this emphasis on manliness, Allen has a deep respect for women. "I always thought women were superior," he related in *MultiVision Cable TV.* "Granted, a lot of decisions outwardly seem to be made by men, but every decision a man makes somewhere is to please a woman or to get a woman's attention." He makes fun of the differences between the sexes but doesn't feel that either sex should feel bad about who they are. For instance, he rejects the idea that men are not as in touch with their feelings as women are, commenting in *MultiVision Cable TV,* "I think men are uncomfortable telling people what they feel, but they're not uncomfortable feeling it."

Allen discusses at length his theories on the differences between men and women—as well as his father's death, the time he spent in prison, and his family—in his 1994 best-seller *Don't Stand Too Close to a Naked Man,* published by Hyperion, Disney's publishing company. Allen also made the jump to the big screen in 1994 when he starred in the Disney film *The Santa Clause,* about a divorced father (Allen) whose son forces him into the role of Santa when the jolly old man falls off their roof on Christmas Eve. With its special effects (Allen grows a huge belly and sprouts white whiskers) and Allen's clowning and complaining, *The Santa Clause,* many believe, is destined to become a Christmas classic.

With the increased success in his life, Allen felt some strain in his personal life. It has sometimes been difficult to sort out the differences between himself, his onstage comic persona, and his sitcom character. He offered some interesting personal observations about this problem in *TV Time*: "Tim Allen, onstage, is a powerful, egocentric guy. He doesn't care about anybody else—he cares about everybody, which means nobody. And Tim Taylor on *Home Improvement* is this goofy guy watching football, and the dialogue that comes out of his mouth is from writers. The real Tim is a smart [aleck] who is also very sensitive and doesn't want anyone hurt if he can avoid it."

Sources

Detroit Free Press, June 7, 1991; November 24, 1991; October 5, 1994; November 11, 1994.

Detroit Monthly, July 1991.

Entertainment Weekly, October 25, 1991; July 17, 1992.

Friends, May/June 1992.

Gentlemen's Quarterly, March 1994.

Hollywood Reporter, February 22, 1991.

Ladies' Home Journal, February 1992; December 1993.

Los Angeles Times, September 17, 1991.

MultiVision Cable TV, December 1991.

Newsday, September 16, 1991.

TV Guide, April 18-24, 1992.

TV Time, November 9-15, 1991.

USA Today, April 15, 1992.

Washington Post TV Week, December 15-21, 1991.

Alicia Alonso

Born December 21, c. 1917
Havana, Cuba

"I live when I dance. I live not just for myself. When I'm on stage with my dancers, I live with them. It is life."

BALLERINA

Alicia Alonso has been fascinating audiences with her performances for more than 50 years. The winner of the Golden Medal of the Gran Teatro Liceo de Barcelona, the Grand Prix de la Ville de Paris, the Anna Pavlova Prize of the Dance University of Paris, and the Cuban Women's Foundation's highest award, the Aria Betancourt, Alonso is a world-class dance artist. She broke cold war barriers to dance *Giselle,* and she even went on to perform the same piece when she was blind. She brought ballet to Cuba, and Cubans to the ballet, when she established the Ballet Nacional de Cuba as well as a national ballet school. Throughout her career, Alonso has tirelessly fought to dance and to give others the same opportunity.

The ballerina was born Alicia Ernestina de la Caridad del Cobre Martinez on December 21 (the year of Alonso's birth has been variously listed as 1917, 1921, and 1922). The petite girl with black hair and eyes was raised in the city of her birth, Havana, Cuba, by her parents, Antonio Martinez and Ernestina (Hoyo) Martinez. Antonio Martinez was a lieutenant in the Cuban army, and he housed his family in the privileged section of the city known as the Vedado. Ernestina Martinez cared for her four children at home; Alicia Alonso credits her mother with encouraging her talent. She recalled in *Dance* magazine, "Mama used to put me in a room with a phonograph and a scarf. That would keep me quiet for a few hours, doing what I imagined was dancing." Alonso's parents did more than leave the girl to develop her talent alone; they provided her with dancing lessons. At the Sociedad Pro-Arte Musical in the capital, the young girl received her first dancing lessons. By age ten Alonso had her public debut when she danced in a waltz in *Sleeping Beauty*.

The best place, at that time, for a gifted dancer to learn and to begin a career was New York City. Alonso and her husband, Fernando Alonso, moved to that city soon after their marriage on February 19, 1937. While Fernando, a fellow dancer Alicia met at the Sociedad, worked with New York's Mordkin Ballet Company, Alicia trained at the School of American Ballet and with some of the best private teachers of classical ballet, including Alexandra Fedorova, Anatole Vilzak, and—later in London—Vera Volkova.

Oddly enough, Alonso did not begin her dance career as a ballerina. Her first performances on stage were as a tap dancer in comedies in the late 1930s. In the musicals *Great Lady* and *Stars in Your Eyes,* the latter starring Ethel Merman and Jimmy Durante, Alonso danced as a chorus girl. By 1939 Alonso was chosen to join the American Ballet Caravan as a soloist and soon thereafter she signed with Ballet Theatre, or the American Ballet Theatre, as a ballet dancer. Alonso's talent was recognized, and she was given solo parts, such as that of the Bird in *Peter and the Wolf* and that of Carlotta Grisi in *Le Pas de Quatre.*

Vision problems hinder career

Alonso was well on her way to success when severe problems with her vision halted her career. The ballerina's retinas became detached, and she was temporarily blinded. The three operations performed to restore her vision were very delicate, and Alonso was confined to bed for one year. She could not turn her head, laugh, or even cry. Despite her physical problems, Alonso did not lose her passion for the ballet. She began to envision herself dancing; by this technique, she learned the movements necessary to dance *Giselle.* When the heavy bandages were removed and Alonso found that she could see, she first had to learn how to walk again. It was not long before she was dancing the very role she had rehearsed over and over again as she lay blind in bed.

Alonso rehearses with John Kriza and Igor Youskevitch for the ballet *Aleko* at the Royal Opera House in London, England.

At the Metropolitan Opera House in 1943, Alonso danced *Giselle* in place of Alicia Markova, who was ill. The ballerina's dance with Anton Dolin was praised by the *New York Times* as "one of the most distinguished performances of the season." Alonso would become famous for her unique interpretation of *Giselle*. Her grandson, Ivan Monreal, said of her years later that, when dancing with her in *Giselle*, he did not think of Alonso as his grandmother. He told the *Saturday Review*, "I think of her as *Giselle*.... Because she is *Giselle*."

After three years of dancing *Giselle* for the Ballet Theatre with Dolin, Andre Eglevsky, and Igor Youskevitch, Alonso was honored with the position of principal dancer. She danced in contemporary ballets such as *Undertow, Fall River Legend, Theme and Variations, Romeo and Juliet,* and *Aleko,* as well as in standard classics such as *Swan Lake, La fille Mal Gardee, Aurora's Wedding, Les Sylphides,* and *The Nutcracker.* Alicia Alonso's reputation as a supreme dancer was growing.

Returns to Cuba to form ballet company

In 1948 Alonso decided to return to her native Cuba to found her own ballet with her husband serving as the general director and his brother working as artistic director. The Ballet Alicia Alonso, as the company was called, provided Ballet Theatre dancers with work and inspired potential dancers and ballet enthusiasts alike throughout South America.

Alonso was not content with this success. Too many of Ballet Alicia Alonso's dancers were non-Cubans. Alonso wanted to give the young people of her native land the opportunity to excel as dancers. In 1950, with the proceeds from her South American tour, a subsidy from the Cuban Ministry of Education, and donations from patrons of the ballet, Alonso was able to open the Alicia Alonso Academy of Ballet in Havana. Alonso had recruited some of the world's best dancers to become instructors at her school; these instructors taught their enthusiastic students well; and soon the ranks of Ballet Alicia Alonso were swelling with young Cuban dancers.

Alonso's dreams of bringing ballet to Cuba had come true. Her company, once consisting of more non-Cubans than Cubans, was now a showcase for Cuban talent. The company staged *Swan Lake, Don Quixote, Aurora's Wedding, Coppelia, Songoro Cosongo, La Fille Mal Gardee,* and, of course, *Giselle.*

Unfortunately, by 1956, Alonso found it necessary to disband her ballet company as well as her school. Fulgencio Batista's regime, which had granted an annual subsidy to Alonso's company, had been decreasing the amount of the subsidy every year. Alonso's dancers, determined to keep dancing despite their low pay, were forced to keep other jobs as well; they were consequently exhausted when it was time to dance. When the government promised Alonso $500 every month if she promised, in return, not to make public the problems with the unsatisfactory subsidy, Alonso refused. She decided that it would be better to shut down operations altogether, and she left the country to dance elsewhere.

Embarks on tour behind iron curtain

Alonso worked as a guest artist with the Ballet Russe de Monte Carlo for the next three years, during which time she was honored with an invitation to dance in the Soviet Union. This highly unusual invitation demonstrated the respect Alonso received throughout the world. No Western dancer had ever before been invited to dance behind the communist iron curtain in the Soviet Union during the cold war, the period of animosity between the Soviet Union and its satellites and Western countries following World War II. For two-and-a-half months in the winter of 1957, Alonso toured cities including Moscow, Riga, Leningrad (now St. Petersburg), and Kiev as she danced in *Giselle* and *Swan Lake.* The great ballerina danced as a guest with the Leningrad Opera Ballet and even appeared on television in Moscow. After this exciting tour, Alonso returned to the United States.

After the Cuban Revolution in 1959, the prima ballerina Alicia Alonso decided to leave the United States and return to her native country. With so many Cubans fleeing their own country to live in America, Alonso's decision was almost unheard of; many people thought that she was making a mistake, and they told her so. Despite their concerns, Alonso was determined to become a part of the revolution that would, supposedly, bring opportunity to all. As a one-time principal dancer with the Ballet Theatre in New York, the first Western ballerina ever invited to dance in the Soviet Union, the winner of *Dance* magazine's award for 1958, and the founder of the Ballet de Cuba, Alonso believed that she could make important contributions to her people now that Fulgencio Batista's regime was out of power.

Provides dance training to Cubans

Fidel Castro, eager to enrich Cuba with cultural and educational organizations, provided Alonso with $200,000 to begin again. She reopened her school, and her new ballet company, the Ballet Nacional de Cuba, and was given official status and guaranteed backing by the federal government. Soon the Ballet could count more than 100 members, and a system of dance schools had been established on the island. As every child was promised a free education in Cuba, any student who was talented and

serious enough could receive ballet instruc-
tion. After an audition, a child could pass to
an elementary-level school which emphasized
training in the arts. The next stage was

Cubanacan, a beautiful academy of the arts near Havana. The final stage
before actually entering the Ballet Nacional was training at Alonso's
school of the Ballet Nacional de Cuba in Havana. Alonso explained the
system in the *Saturday Review* in 1979: "A rural child has an equal opportunity with the city child. If there is dance talent, we will find it; if the
child has a desire to dance, we will give him every chance to develop his
talent." As one example of the system, *Saturday Review* reminded its read-
ers that Jorge Esquivel, who was Cuba's premier danseur and Alonso's
usual partner despite his youth, was once a "forgotten orphan."

The government's enthusiasm for Alonso's work enabled her to bring
ballet to the Cuban people in other ways as well. Choreographers were
encouraged to create original works for the Ballet Nacional, and the best
of these works were performed along with such classics as *Coppelia, La
Fille Mal Gardee, The Nutcracker, Les Sylphides,* and again, *Giselle.* Those
who stood more to gain from watching than from creating also benefited
from the government's support of the Ballet. The company traveled to
perform in front of all kinds of audiences—the poor and the rich alike
enjoyed the ballet in parks, schools, and even factories.

The only audience for which the company was prohibited from performing was the one in the United States. The Ballet Nacional de Cuba
went instead to many countries which were, at the time, Communist. The
People's Republic of China, Mongolia, North Vietnam, and countries in
Central and South America were treated to performances.

Alonso herself traveled elsewhere as a guest artist with many companies. These included the Grands Ballets Canadians and the Royal Danish
Ballet. Alonso danced *Giselle* at Montreal's Expo 67 and received standing
ovations. Although Alonso had been a star of the Ballet Theatre in the
United States, she was not allowed to dance there for some years. When
cold war tensions were peaking, the U.S. State Department would not
allow Alonso to enter the country because of her support for the Communist administration of Fidel Castro.

Tours North America

It was not until 1971 that the Ballet Nacional de Cuba could make a North
American tour. Alonso danced a piece from *Swan Lake, Oedipus the King, La*

Dame aux Camelias, Carmen, and *Giselle.* After viewing Alonso's performance in *Giselle,* a critic from the *New York Times* reported, "In some respects the physical command is not so certain as it was years ago, but [Alonso] is now a far better dancer than she was. The nuances and grace notes that distinguish great classic dancing from the superbly accomplished are now very evident, and her musical phrasing is as individual as ever."

The fact that Alonso performed so beautifully was a testament to her great skill and talent; the dancer was almost completely blind. She had to be led onto the stage—once she was there, she found her position with the aid of bright spotlights. After her performance she had to follow a voice to get off the stage. Alonso did not want people to view her performance in light of this handicap, and she insisted that the dance should be enjoyed without external considerations. Her vision was restored by Barcelona surgeons in 1972, and she was healthy enough to perform by 1975. During the latter half of the 1970s she danced as a guest performer throughout the United States, and of course, in Cuba with the Ballet Nacional.

Besides touring with the Ballet Nacional and on her own, Alonso has been involved in many other activities during the years since 1958. She has choreographed works such as *Ensayo sinfonica, The Circus, Lidia,* and *The Little Thief.* Alonso trains students and decides which should advance to the next level of the training system. She has been a member of the World Council for Peace since 1974 and has served as vice president of the National Union of Cuban Writers and Artists. Alonso also does her share of the work that is delegated to all Cubans—she toils, along with members of the company, in the coffee fields to fulfill her agricultural duties. In addition, Alonso spends time with her family. By 1977 she had divorced Fernando Alonso and married a writer and lawyer named Pedro Simon. Her daughter, Laura Alonso, is a soloist with the Ballet Nacional; she trains her mother every morning, correcting the veteran dancer as if she were a beginner when she misses a step.

In 1990 Alicia Alonso, at the approximate age of 70, gave a performance of the pas de deux from *Swan Lake,* Act II, at the American Ballet Theatre's 50th anniversary celebration. While it was "an excruciatingly slow and rickety performance," as Laura Jacobs wrote in the *New Leader,* it was also passionate. According to Jacobs, Alonso's "'40s technique of soft turn-out and sachet-like port de bras gave the ballet a glow that was missing from every performance by ABT's young beauties in their spanking new *Swan Lake* last spring." And in Chile in 1991 after a performance of Alberto Mendez's *La Diva,* a reviewer for *Dance* magazine wrote "Thirty-two years after her last visit to Chile, Alicia Alonso's artistry is unimpaired." Despite her age, the beauty of Alonso's dance will never fade. Dancing, to the ballerina, is in fact what revives her. She was quoted in the *Saturday Review:* "Dance works on the total being. By that I mean the mind and the spirit as well as the purely physical parts, and I think of dance as the total antibiotic for healing."

Sources

Dance, December 1953; June 1980; November 1981; April 1982; June 1982; October 1982; January 1983; January 1985; August 1987; September 1989; August 1990; November 1991.

New Leader, March 5, 1990.

New York Times, November 3, 1943; June 21, 1971.

Saturday Review, January 6, 1979.

World Press Review, April 1982.

Maria Conchita Alonso

Born in 1957
Cuba

"It doesn't matter how I am in my daily life; what I can do as an artist is something else. When I act, I can become whatever my role requires."

ACTRESS AND SINGER

Entertainer Maria Conchita Alonso has accomplished the difficult task of balancing a thriving career as a Hollywood film actress with success in Spanish pop music. In addition to making records and movies, she has worked as a magazine model and a television actress and has created her own film production company. For her contributions to both the entertainment industry and to the Hispanic community, Alonso was named Hispanic Woman of the Year by the Mexican American Opportunity Foundation in 1990, and in 1992 she was named Hispanic Entertainer of the Year for the Cinco de Mayo celebration.

Alonso was born in Cuba to Jose and Conchita Alonso. The Alonso family, which includes older brothers Ricardo and Roberto (whom Alonso refers to as her "biggest fans"), immigrated to Venezuela when the actress was still a child. When she was growing up, Alonso's parents sent her to schools in France and Switzerland; although she loved her years in

Europe, Alonso remains proud of both her Cuban blood and her Venezuelan upbringing.

Alonso's artistic calling came early. By age 14, she was modeling and doing television commercials. In 1971 Alonso was named "Miss Teenager of the World" and in 1975 she represented Venezuela in the "Miss World" Pageant. In an interview with the *Los Angeles Times,* she recalled her stay in London for the Miss World Pageant: "I love food. I love to eat. Because I was nervous about the contest, I ate and ate. So much so that when it came to the night of the contest, I couldn't even get into the dress I'd bought." She still walked away from the pageant as sixth runner-up. Her parents provided a balanced perspective on her success as a beauty contestant that helped Alonso in later endeavors. "They kept my feet firmly on the ground," she recalled in an interview. They helped her realize that "it's not looks, it's what is inside you, it's what you do with your life that's important."

Alonso returned to Venezuela and went on to star in ten Spanish-language television "soap operas" (shown throughout Latin America and the United States) while also carving a niche for herself as one of the hottest singers in Spanish pop-rock music. Although she quickly became a favorite with Hispanic audiences, she opted to expand her career and try her luck in the United States. In 1982 she moved from Caracas to Los Angeles. Her motto: "Dare to try new things." Her goal: the movies.

Move to Hollywood pays off

The gamble paid off when she was cast as Robin Williams's Italian immigrant girlfriend in the film *Moscow on the Hudson.* Her onscreen charm and spirit caught the eye of Hollywood filmmakers and landed her roles in nine more films, including *Colors,* starring Robert Duvall and Sean Penn, and *Running Man,* in which Alonso played opposite Arnold Schwarzenegger. Other movies featuring Alonso are *Extreme Prejudice, Touch and Go, Blood Ties, A Fine Mess, Vampire's Kiss, Predator II,* and *McBain.* Although not box-office blockbusters, the films established her as a capable actress in both comedy and drama who could hold her own against Hollywood's top leading men.

Alonso looks to Arnold Schwarzenegger (her co-star in *Running Man*) as a type of role model, a fellow foreigner in the American film industry. She considers him "number one in the world, yet he is a foreigner.... And with an accent heavier than mine. And with a name more difficult to pronounce than mine!" In a more serious tone she added, "I would like to reach the place Arnold's at, or even further.... I don't think he'll ever be nominated for an Academy Award because the type of movies he makes are not for that. I do want to be nominated for an 'Oscar.' In this aspect, I'd like to surpass him."

Alonso has worked as a television actress as well. In 1989 she starred in the short-lived NBC-TV series *One of the Boys,* which related the experiences of a young Hispanic girl newly arrived in the United States. When asked in an interview if she enjoyed the experience, Alonso recalled: "We got ratings, but NBC didn't think it would be a long running hit and they canceled it. I was happy because I don't want to do that type of television yet. Perhaps when I'm older, but for now I want to do my movies, my concert tours."

The entertainer's sparkling personality and witty repartee make her a favorite guest on the television talk-show circuit, where she is frequently asked about the difficulty of working in Hollywood as a Hispanic. She related to *Hispanic* magazine that when television host David Letterman once inquired if she minded playing Hispanic roles, Alonso replied, "Why not? That's what I am. The important thing is that they be good parts." Alonso does not believe being a Hispanic makes the challenge more difficult: "I always try not to say 'for a Hispanic' because I don't believe being Hispanic has anything to do with the fact we don't get much work. It has to do with being a foreigner, to speak with a different accent, to have a different 'look.'" Reflecting on the particular obstacles for a woman in acting, Alonso stated, "There are fewer roles for women than for men. And there are two or three actresses who usually corner the female role in movies."

Musical talent wins Grammy nominations

As a singer and live performer, Alonso's musical career has kept pace with her film work. In 1988 she was nominated for a Grammy Award for Best Latin Pop Performance for the single "Otra Mentira Mas." This was her second Grammy nomination. In 1985 she was short-listed for Best Latin Artist for her self-titled album *Maria Conchita.* The record was certified platinum internationally and her previous four albums, including *O Ella o Yo,* went gold. Another album, *Hazme Sentir,* coproduced by Alonso and K. C. Porter, garnered gold records in several countries after the release of only two singles. Alonso looks forward to recording in English, but has turned down offers from two separate labels because the companies were interested in a type of music that is different from what she likes to do.

In 1991 Alonso signed a 52-show contract with Channel 13, the Mexican government's commercial TV channel, to star in *Picante!* (which means "spicy"), a weekly prime time variety program. The show, coproduced by Alonso, was conceived and shaped to showcase her many talents—singing, dancing, acting, comedy, and interviewing guest stars. Because it coincided with the series debut, and because she "felt like it," she appeared in the December 1991 issue of *Playboy, Mexico* which, according to Alonso, ran a set of "sexy but not nude" photos. Alonso had rejected prior offers from *Playboy, USA* because "they show more." In addition to her television work, Alonso created her first video in 1992. The dance and fitness program was released in Spanish as *Bailalo Caliente!* and in English as *Dance it Up!* She is currently working on an autobiographical video entitled *Asi Soy Yo.*

Reflecting on the unique challenges of maintaining two careers, Alonso admitted, "I'm very dispersed. My dedication is placed in many things." She also feels she's sacrificed some of her Hispanic career by doing American movies: "Yes, I've lost some ground. My name in the Hispanic market has maintained itself, but I've lost in the sense that other artists in the Latin market, for instance singers, that's all they do. And they spend 24 hours a day, 12 months a year doing that—their record, their concert tour, their promotions. They dedicate their mind, their energy, everything exclusively towards that goal. Same thing with Hispanic soap opera actors. They do one soap here, another there. That's the only thing they do. Instead I do too many things.... So, of course, I've probably lost some following ... in my movies, in my television program, in records, in modeling, in other side businesses I have."

Alonso, who is single, admitted in an interview that she has sacrificed much of her private life in order to maintain multiple careers "because if you're not working on one thing, you're working on another." She does spend some time on outside interests. An animal lover, Alonso has her two pet Yorkshire terriers travel with her whenever possible. She favors laws protecting the rights of animals and several years ago changed her eating habits to become a semi-vegetarian. She also spends time at her homes in Los Angeles, Caracas, Miami, and Mexico City.

How Alonso Succeeds on Two Continents

"It is important not to have a big ego. No Hispanic artist is likely to be valued or respected in the American market as they are valued and respected in the Hispanic market. That's why the majority of Latin stars don't do anything in the U.S. Because they can be a big star elsewhere, but be a nobody here. An artist's ego is very big and they can't take rejection. I think you need a very tranquil ego, very controlled. You also have to be a hard worker."

Speaking out brings risks and rewards

Both the Hispanic entertainment community and Hollywood insiders have labeled the multi-faceted artist a true fighter, though her bubbly, free-spirited image tends to disguise the intensity of her mission. Alonso concedes that her maverick spirit has lost her some movie roles. She explained in an interview: "I find that my personality—because I am a bit rebellious, very spontaneous, very open—many producers don't see beyond that. I've had problems in getting certain roles because they don't realize that my personality can be the way it is, but as soon as I begin to act I can become whatever I want to be."

But her spunk and ingenuity have also won her roles. Auditioning for the comedy movie *A Fine Mess,* where she was to play the Chilean wife of a gangster, Alonso's natural temperament caught producer Blake Edwards's attention. She drove up to the audition in a classic Jaguar convertible and, just as it rolled to a stop, the car burst into plumes of steam and smoke. Alonso leaped out, looked under the hood and, enveloped in clouds of smoke and steam, flung her arms up in frustration. Edwards found this so funny that he gave her the role on the spot.

Explaining her apparently boundless bravado, Alonso expressed to *Time* magazine that "we Latins have this fire inside us, in our hearts, in our skin, the flesh. You just go for it." She does not worry that her Spanish-flavored English may limit her roles. "Who cares? I know plenty of actresses who speak without accents. They're not working, I am."

Alonso's professional choices are not based on money but on personal instinct. Often one path is pitted against another. But she insists "that's the way it is and I don't want to change." She is constantly becoming involved in new projects, even in the business end of "show business." A savvy entrepreneur, Alonso has formed a production company to develop film and television properties, in English and Spanish.

Sources

Hispanic, May 1989.

Hispanic Business, July 1992.

Los Angeles Times, August 9, 1986.

Time, July 11, 1988.

Fred Astaire

Born May 10, 1899, Omaha, Nebraska
Died June 22, 1987, Beverly Hills, California

DANCER AND ACTOR

Fred Astaire is in a class by himself. Of all the movie legends of the golden era of the 1930s and 1940s, he is perhaps the most universally accepted as unquestionably great. His film career encompassed more than 50 years as a top star, and his theater and television work have also been recognized as outstanding. The name "Fred Astaire" not only means "dance on film"; it also stands for quality, longevity, and that most elusive characteristic of an artist—a true personal style. According to the *New Yorker*, "[Astaire] transformed forever the ideal of a gentleman. He replaced a Continental model of poise and assurance and rectitude ... with an American restlessness and expectancy and exhilaration of movement, and then found in those things a poise and assurance and rectitude of their own."

"I never broke down on closing night. The cast would be sobbing and weeping, but I always planned on going on to something new."

Astaire was one of a small group of actors who have been able to shape their own movies and make a distinct contribution to film history beyond the level of entertainment or personality. His perfectionism and

Fred and Adele Astaire spent two years in public school in Weehawken, New Jersey; that was the only formal education the pair ever received. Their mother, Ann, was responsible for tutoring them the rest of the time.

his insistence on control of his own dance work expanded his influence on films. Not only did he create his own choreography in most of his films, he also participated in the decision-making process of how his dances would be scored, photographed, and edited. The careful matching of dance and image seen in his best numbers was a direct result of his desire for the best in every aspect of his work. Astaire pioneered the serious presentation of dance in motion pictures, both by his on-screen influence and his behind-the-scenes collaboration.

Began dancing at an early age

Astaire was born to Frederic and Ann Austerlitz on May 10, 1899, in Omaha, Nebraska. His father had emigrated from Austria and become a beer salesman in the United States. Astaire was first introduced to dance when he was four and enrolled in the same school of dance as his older sister, Adele. Shortly thereafter his parents decided to move to New York City so that the children could have the best dance teachers available. After less than a year, the two siblings had changed their name to Astaire (a name both their parents thought more appropriate for the stage) and given their first professional performance. Before long they were appearing in vaudeville—a type of entertainment, popular at the turn of the century, that combined songs, dances and comic skits. Billed as "Juvenile Artists Presenting an Electric Toe-Dancing Novelty," the two toured professionally for five years. When Adele began to look like a young woman and Fred still a skinny kid, the family decided that the act would no longer work and they settled down for a while in Weehawken, New Jersey.

In 1917, after a two-year break, Fred and Adele Astaire returned to the stage as adults. Their reception was fantastic and they soon began performing on Broadway. Throughout the 1920s the two reigned as the King and Queen of dance. Both U.S. and English audiences flocked to their performances and the rich and powerful courted them—including British royalty. But by 1932, their reign had come to an end with their final performance, the musical *The Band Wagon*.

When the show closed Adele announced her retirement and upcoming marriage to Lord Charles Cavendish, the son of the ninth Duke of Devonshire. Soon after his sister's announcement, Astaire met and married the New York socialite Phyllis Potter. They remained happily married until 1954 when she died of cancer. The two raised a son by her previous marriage as well as their own son and daughter.

Heads for Hollywood

After his sister's retirement, Astaire faced the prospect of performing alone for the first time in his life. He decided to head for Hollywood and try his luck in films. After Astaire's initial screen test, a Hollywood executive made a now infamous proclamation concerning Astaire's talent: "Can't act. Can't sing. Balding. Can dance a little." Astaire soon proved the executive wrong and his films are now considered classics.

Astaire's film debut was in a minor role as himself in a Joan Crawford-Clark Gable film entitled *Dancing Lady*. His first real success came when he was paired with Ginger Rogers for a series of elegant musicals produced in the 1930s for RKO studios. (The pair was reunited later for their last film, *The Barkleys of Broadway*.) The RKO films, with their charmingly complicated plots, excellent music, and remarkable dances, represent the high point of the 1930s musical format. Although Astaire was paired thereafter with many beautiful women who were also fine dancers—Rita Hayworth, Vera-Ellen, and Cyd Charisse—most critics agree that his most compatible partner on film was Ginger Rogers, whose looks and personality seemed to make a perfect contrast and complement to his own.

During the 1940s and 1950s Astaire appeared in several outstanding musical films produced at the Metro-Goldwyn-Mayer studio. He continued his career past his dancing years, playing light comedy and dramatic roles in both television and film with equal success. Although Astaire is associated with a certain European elegance of casual dress, his personality on film is actually that of a brash American who makes wisecracks and cons his way forward toward his true moment of self-expression: the dance. Astaire's typical film character was saved from the brink of unpleasantness by the joy, the tenderness, and the sexual tension of his dancing. The easy way in which he moved seemed to suggest to viewers that we could all be dancers, that music and dancing could and should be natural parts of self-expression. In this way, he helped to popularize and develop dance as an art form.

Astaire's screen work involved all kinds of dancing, including tap, ballet, acrobatic, and jazz. Many of his routines were simple and elegant, and the photography was designed to match that quality. In some films, however, he executed tricky routines that might be called experimental—

Ginger Rogers and Astaire in *Carefree*, 1938.

dancing on the ceiling in *Royal Wedding,* slow motion in *Easter Parade,* dancing on air in *The Belle of New York,* and with empty shoes in a shoe repair shop in *The Barkleys of Broadway.* But simple or experimental, Astaire's routines were always perfectly danced and perfectly presented onscreen. His command of cinema was as great as his command of dance. As a result, he constitutes a major revolutionary force in the development of musical films.

At the age of 75 Astaire became so intrigued by skateboards that he attempted to ride one and ended up breaking his wrist.

Marries jockey

When Astaire's wife died in 1954 he was devastated, and for a long time it appeared that he would never remarry. Then, in 1973, he met Robyn Smith, a successful 31-year-old jockey. The two were married in 1980 and they spent their time playing backgammon and going to the race track. Astaire's agent commented on their marriage in *People*: "Because of Robyn his last years were so happy. She was a constant companion." On June 12, 1987, Astaire was admitted to Los Angeles Hospital for a bad cold. He developed pneumonia and died ten days later in his wife's arms. "He died in my arms," stated Robyn Astaire in *People*, "and that's the way he wanted it. He died holding on to me."

Astaire won almost every major award in film. His place in film is not just assured; it is cemented. There is no one to equal him, but his own assessment of his contribution is reflective of his personal modesty, simplicity, and elegance. "I have no desire to prove any thing by it," he wrote in his autobiography, *Steps in Time*. "I just dance."

Sources

Astaire, Fred, *Steps in Time*, New York, 1959; revised edition, 1981.

Dance Magazine, November 1987; November 1993.

Maclean's, July 6, 1987.

New Yorker, July 6, 1987.

People, July 6, 1987.

Time, July 6, 1987.

Joan Baez

Born January 9, 1941
Staten Island, New York

SINGER, SONGWRITER, AND ACTIVIST

"Baez's 20-year metamorphosis from popular folk singer to 80's survivor provides an instructional tale from which one could view the changes in values in our society in the past two decades."
—Barbara Goldsmith

S inger, songwriter, and activist Joan Baez was an important figure of the 1960s' counterculture in America. During that decade she appeared on the cover of *Time* magazine, sang to a crowd of 350,000 gathered at the Lincoln Memorial for Martin Luther King, Jr.'s "I Have a Dream" speech, toured with legendary entertainer Bob Dylan, campaigned against the Vietnam War, and performed at Woodstock. Yet, despite her connection with so many of the important events and personalities of the 1960s, she refuses to see herself as a symbol of that era. In a *Rolling Stone* interview with Mike Sager she maintained that she would rather be seen as an example "of following through on your beliefs, using your talents to do so."

Baez's belief and her talents have brought her considerable fame during a 30-year career that found its start in early childhood influences. She was born Joan Chandos Baez on January 9, 1941, in Staten Island, New

York, to Joan Bridge Baez, originally from Scotland, and Albert Baez, who came to the United States from Mexico. From her parents the singer inherited both a rich multicultural background and the nonviolent Quaker religious beliefs that inspired her own interest in issues of peace and justice. Her father was a physicist whose moral concerns caused him to turn down well-paying defense work and devote his life to academic research. Commenting on the consequences of her father's decision in her 1987 autobiography, *And a Voice to Sing With,* Baez noted: "We would never have all the fine and useless things little girls want when they are growing up. Instead we would have a father with a clear conscience. Decency would be his legacy to us."

Because of her Hispanic roots, Baez was introduced to racial inequality at a young age. In her autobiography she recalled being taunted as a child because of the color of her skin and related her experiences in junior high school where she felt isolated from both the Mexican and white children. She wrote: "Few Mexicans were interested in school and they were ostracized by the whites. So there I was, with a Mexican name, skin, and hair: the Anglos couldn't accept me because of all three, and the Mexicans couldn't accept me because I didn't speak Spanish." She was also considered strange because of her pacifist beliefs. While other students spoke with fear of the Soviet Union and echoed anticommunist feelings firmly held by most adults at the time, Baez took an antimilitary stance that she learned from family discussions and Quaker activities.

Baez admits that loneliness was an important factor in her desire to become a singer. Seeing music as a path to popularity, she spent a summer developing her voice and learning to play the ukulele. She soon gained a reputation as an entertainer and made her first stage appearance in a school talent show. She was also known among her peers as a talented artist who could sketch Disney characters and paint school election posters with ease. At 14 she wrote a short, self-illustrated essay entitled "What I Believe" in which she related her beliefs on many topics. The essay expressed many of the truths that would serve as a moral guide for Baez's actions throughout her life. The excerpt she included in her autobiography ends with her musing, "I think of myself as hardly a speck. Then I see there is no use for this tiny dot to spend its small life doing things for itself. It might as well spend its tiny amount of time making the less fortunate specks in the world enjoy themselves."

Discovers Boston folk scene

A family move from California to the Boston area after her high school graduation provided the circumstances that eventually allowed Baez to help "the less fortunate specks" mentioned in her essay. Although she started classes at Boston University, intellectual pursuits were quickly replaced by her growing interest in folk music. Bolstered by the popularity of such folk musicians as Pete Seeger and the Kingston Trio, the genre had experienced a revival during the late 1950s. Coffeehouses that featured local singers became popular gathering spots for college students throughout the country. At first Baez and a roommate sang duets ("Fair and Tender Maidens" was their specialty) at coffeehouses in the Boston area, but Baez soon went solo. She accepted an invitation to perform two nights a week at Club Mt. Auburn 47, a Harvard Square jazz club that was hoping to add folk enthusiasts to its regular audience.

In 1959 Baez had gathered enough of a following to record her first album, *Folksingers 'Round Harvard Square.* That same year she sang for a couple of weeks at The Gate of Horn, a Chicago nightclub. While there she met popular folk singer Bob Gibson, who invited her to appear with him at the first Newport Jazz Festival that August. Her three-octave soprano voice captivated the festival crowd of 13,000 and made her an instant celebrity. Although she returned to her coffeehouse engagements after the festival, Baez sensed the increasingly important role that music would play in her life.

Turning down more lucrative deals with larger record companies, Baez chose to sign her first contract with Vanguard, a small label known for its quality classical music recordings. Her first solo album, simply titled *Joan Baez,* was released near the end of 1960. Made up entirely of traditional folk songs, the album was a success, reaching the number three spot on the sales charts. Near the time of the record's release, Baez moved to California's Pacific coast.

From her new home in California, Baez often commuted to the East Coast, playing colleges with other folk artists in auditoriums seating 200-500 people. In November 1960 she played her first solo concert to an audience of 800 in New York City. By 1963 her third album had come out and she was playing at the Forest Hills Music Festival and Hollywood Bowl with as many as 20,000 in attendance. As her career seemed to take over her life, she began to think about the essay that she had written as a teenager and what was truly important to her. In her autobiography she wrote, "I was in a position now to do something more with my life than just sing. I had the capacity to make lots and lots of money. I could reach lots and lots of people. It would be a while before this sentiment would take root and grow into something tangible, but the intent was now evident and becoming stronger by the day."

Becomes active in Vietnam War protest

The Vietnam War protest became the cause to which Baez would devote an increasingly larger amount of energy as the 1960s progressed. In 1964 she announced that she would stop paying the 60 percent of her federal income tax that she figured went to financing the U.S. Defense Department. The following year she founded the Institute for the Study of Nonviolence (now called the Resource Center for Nonviolence) in Palo Alto, California. Her political beliefs at times affected her career. In 1967, citing the singer's strong antiwar stance, the Daughters of the American Revolution (DAR) refused Baez the permission to play at their Constitution Hall in Washington, D.C. When news of the refusal received sympathetic coverage in the press, Secretary of the Interior Mo Udall gave Baez permission to play an outdoor concert at the base of the Washington Monument, where an estimated 30,000 people came to hear her sing. Several months later she was arrested and jailed for her active opposition to the Vietnam War draft. The following year she married David Harris, a leader in the draft resistance movement.

Bob Dylan and Woodstock

Despite her mounting political involvement, Baez shared her voice with others in concert appearances and on numerous albums during the 1960s. Reluctant to leave traditional melodies behind, she slowly added more contemporary music to her repertoire. Her fourth album, *Joan Baez in Concert Part Two,* released in 1963, included a Bob Dylan song, "Don't Think Twice, It's Alright." That same year she helped Dylan's career by inviting him to appear with her during her concert tour. The two singers eventually toured together with equal billing and Baez later recorded *Any Day Now,* a double album of Dylan tunes. She further expanded the scope of her musical offerings during the decade with *Baptism,* an album of spoken and sung selections from the poetry of Arthur Rimbaud, Federico García Lorca, James Joyce, and others, and an album of country and western music called *David's Album.* In one of the highlights of her career, Baez appeared at the Woodstock Music Festival. The five-day, now-legendary event was held in 1969 in upstate New York and brought together some of the most important and influential musicians of the decade.

The seventies saw Baez emerge as a songwriter on her album *Blessed Are ...,* which featured several songs based on her experiences as a wife and mother, including "A Song for David" and "Gabriel and Me," a lullaby written for her son. In 1971 Baez and Harris were divorced and she decided

Baez and Dylan

Baez and Dylan toured together in the mid-1970s. Her performance of his "Blowin' in the Wind" was included on the Grammy Award presentations of 1983 to illustrate that "Music has a message." Other Dylan songs, such as "Don't Think Twice, It's Allright" and "A Hard Rain's a-Gonna Fall," remain in her repertory.

to end her association with Vanguard. "The Night They Drove Old Dixie Down," a cut off *Blessed Are ...*, became one of the most popular songs of 1972 and Baez's biggest commercial success. Continuing her political activism that same year, she and a small group of friends toured (what was then North) Vietnam to witness the effects of the continuing war on the Vietnamese people. During 11 of the 13 days, Baez stayed in the capital city of Hanoi, where the United States carried out the heaviest raids of the war. On her return home, Baez edited 15 hours of tapes she had recorded during her trip and made them into her 1973 album, *Where Are You Now, My Son?*, a very personal plea for an end to the war.

Baez remained active in political and social concerns in the United States as well. The same year as her Vietnam visit, she organized a gathering of women and children who joined hands around the Congress building in Washington, D.C., to protest continued U.S. involvement in Vietnam. Baez has served on the national advisory board of Amnesty International, a worldwide organization that works for the release of people imprisoned for their religious or political beliefs, and she was instrumental in founding Amnesty West Coast, the group's California branch. In 1979 she founded Humanitas International (for which she still serves as president). Based in Menlo Park, California, the organization promotes human rights, disarmament, and nonviolence through seminars and other educational opportunities.

Career sees resurgence

In her autobiography, Baez noted how sometime during the late 1970s she "began the painful and humiliating process of discovering, ever so slowly, that though I might be timeless in the world of music, at least in the United States I was no longer timely." Her waning popularity received a boost in 1985 when she was asked to open the U.S. portion of Live-Aid, a multi-act rock concert designed to raise funds for relief of African famine victims. In 1986 she took part, along with fellow musicians Sting, U2, and Peter Gabriel, in the "Conspiracy of Hope" concert tour celebrating Amnesty International's twenty-fifth anniversary.

In 1987, *And a Voice to Sing With* was reviewed in a number of major periodicals in the United States and once again brought Baez's life and music to the attention of the national media. In the book, and in the interviews that followed its publication, Baez spoke of the materialism she saw pervading society. In a *Christian Science Monitor* review, Amy Duncan referred to the fact that "Baez writes a bit dispiritedly about the '80s, and decries particularly the 'me generation' mentality and what she sees as a lack of ethical and humanitarian values." In a conversation with Alvin P. Sanoff appearing in *U.S. News and World Report,* Baez contrasted the politically concerned music of her early career to the music of today, stating, "The prevailing ethos is: No negative thoughts, and everything is beautiful!" Baez continued, "You just jog, eat enough of the right yogurt, and everything is going to be all right."

Social historian Barbara Goldsmith, writing for the *New York Times Book Review,* characterized Baez's work as the story of not just one person but of an entire society. "Baez's 20-year metamorphosis from popular folk singer to 80's survivor provides an instructional tale from which one could extrapolate the changes in values in our society in the past two decades." However, whatever changes Goldsmith detected in Baez's value system, Baez herself minimizes. As Cathleen McGuigan pointed out in *Newsweek,* "Baez's music may have gone out of style, but according to her book, she never altered her art or her politics to suit fashion."

Baez continues to attract public attention with both her voice and her activism. In a 1989 *New York Times* review of a Baez concert that coincided with the 30th anniversary of the album *Joan Baez,* Stephen Holden wrote: "Her voice, though quite different in texture from the ethereal folk soprano of her first albums, remains a powerful instrument." In celebration of the anniversary, Baez released *Speaking of Dreams,* an album of social commentary. In 1993 Baez released the album *Play Me Backwards,* which received critical acclaim. *Stereo Review* hailed it as "one of the finest records of her career," and *Rolling Stone* praised her voice, saying, "Baez's voice has reached new levels of mature expressions. The texture of her voice may have darkened, but its beauty remains untarnished."

In addition to maintaining her music, she continues to dedicate her time to causes in which she believes. In the late 1980s Baez toured Israel and the occupied territories of the Middle East, seeking a peaceful end to the conflict there. She has survived what she calls in her autobiography, "the ashes and silence of the 1980s," and appears to be firm in her dedication to do what she can to make life easier for "the less fortunate specks in the world."

Sources

Baez, Joan, *And a Voice to Sing With,* Summit Books, 1987.

Baez, Joan, *Daybreak,* Dial, 1968.

Christian Science Monitor, September 3, 1987.

Los Angeles Times, February 3, 1991.

Newsweek, July 20, 1987.

New York Times, November 7, 1960; November 13, 1961; December 12, 1989.

New York Times Book Review, June 21, 1987.

Rolling Stone, November 5, 1987; January, 1993.

Stereo Review, April 1993.

Time, June 1, 1962; November 23, 1962.

U.S. News & World Report, June 29, 1987.

Mikhail Baryshnikov

Born January 27, 1948
Riga, Latvia, U.S.S.R

*"Baryshnikov has always embraced the
curious, contradictory, and explosive
combination of sporadic rebellion and
diligent submission to duty that not only
creates a great dancer but extends the
horizons of what is possible in dance."*
—John Fraser

DANCER AND ACTOR

Widely recognized as the premiere dancer of his generation, Mikhail Baryshnikov was thrust into the international spotlight when he defected in 1974 from the Soviet Union, where he was already highly acclaimed. Baryshnikov's electrifying masculine presence and flawless technique led to worldwide recognition and fame soon after his defection. Many credit him with inspiring a renewed interest in classical dance. Although Baryshnikov was originally trained in ballet, he began to explore the work of contemporary choreographers when he arrived in New York. Most recently Baryshnikov has spent his time and energy working with the White Oak Dance Project—a group that he founded in 1990 that works exclusively with modern choreographers.

Troubled youth

Baryshnikov was born in Latvia, a country invaded and occupied by the Soviet Union under Joseph Stalin during World War II. The Soviet Union continued to occupy Latvia after the war; Baryshnikov's father was a military officer and part of the occupying forces and so Baryshnikov was somewhat of an outsider during his youth. Although he was never sure of the extent of his father's role in the occupation, Baryshnikov did know that his father was an anti-Semite (a hater of Jews) and a hater of the Latvian people. Perhaps out of rebellion, or perhaps out of necessity, Baryshnikov drew his father's disapproval by seeking out Latvian and Jewish friends.

Because Baryshnikov was embarrassed by his father's bigoted views, he kept his friends away from his home. The only time they came over was when his mother was there alone. While his relationship with his father was strained, Baryshnikov has always recalled his mother with great warmth and affection. It was she who introduced high culture to her son by taking him to the opera and the ballet.

At the age of ten, Baryshnikov began taking folk dancing lessons, and at 11 he auditioned for a local choreographic school. While his father had appreciated the folk dancing, he disapproved of Baryshnikov's serious study of dance. Instead, his father pressured Baryshnikov to follow in his own footsteps and become a military officer. But to do that Baryshnikov would need to do well at school and, much to his father's disgust, Baryshnikov was a poor student who cared little for schoolwork and exhibited no desire to excel. In the midst of all this turmoil, Baryshnikov's mother committed suicide. The reasons behind her decision to kill herself are unclear, but the act itself traumatized Baryshnikov and he still bears the scars of her death.

An article for *Saturday Night* described a 1986 party that Baryshnikov attended, where a photograph on a book's dust jacket reminded him of his mother. The woman on the cover was young, beautiful, tall, and probably blonde. Grabbing the book, Baryshnikov reflected: "That's how I remember her the final day, the last time I ever saw her. We were all supposed to be going away for a holiday, but at the last minute I learned Mother wasn't coming. There seemed to be no reason for this, and Father wasn't the sort of man to answer any questions. Somehow I didn't really understand she wasn't coming until I was actually on the train with Father and turned around to see Mother was still on the platform. She was crying and the tears were pouring down her face. And I started crying too. I couldn't stop my own tears. Then the train began to move and she walked a little way beside it. Finally she just stopped walking, and we became farther and farther apart. She kept waving, and in my mind she was never more beautiful. That was it, I never saw her again. By the time I returned, she was dead. For me at the time, it was the end of my life."

Throws himself into the dance

Baryshnikov began to devote himself to the study of dance. He had three

Baryshnikov dancing with Alessandra Ferri in *Giselle* at the Auditorium Theater in Chicago, Illinois, February 3, 1986.

intensive years of training in the basics of ballet technique. His relationship with his father was at the point where they acknowledged each other politely, but that was all. At the age of 15, Baryshnikov had outgrown the teachers available to him in Latvia and he enrolled at the Leningrad ballet school. There he came under the tutelage of Alexander Pushkin, a renowned ballet instructor who became a father figure to his young student. Pushkin offered Baryshnikov the kind of warmth and encouragement his father denied him, and teacher and pupil soon made a very successful team.

The Leningrad school was extremely strict, and Baryshnikov's days were filled with nothing other than the rigorous demands of classical ballet training. Pushkin recognized Baryshnikov's incredible talent and he challenged him to fulfill his potential. Whereas other teachers might have considered Baryshnikov's small stature an obstacle to dancing the great romantic roles, Pushkin refused to let the Soviet ballet world overlook Baryshnikov. "Pushkin always believed I would be a classical dancer," Baryshnikov told *Saturday Night.* "Nobody else thought so, because I was so tiny with a baby face. But he said, 'Just keep going, keep going.' He gave me incredible love."

In 1966, at the age of 18, Baryshnikov competed at the Varna Competition where he won top honors. At the Moscow International Ballet Competition in 1969 he won a Gold Medal. He soon became a star in the Kirov Ballet and was exposed to the West when he began to tour. Baryshnikov began to dream of a life in America. While he had plenty of material goods in Russia, he longed for the freedom of thought and expression that the United States represented. And so, in the late spring of 1974, Baryshnikov eluded the KGB (the Soviet security police) and found a safe haven in Toronto, Ontario, Canada.

Joins ABT

His first order of business was to find a ballet company he could join. The American Ballet Theatre (ABT) in New York was the perfect home, for they had a history of embracing "foreign" stars, and Baryshnikov knew most of their repertoire. Despite his fondness for America, Baryshnikov couldn't help but feel a loss when he remembered his native country. "The phantom of Russia pursued and haunted me like a hangman," Baryshnikov told *Saturday Night.* "It was always invisibly watching my steps and made my life almost unbearable." In order to shed this phantom Baryshnikov worked incessantly. He desperately wanted to stretch himself as an artist and he worked with a great number of choreographers, from the classical to the avant-garde. He even left ABT so that he might work with the famous choreographer George Balanchine, in the New York City Ballet. After 15 months Baryshnikov returned to ABT as artistic director.

Baryshnikov has a daughter, Aleksandra, with film actress Jessica Lange. He credits Aleksandra with finally giving him the sense of belonging in America.

From 1980 until 1990 Baryshnikov served as the artistic director for the American Ballet Theatre. Although many doubted his ability to oversee a major company, his tenure was such a success that his dancers were devastated when he announced he was leaving. While there Baryshnikov restaged such classics as *Swan Lake* and *Giselle*. He also invited such modern dance choreographers as Mark Morris, Paul Taylor, and Merce Cunningham to create new works for his dancers—an idea the old ABT would never have entertained. He even named postmodernist dancer and choreographer Twyla Tharp as artistic associate. After a disagreement with the company's executive director, Baryshnikov left ABT sooner than he'd planned.

White Oak Dance Project

His next project was the formation of the White Oak Dance Project. The group was originally founded in 1990 as a vehicle for the works of Mark Morris—one of Baryshnikov's favorite choreographers. Comprised of eight members (four men and four women), the group is a cooperative that decides together what new dances they will pursue. In an interview with *Dance Magazine,* Baryshnikov described the company: "White Oak's not a company in the true sense. We don't have a particular philosophy. We are all mature dancers, and we are more involved with the everyday particulars of the company than most dancers might expect to be. We work with people we admire, discuss around a table how long we want to work, what we want to do, where we want to go, and how many performances we want to dance.... We respect each others' opinions, as well as one another as artists."

Another factor that distinguishes this group is the age of the performers. Half of the group is over 40—an unheard of phenomenon in the dance world, where prima ballerinas are often in their teens and most performers retire by their late thirties. Because of Baryshnikov's reputation, the performances usually sell out and there's no need for the incessant fundraising that burdens so many dance troupes. As for Baryshnikov, he seems more fulfilled now than at any other point in his long career. "It's been my primary thing for these last four years," Baryshnikov told *Dance Magazine,* "the most productive time in my career—and the most interesting from my point of view. I've very much narrowed my interests to what I can do best—and I believe *this* is the best I've ever done."

Sources

Dance Magazine, January 1990; January 1992; March 1994.

Entertainment Weekly, May 22, 1992.

Life, November 1988.

Newsweek, February 28, 1994.

Premiere, March 1991.

Rolling Stone, October 8, 1987.

Saturday Night, December 1988; March 1993.

Time, March 14, 1994.

Vogue, December 1992.

The Beatles

ROCK GROUP

The Beatles "played the songs for the best time of our lives, and always will."
—Neil Munro

On February 7, 1964, the Beatles arrived at Kennedy International Airport in New York City, met by 110 police officers and a mob of more than 10,000 screaming fans. The British Invasion—and in particular, "Beatlemania"—had begun, and the "mop-topped" Beatles (John Lennon, Paul McCartney, George Harrison, and Ringo Starr) wasted no time in endearing themselves to American fans and the media, though many adults remained skeptical. According to the February 24, 1964, *Newsweek* cover story, the Beatles' music, already topping the charts, was "a near disaster" that did away with "secondary rhythms, harmony, and melody." Despite such early criticism, the Beatles garnered two Grammy awards in 1964, foreshadowing the influence they would have on the future of pop culture.

Inspired by the simple guitar-and-washboard "skiffle" music of Lonnie Doengan and later by U.S. pop artists such as Elvis Presley, Buddy Holly, and Little Richard, John Lennon formed his own group, the Quar-

Individual members of the Beatles were decorated with the Order of the British Empire in 1965.

rymen, in 1956 with Pete Shotton and other friends. Expertise helped guitarist Paul McCartney, whom Shotton introduced to Lennon in 1957 at a church function, find a place in the band, and he in turn introduced Lennon to George Harrison. Only 14, Harrison, though a skilled guitarist, did not overly impress 17-year-old Lennon, but his perseverance finally won him a permanent niche in the developing ensemble. Stuart Sutcliffe, an artist friend of Lennon's, brought a bass guitar into the group a year later. Calling themselves Johnny and the Moondogs, the band eventually won a chance to tour Scotland, backing a little-known singer named Johnny Gentle. Renamed the Silver Beatles, they were well received, but the pay was poor, and the end of the tour saw the exit of a disgusted drummer and the arrival of Pete Best.

With the help of Welshman Allan Williams, club owner and sometime manager for many promising bands playing around Liverpool in 1960, the Beatles found themselves polishing their act at seedy clubs in Hamburg, West Germany. Living quarters were squalid, working conditions demanding, but instead of splintering the group, the experience strengthened them. Encouraged by their audiences' demands to "make show," they became confident, outrageous performers. Lennon in particular was reported to have played in his underwear with a toilet seat around his neck, and the whole band romped madly on the stage. Such spectacles by the Beatles and another English band, Rory Storme and the Hurricanes, ultimately caved in the stage at one club. The Beatles' second trip to Hamburg, in 1961, was distinguished by a better club and a series of recordings for which they backed singer Tony Sheridan. These recordings proved critical in gaining them a full-time manager. At the end of that stay, Sutcliffe remained in Hamburg to marry, having given bass duties to McCartney. He died tragically the following spring, shortly after the Beatles joined up with Brian Epstein.

Sign with Brian Epstein

Intrigued by requests for Tony Sheridan's "My Bonnie" single, featuring the Beatles, record shop manager Brian Epstein sought the band at Liverpool's Cavern Club. Within a year of signing a managerial agreement with Epstein, the Beatles gained a recording contract from E.M.I. Records producer George Martin, and on the eve of success shuffled yet another drummer out, causing riots among Pete Best's loyal following. The last in a line of percussionists came in the form of the Hurricanes' sad-eyed former drummer, Ritchie Starkey—Ringo Starr.

The Beatles performing on *The Ed Sullivan Show*, June 1966.

Despite initial doubts, Martin agreed to use Lennon and McCartney originals on both sides of the Beatles' first single. "Love Me Do," released on October 5, 1962, did well enough to convince Martin that, with the right material, the Beatles could achieve a number one record. He was proved correct. "Please Please Me," released in Britain on January 12, 1963, was an immediate hit. The biweekly newspaper *Mersey Beat* quoted Keith Fordyce of *New Musical Express,* who called the song "a really enjoyable platter, full of vigour and vitality," as well as Brian Matthew, then Britain's most influential commentator on pop music, who proclaimed the Beatles "musically and visually the most accomplished group to emerge since the Shadows." The Beatles' first British album, recorded in one 13-hour session, remained number one on the charts for six months.

The United States remained indifferent until, one month before the Beatles' arrival, E.M.I.'s U.S. subsidiary, Capitol Records, launched an unprecedented $50,000 promotional campaign. It and the Beatles' performance on *The Ed Sullivan Show,* which opened their first American tour, paid off handsomely. "I Want to Hold Your Hand," released in the United States in January 1964, hit number one within three weeks. After seven weeks at the top of the charts, it dropped to number two to make room for "She Loves You," which gave way to "Can't Buy Me Love." As many as three new songs a week were released, until on April 4, 1964, the Beatles held the top five slots on the *Billboard* list of top sellers, another seven in the top 100, and four album positions, including the top two. One week later, 14 of the top 100 songs were the Beatles'—a feat unmatched before or since.

Make feature films

Also in 1964, long before music videos had become commonplace, the Beatles appeared in the first of several innovative full-length feature films. Shot in black-and-white and well received by critics, *A Hard Day's Night* represented a day in the life of the group. Its release one month before the Beatles began their second U.S. tour was timely. *Help,* released in July 1965, was a madcap fantasy filmed in color. Exotic locations made *Help* visually more interesting than the first film, but critics were less impressed. Both albums sold well, though the U.S. versions contained fewer original songs.

The 1965 and 1966 albums *Rubber Soul* and *Revolver* marked a turning point in the Beatles's recording history. The most original of their collections to date, both combined Eastern, country-western, soul, and classical motifs with trendsetting covers of songs by others, breaking any mold that seemed to contain "rock and roll." In both albums, balladry, classical instrumentation, and new structure resulted in brilliant new concepts just hinted at in earlier works like "Yesterday" and "Rain." Songs such as "Tomorrow Never Knows," "Eleanor Rigby," and "Norwegian Wood" made use of sophisticated recording techniques—marking the beginning of the end of the group's touring, since live performances of such songs were technically impossible at the time. The Beatles became further distanced from their fans by Lennon's comments to a London *Evening Standard* writer: "Christianity will go. It will vanish and shrink. I needn't argue about that, I'm right and will be proved right. We're more popular than Jesus Christ now. I don't know which will go first, rock 'n' roll or Christianity. Jesus was all right, but his disciples were thick and ordinary. It's them twisting it that ruins it for me." While the British dismissed the statement as another "Lennonism," American teens in the Bible Belt of the South took Lennon's words literally, ceremoniously burning Beatle albums as the group finished their last U.S. tour amid riots and death threats.

Acclaimed by critics, with advance sales of more than one million, the tightly produced "conceptual" album *Sgt. Pepper's Lonely Hearts Club Band* was perhaps the high point of the Beatles' recording career. No longer a "collection" of Lennon-McCartney and Harrison originals, the four-Grammy album was, in a stunning and evocative cover package, a thematic whole so artfully pleasing as to remain remarkably timeless. Imaginative melodies carried songs about many life experiences, self-conscious philosophy, and bizarre imagery, as in "A Day in the Life"—a classic sixties studio production. The Beatles' music had evolved from catchy love songs to profound ballads, social commentary, and work clearly affected by their growing awareness of and experimentation with Eastern mysticism and hallucinogenic drugs. Songs like "Lucy in the Sky With Diamonds" were pegged as drug-induced (the initials, supposedly, stood for the drug LSD), and even Starr's seemingly harmless rendition of "A Little Help From My Friends" included references to getting "high." Broadening their horizons seemed an essential part of the Beatles' lives and, influenced greatly by Harrison's interest in Indian religion, the Beatles visited the Maharishi Mahesh Yogi in Bangor, Wales, in 1967. It was there that news of Brian Epstein's drug-induced death reached them.

The group's next cooperative project was the scripting and directing of another film, *Magical Mystery Tour*, an unrehearsed, unorganized failure. Intended to be fresh, it drew criticism as an undisciplined compilation of adolescent humor and gag bits, generally resulting in boredom. The accompanying album, however, featured polished studio numbers such as McCartney's "Fool on the Hill" and a curiosity of Lennon's entitled "I Am the Walrus." The American LP added tracks including "Penny Lane,"

"Hello Goodbye," and "Strawberry Fields Forever," which were immortalized on short films broadcast by Ed Sullivan. Solo projects in 1967 and 1968 included the acting debuts of Lennon in *How I Won the War* and Starr in *Candy*, Harrison's soundtrack to the film *Wonderwall*, and Lennon's eventual release of his and Yoko Ono's controversial *Two Virgins* album.

The group was growing apart, early evidenced in 1968 on their two-record set, *The Beatles*, the first album released by the group's new record company, Apple. *The White Album*, as it was commonly known, showcased a variety of songs, mostly disjointed, often incomprehensible. According to George Martin, as quoted in *The Beatles Forever*, "I tried to plead with them to be selective and make it a really good single album, but they wouldn't have it." The unity seen in earlier projects was nudged aside by individuality and what appeared to be a growing rift between Lennon and McCartney. Whereas the latter contributed ballads like "Blackbird," the former sang antiwar statements and continued to experiment with unusual production. Harrison, on the other hand, shone in "While My Guitar Gently Weeps," aided by Eric Clapton's tasteful guitar solo. Starr, for the first time, was allotted the space for an original, the country-western "Don't Pass Me By," which became a number one hit in Scandinavia where it was released as a single. Overall, critics found the *White Album* a letdown after the mastery of *Sgt. Pepper*, though Capitol claimed it was the fastest-selling album in the history of the record industry.

The Beatles regained some of their lost status with *Yellow Submarine*, an animated feature film released in July 1968. A fantasy pitting the big-eyed, colorfully clothed Beatles against the small Blue Meanies, the film was visually pleasing if not initially a big money-maker. The group spent minimal time on the music, padding it with studio-session throwaways and re-releases of "All You Need Is Love" and "Yellow Submarine" itself. The remainder of 1968 and 1969 showed the individual Beatles continuing to work apart. Starr appeared in the film *The Magic Christian*, and Lennon performed live outside the group with Yoko Ono, whom he had married, and the Plastic Ono Band.

Recapture magic with Abbey Road

After spending months filming and recording the documentary that would later emerge as the *Let It Be* film and album, the Beatles abandoned 30 hours of tape and film to producer George Martin. Since editing it down would make release before 1970 impossible, the album was put on hold. Instead, for the final time, the Beatles gathered to produce an album "the way we used to do it," as McCartney was quoted as saying in Philip Norman's book

Shout! The result was as stunning as *Sgt. Pepper* had been. With *Abbey Road*, the Beatles were at their best. Wrote Nicholas Schaffner in *The Beatles Forever*, "The musicianship is always tasteful, unobtrusive, and supportive of the songs themselves. The Beatles never sounded more together." Yet another Grammy winner, it was a triumphant exit from the 1960s.

American producer Phil Spector took over the *Let It Be* clean-up project from George Martin in 1970. The resulting album, brought out after 15 months of apathy, fighting, and legal battles, was a mixture of raw recordings, glimpses of the Beatles in an earlier era, and heavily dubbed strings and vocals—as on McCartney's "Long and Winding Road." Though most tracks were tightly and effectively edited, critics said the album lacked the harmony of earlier endeavors. According to Schaffner, Lennon later told *Rolling Stone*, "We couldn't get into it.... I don't know, it was just a dreadful, dreadful feeling ... you couldn't make music ... in a strange place with people filming you and colored lights." The film, which strove to show the Beatles as honestly and naturally as possible, gave further evidence of disintegration. Band members were shown quarreling, unresponsive to McCartney's attempts to raise morale. Said Alan Smith of the *New Musical Express*, as quoted by Roy Carr and Tony Tyler in *The Beatles: An Illustrated Record*, "If the Beatles soundtrack album *Let It Be* is to be their last, then it will stand as a cheapskate epitaph, a cardboard tombstone, a sad and tatty end to a musical fusion which wiped clean and drew again the face of pop music."

By the end of 1970, all four Beatles had recorded solo albums, and, in 1971, McCartney sued for the termination of the group. Throughout the seventies, promoters attempted to reunite them without success. The closest approximation of a reunion was Starr's *Ringo* album in 1973—though never together in the studio, Lennon, Harrison, and McCartney contributed music, vocals, and backing. Any lingering hope of a joint performance or album ended with the tragic murder of John Lennon on December 8, 1980. A year before, Neil Munro, in an *Oakland Press Sunday Magazine* article, provided what might make a fitting epitaph, setting the Beatles into their place in history: "Their musical imagination was startling. They lived on it.... They played the songs for the best times of our lives, and always will."

Sources

Carr, Roy, and Tony Tyler, *The Beatles: An Illustrated Record*, Harmony Books, 1978.

Evening Standard, March 4, 1966.

Mersey Beat, January 31–February 14, 1963.

Newsweek, February 24, 1964.

Norman, Philip, *Shout! The Beatles in Their Generation*, Simon and Schuster, 1981.

Oakland Press Sunday Magazine, February 4, 1979.

Schaffner, Nicholas, *The Beatles Forever*, McGraw, 1978.

Schaumburg, Ron, *Growing Up With the Beatles*, Harcourt, 1976.

Time, December 22, 1980.

Candice Bergen

Born May 9, 1946
Beverly Hills, California

ACTRESS

F ew children brought up in the glittery world of 1940s Hollywood had a tougher act to follow than Candice Bergen. As the only daughter of Edgar Bergen, the famed ventriloquist of film and radio, Bergen was dubbed "Charlie McCarthy's sister" by the press, after her father's equally renowned dummy. Realizing early that there was no competing for laughs with Edgar Bergen's wooden dummy, Bergen suppressed her love of comedy and sought dramatic roles. Since the mid-sixties, she has worked as a model, writer, and photojournalist but is best known for her career as an actress. Said to epitomize the classic American cool blonde, Bergen's looks are so striking that some have deemed her movie star Grace Kelly's successor. But her beauty and her father's legacy have brought mixed blessings to an actress whose efforts to prove herself in comic roles have finally been rewarded. For

"I'm not a Republican, but I believe there are a lot of Republicans ... qualified to be president. And I don't disagree with the Republican message about values. I do fear this country is being shredded apart. But poverty is contributing to an erosion of family values far more than the media are."

Candice Bergen, the path to personal and professional contentment has been paved with both bitter and sweet experiences.

Bergen was born on May 9, 1946, to her famous father and Frances Westerman Bergen, a former fashion model from Alabama. A son, Kris, was born 16 years later, and Bergen has sustained an extremely close relationship with her brother despite their age difference. According to *American Film*, Bergen uses the phrase "children of paradise" to characterize herself and her contemporaries growing up in this fairy tale era of Hollywood. She lived in the exclusive neighborhood of Bel Air, and her friends included Liza Minnelli, Marlo Thomas, and the sons of Jimmy Stewart and David Niven. Bergen's memories of riding a train in Walt Disney's backyard and watching her mother dance with Fred Astaire at the family's elaborate Christmas parties, however, only emphasize her disillusionment with present-day Hollywood. "To me there is a grotesqueness about the way people flaunt money here," she told Maureen Orth of *Vanity Fair*. "It wasn't about money when I was growing up. The magic was really more in the people."

Competes with Charlie for attention

Yet Bergen's rosy recollections of this aspect of her childhood are undercut by compelling memories of life with Edgar Bergen, and, inevitably, Charlie McCarthy. "Charlie was the focal point, the core of the family," Bergen explained to *Vanity Fair*. "He got the laughs. He got the fan mail. He was my competition." In *Knock Wood,* Bergen's best-selling memoir published in 1984, she describes a ritual that took place in the Bergen household on Sunday mornings: Edgar Bergen would prop up Charlie on one knee, his daughter on the other, and, with his hands on the back of their necks, speak for each of them. And although Bergen received Charlie's room when she was born, he was moved to the larger, grander guest room. While Bergen jokes in *Knock Wood* that these experiences enabled her to identify with the Muppets, she admits that for her the dummy's power was not demystified until years later when she saw the original Charlie on display at the Smithsonian, lifeless and encased in glass.

If Candice Bergen played second fiddle to a puppet as a child, she certainly managed to capture her parents' attention during adolescence. In an interview with *Parade*'s Cleveland Amory, she recalled: "I was a regular little princess, and I grew up in a very fast lane. After all, my friends were the sons and daughters of the rich and famous. The only poor people we knew were our teachers." Having picked up the basics of voice impersonation from her father by the time she entered Westlake School

Gains respect with Carnal Knowledge

Bergen gained some professional ground in 1971 when Mike Nichols cast her in his controversial film *Carnal Knowledge*. While the critics did not embrace her portrayal of a Smith coed involved with both Art Garfunkel and Jack Nicholson, they agreed that she could stop worrying about her talent. Seemingly, Bergen had already stopped worrying, for she was engrossed in launching her photojournalism career. She began by amassing an admirable list of interviews, including ones with Paul Newman and Lee Marvin, and later displayed some of her photographs on NBC-TV's *Today Show*. An assignment for *National Geographic* fueled Bergen's appetite for adventure by taking her to Kenya to report on a Masai tribe ritual. Returning to Africa to spend a week with renowned ethologist (a scientist who studies the behavior patterns of animals) Dr. Jane Goodall, she observed chimpanzees in their natural habitat at a stream reserve on Lake Tanganyika. In the United States, Bergen made her mark as the first female photojournalist to spend four days at the White House with then president Gerald Ford and his family.

The seeds of political activism that blossomed simultaneously with Bergen's photojournalism career were sown years earlier. A product of sixties sensibilities, she had joined a society that espoused the ethical treatment of animals. Recalling that it set off one of her family's biggest arguments, Bergen told *Parade:* "It started with my berating my mother for wearing furs and my father for shooting ducks. When I told them I had invested my money in a nonviolent leather company ... that was the final [straw].... My father said, 'Now this—and with your inheritance too.'" Inheritance or not, Bergen plunged headlong into a number of social causes. She demonstrated at Alcatraz to protest the plight of Native Americans, campaigned for antiwar candidates, condemned restrictive abortion laws, and became a board member of Friends of the Earth. Further inspiration for political activity came from film producer Bert Schneider. Together they spent time with the revolutionary Black Panthers and got arrested at a lie-down in the Senate corridors protesting the Vietnam War.

A difficult period for Bergen, the late seventies were a time for shedding old skins and taking self-inventories. She admitted to trading her globetrotting ways for the peace and solitude of her New York apartment. "A delayed bomb. You are thirty," she told *Vanity Fair*. "Your twenties have been spent and what have you got to show for it?" The death of her father in 1978 was not without relief for Bergen, who had nevertheless made peace with him years earlier. Freed from the need to capture even his negative attention, she was finally able to take herself seriously. The year 1979 marked a fresh start. Burt Reynolds offered her the part of Jessica, his vain and nasty wife in *Starting Over*. Although she initially wanted Jill Clayburgh's more sympathetic role, she was quickly charmed by the prospect of playing a comic character. Bergen confided to writer William Styron in an *Esquire* interview: "As soon as I really made the commitment to play someone slightly foolish ... there was much more of that character in me than I would have ever dared admit. There was something thrilling about getting to do that."

Marries Louis Malle

Bergen's professional success, however, did not make up for the void she felt in her personal life. "I have this fantasy that someday I will have a handsome man-size dummy whom I can sit on my knee," she told *Vanity Fair* in 1979. "He will be everything I'm looking for in a man." A real-life answer came in 1980 in the form of French film director Louis Malle. Long before they had even met, Bergen recalled, a mutual friend predicted their marriage. But both were gun-shy and they spent much of their first date at the New York restaurant the Russian Tea Room discussing their confirmed bachelorhoods. All the same, the lunch lasted four hours, and later that year they got married. "Louis and I really saved each other," she explained to *Vanity Fair*. "We're almost reverential about our marriage."

With a loving and supporting family, and another successful comedy called *Rich and Famous* behind her, Bergen had summoned enough energy by the late eighties to embark on the biggest project of her career thus far: the title role in the smash-hit television series *Murphy Brown*, which debuted in 1988. Producers Diane English and Joe Shukovsky had some reservations about the patrician image associated with Bergen's dramatic roles but knew they had found their match when, according to the *New York Times*, she shared their "whoopie-cushion, slip-on-the-banana-peel sense of humor." Hardly slapstick, though, *Murphy Brown* is about a hugely successful anchorwoman known for her brassy quips, whose private loneliness is evidenced by her battle with alcoholism and frequent nights alone belting out Aretha Franklin songs.

While *Newsweek* hailed the show for "reshaping male and female images on the screen," its success has been measured in other ways. *W* magazine, for example, featured a story on female anchors Jane Pauley, Kathleen Sullivan, and—Murphy Brown. And after an episode in which Murphy's ticket to the presidential inauguration got lost, President Bush extended Bergen a personal invitation. Having proven that she can handle a comedic role with

Even though Bergen works on the set of *Murphy Brown* 21 weeks a year, she still manages to make time for her daughter, Chloe. In the summer the two stay with Malle on a farm in the south of France, and Malle often spends time in Los Angeles.

the depth and range of a complex character, Bergen nonetheless suspects that her flawed heroine would not survive in the real world of television news. "I love that she's a loose cannon," Bergen told the *New York Times*, "but television rewards mediocrity. I just don't think they want people with rough edges."

Perhaps the most publicized issue associated with *Murphy Brown* was Vice-President Dan Quayle's statement that the show belittled family values. During the 1991-92 season Murphy Brown became pregnant and decided to face the challenges of single parenthood. Quayle attacked the show for glorifying a woman who chose to raise a child without a husband, feeling that such an act symbolized the abandonment of traditional family values. His statements caused an uproar, with single parents across the country protesting that the absence of a spouse didn't make them any less fit as parents. Bergen herself was surprised at Quayle's attack. When questioned in *Time* about her reaction, Bergen replied: "I don't know what goes on inside Dan Quayle's mind, and I'm very happy for that mystery to remain intact. It's a landscape I don't especially want to explore."

It has been Bergen's own rough edges that have made her personal and professional life a success. "As you get older, you feel lucky, and you get grateful," she told Georgia A. Brown of *American Film.* "Now when I work, I do it conscientiously, I try to be as brave as I can be, I try to take chances."

Sources

American Film, October 1981.

Esquire, January 1982; August 1992.

Newsweek, March 13, 1989.

New York Times, November 20, 1988.

New York Times Book Review, April 8, 1984.

Parade, July 23, 1989.

Time, September 21, 1992.

TV Guide, September 19, 1992.

Vanity Fair, February 1989.

Rubén Blades

Born July 16, 1948
Panama City, Panama

SINGER, ACTOR, LAWYER, AND
POLITICIAN

Rubén Blades is a multitalented celebrity whose interests range from music to film to politics. He grew up in Panama City, Panama, but immigrated to New York in 1974 with only $100 in his pocket. During the next 20 years, he became an international entertainer and earned a law degree from Harvard University. His "salsa" music originally gained attention for its political themes—many of which were controversial. Although Blades has often been separated from his native Panama, his interests have remained with its government and its people. In May 1994 he made a strong run for the presidency of his homeland.

"I made money by singing about social issues, and I ended up living better than the subjects of my songs. If I sang about people who needed a break, then why not try to give them a break?"

Blades's parents met in the 1940s while both were performers in Panama City nightclubs. His mother, Anoland Benita, was a cabaret singer, while his father, Rubén Dario Blades, was a conga player in a band. Born in 1948 in a poor neighborhood in Panama City, Blades grew up listening not only to his parents' music but also to that of Elvis Presley and the Beatles. He wanted to become a musician, but his father—who was also a policeman—insisted that the young Blades attend college to study law. Blades kept up with his music by singing with local Latin bands while studying for law classes at the University of Panama. After he graduated and passed the bar (an exam allowing lawyers to practice), he became a lawyer for the Bank of Panama. He then headed to the United States for a visit.

The visit turned out to be longer than Blades had expected. While in New York City, he hovered between careers for a time, still weighing his love for music against his interest in law. The growing popularity of salsa finally won him over. *Salsa* (Spanish for "sauce") is a musical blend of various Afro-Caribbean folk styles. In the 1970s, Latin record producers in New York City began to promote the spicy dance music. After working for a while in the mailroom of Fania Records, a leading salsa label, Blades signed a contract with the company. In 1978 he and trombonist Willie Colón recorded *Siembra*, one of the best-selling salsa albums of all time.

Protest songs bring danger and success

Blades began to experiment with salsa music. He added elements of jazz and rock to the Latin beat, replacing the sound of the standard horns with that of a synthesizer. In writing his own songs, he moved away from tired love themes to tales of life in the barrios (Spanish neighborhoods) of New York. He borrowed ideas from his friend, Colombian novelist Gabriel García Márquez, and explored political issues in song. As Anthony DePalma noted in the *New York Times Magazine*, "The words [Blades] sings are not of partying, but of protest, of indignance against greed, corruption, and spiritual [laziness]."

Blades's resulting work stirred up controversy. In 1980 he wrote "Tiburon," a song that condemned superpowers for interfering with the political affairs of smaller countries. Many people were outraged, interpreting the song as a direct criticism of U.S. involvement in the problems of Panama. The song was banned on Miami's Latin-music radio stations and Blades had to wear a bulletproof vest while performing there.

Despite these negative reactions, Blades's musical popularity grew. He became a leader of the *Nueva Cancion* ("New Song") movement that blended poetry and protest politics with a Latin rhythm. In an attempt to reach a larger audience, Blades signed with mainstream record company Elektra/Asylum in 1984, becoming the first Latin artist to do so. With each successive album, Blades has stretched the limits of Latin music. In the process, he has won two Grammy awards. On his albums, he has recorded duets in Spanish with such artists as Linda Ronstadt and Joe Jackson. In 1988 he surprised the Latin-music world by releasing a record in English, *Nothing but the Truth.*

Doesn't recognize barriers

Some Hispanics criticized Blades for abandoning his roots, but he told Guy D. Garcia of *Time* that he was open to exploring everything before him: "I refuse to acknowledge a barrier. I think the barriers are in the mind and in the heart." His desire not to remain still had become evident in 1984. That year he had put his rising musical career on hold while he studied for a master's degree in international law from Harvard University. Having completed his year-long studies, Blades changed course again and delved into acting.

In 1985 he starred in the film *Crossover Dreams,* the story of a Latin singer who leaves his family and friends behind as he switches to mainstream music. When the singer's efforts fail, he is left with nothing. Since that beginning, Blades has acted in several major films, including Robert Redford's *The Milagro Beanfield War* (1986), *Fatal Beauty* (1987) with Whoopi Goldberg, and *Predator II* (1991).

Blades's celebrity status has not prevented him from keeping a close eye on the politics in Panama. He has been displeased by corruption in Panama's government and poor living conditions among its people. In 1989 he was critical of the United States when it invaded Panama and ousted corrupt president Manuel Noriega. With hopes of bringing democracy back to a country long ruled by dictators, Blades helped found a political party in Panama in 1991 called *Papá Egoró* ("Mother Earth" in one of Panama's native languages).

Makes a bid for presidency

At first, Blades did not say whether he would run for the Panamanian presidency. He told Garcia he simply hoped to create "what up to this point has been a mythical place: a Latin America that respects and loves itself, is incorruptible, romantic, nationalistic, and has a human perception of the needs of the world at large." Some Panamanian politicians, however, said Blades had no business returning to interfere in their government. In a 1993 speech, Blades responded to his critics: "A country is not abandoned because we are far from its territory," he said, "a country is aban-

When campaigning, Blades admitted to missing his wife, actress Lisa Lebenzon. "My wife and I understand each other's needs and spaces and silences," Blades said. "It's very difficult to be here by myself. We used to drink coffee together, work crossword puzzles, walk. I miss our routine."

doned when we remove it from our heart." Later that year, he officially announced his run for the presidency.

In the months before the May 1994 election, Blades led the presidential campaign polls. But the election showed different results as Ernesto Pérez Balladeras became Panama's new president. Blades came in second, receiving almost a fourth of the vote. He returned to the United States to resume his music and film career.

Sources

Marton, Betty A., *Ruben Blades,* Chelsea House, 1992.

New Republic, November 1, 1993.

New York Times, March 17, 1994; May 9, 1994.

New York Times Magazine, June 21, 1987.

People, May 9, 1994.

Time, January 29, 1990.

Garth Brooks

Born in 1962
Tulsa, Oklahoma

SINGER AND SONGWRITER

G arth Brooks is not simply one of the most popular recording artists in country music; instead, he ranks among the most popular recording artists in any field. In the first week after his 1991 album, *Ropin' the Wind*, was released, it "made music history by becoming the first album to enter both *Billboard*'s country and pop charts at No. 1," reported *People* magazine. Because of his broad popular appeal, "Brooks has moved more records with greater velocity than anyone ever in Nashville," wrote *People*'s Jim Jerome. After releasing just three albums, his combined record sales "[approached] a staggering 10 million units."

"I surrounded myself with people who knew me long before I happened. So if I start acting different, man, they'll square me in a minute."

Brooks was born in Tulsa, Oklahoma, in 1962 but was raised in small-town Yukon, Oklahoma. His father, Troyal, an oil company engineer, and mother, Colleen, had six children. Family life was very modest on Troyal Brooks's $25,000 annual salary. Brooks and his brothers and sister learned how to pick guitars and sang with their mother, who had a brief career as a country singer in the 1950s.

In high school, Brooks's major passion was sports; he was a four-sport athlete, participating in football, basketball, baseball, and track and field. Eventually his athletic talent won him a track scholarship to Oklahoma State University. Despite his heavy involvement in sports, however, Brooks maintained an interest in music and still found time to play in a band during his high school years.

Inspired by George Strait

Brooks's musical influences include traditional country-music stars George Jones and Merle Haggard, pop singers Billy Joel, James Taylor, and Dan Fogelberg, and the world of rock and roll in general. But a short time before starting college, Brooks "heard [country singer George] Strait do 'Unwound' on [his] car radio, and that's the exact moment it all changed," he told *People*'s Jerome; Brooks was profoundly affected by the new, yet traditional-sounding country musician, and by his own admission "became a George wannabe and imitator for the next seven years."

As a track star at Oklahoma State, in Stillwater, the 6'1", 225-pound Brooks was a javelin thrower. In the classroom, he studied advertising, "hoping to adapt his original music to jingles and creative copy," revealed *Entertainment Weekly* contributor Alanna Nash. Brooks also played his music around campus, performing duets with roommate Ty Englund and, for a while, performing in a bluegrass band.

He also worked odd jobs to help support himself. One of these was as a bouncer at a club called Tumbleweeds. It was there that Brooks met his future wife, Sandy Mahr. She had gotten into a brawl in the Tumbleweeds ladies' room one night; when Brooks rushed in, he found her with her fist through the wall. "All she said was, 'I missed,'" recalled Brooks to Jane Sanderson of *People*. "I thought, 'Man, this is nuts.' Then I told her she had to leave, but as I was takin' her outside, I kept thinkin' about how good-lookin' she was." Sandy was a fellow student, and she and Brooks soon began dating. Before long, romance blossomed.

Pursued music when athletic career foundered

While in college, however, athletics were still the driving force in Brooks's life—he wanted to be the best in the javelin throw. As *People*'s Jerome noted, "His dreams then were more likely about gold medals and the for Girls, Bergen regularly called the registrar's office pretending to be her mother to get the day off. Living in the fast lane meant "makeup at eleven, high heels at twelve, dates at thirteen, and going steady at fourteen," reported *Parade*. If her parents hoped that sending Bergen to a Swiss boarding school would make her less precocious, they were in for a shock: when they visited her at Christmas break, she suggested they talk over cocktails. Bergen told Amory, "They couldn't wait to get me back to Beverly Hills."

Enrolling in the University of Pennsylvania to study art history in 1963, Bergen received campus-wide recognition as Miss University and for her performance in the Tennessee Williams play *Summer and Smoke*. Even Edgar Bergen, who had once discouraged his daughter from acting after giving her some test lines to read, was impressed. But his glow of pride faded when at the end of her sophomore year Bergen was asked to leave the university due to poor grades. "I was devastated," Bergen deadpanned in her interview with *Parade*. "I went around showing the letter to my friends. 'Nobody,' I told them proudly, 'flunks art and music.'" Bergen immediately headed for New York City, where she became an instant success at modeling, her face on the covers of several national magazines.

It was in New York that film director Sidney Lumet discovered Bergen and cast her in his 1966 film *The Group*, based on Mary McCarthy's best-selling novel. She was said to have accepted the role of the lesbian Lakey to raise money for a new career in photojournalism and because she relished the audacity of the gesture. Her efforts, however, went unappreciated by both her parents—who had hoped she would play an ingenue—and the critics. According to *Vanity Fair*, reviewer Pauline Kael called Bergen "inordinately beautiful," but panned her debut: "She doesn't know how to move, she cannot say her lines so that one sounds different from the one before. As an actress, her only flair is in her nostrils."

A similar mixture of praise for Bergen's beauty and scorn for her talent characterized much of the critical response to several of her early films. In 1966 she played a missionary schoolteacher in *The Sand Pebbles*, a portrayal that one critic said bore no resemblance to acting and another found flawless and beautiful. A series of undistinguished films followed, including *The Day the Fish Came Out, The Adventurers, The Wind and the Lion*, and *T. R. Baskin*. According to *American Film*, even then Bergen remained unflinchingly honest. Referring to filming in exotic places such as Greece and Taiwan, she once said, "It doesn't make for a fine body of work, but it does make for some great travel."

Olympics than gold records and the Opry." But Brooks's dreams of athletic glory were dashed when he failed to make the Big Eight Conference finals his senior year. "A coach came by and said, 'Well, now you can get on with what matters in life,'" Brooks told *People.* "I wondered, 'What the hell could that be?'"

> "There are lots of artists who can sing but who can't impart the emotion and personality that make an entertainer shine. Garth pulls it off."—Reba McEntire

After graduation in 1985, Brooks decided to head for Nashville to take his shot at country-music stardom. He lasted only a short time in the country-music capital. "I had thought the world was waiting for me," he told *People* contributor Sanderson, "but there's nothing colder than reality." Brooks went back to Stillwater, and he and Sandy worked various jobs while he polished his musical skills. They married in 1986 and, a year later, put together their last $1,500 to try Nashville a second time. Once again, however, Nashville was not eager to have Brooks. He struggled to get his music heard, pitching his songs all over town for months. He finally got his big break when he was added to a newcomer showcase at a club when another act failed to show. Brooks was noticed by a talent scout from Capitol Records and was soon signed to a recording contract.

Lightning struck

His debut album, *Garth Brooks*, was released in 1989. The album generated four Number One country singles and "raised Brooks from honky-tonker to concert headliner almost overnight," wrote Sanderson, who called the tunes on *Garth Brooks* a mixture of "soft laments and raucous cowboy rock." Citing the singer's "gift for finding something fresh in the familiar, something timely in the predictable and timeworn," Jay Cocks of *Time* explained that Brooks makes "a direct assault on the heartstrings, singing in a kind of simonized tenor suitable for both serenades and bustouts."

In 1990 Brooks won the Country Music Association's Horizon Award for most promising newcomer. He also won a Video of the Year award for his song "The Dance." Also that year, he released his second album, *No Fences.* Sales of this follow-up recording zoomed, launching more Number One country singles and reaching as high as Number Four on *Billboard*'s pop chart. In the spring of 1991 Brooks won an unprecedented six Academy of Country Music awards—top male vocalist, single, song, album, video, as well as entertainer of the year. Later that year, Brooks's debut album passed the 2 million sales mark. *No Fences* passed 4 million, and the rising star's expected third album brought in advance orders of 2 million.

Topped the pop charts

When, in the fall of 1991, Brooks's album *Ropin' the Wind* opened at the top of the *Billboard* pop charts—unheard of for a country act—Brooks was indisputably hailed as the new champion of the music business. *Entertainment Weekly* contributor Nash proclaimed him "the most popular male singer of any kind in the business today." *Stereo Review* called *Ropin' the Wind* "his best yet." The magazine allowed that *No Fences*, "with its provocative mix of styles and subjects, went a long way toward making [Brooks] stand out. But it [was the] third album that [told] the tale, primarily through the breadth of Brooks's songwriting in a program that ranges from bluegrass ... to Western swing ... and pop." Discussing his third release with Celeste Gomes of *Country Song Roundup*, Brooks said, "I am the kind of person who can be happy with it if the people are. The purpose of *Ropin' the Wind* is to hopefully convince people that *No Fences* was not a fluke. And hopefully to convince people that if they buy a Garth Brooks product, it's ten songs, not three singles and filler."

Brooks has managed to maintain his success with the 1992 *The Chase* and the 1993 *In Pieces.* In 1992 Brooks sold more albums than any other musician in any other music category. Brooks admitted to Nash that he is quite surprised at the enormity of his success. "I really don't have a clue why it happened to me," he said. "Because what I deserve and what I've gotten are totally off balance.... All I can say is that it's divine intervention." Nash, however, noted that there are "earthly explanations." Among the new generation of country stars, "Brooks is the performer who most understands common folk. A chubby, balding Everyman with boy-next-door appeal, he has exceptional taste in songs—both his own and those of others. It's real-life music to which nearly everyone ... can relate."

Kills 'em in concert

An exuberant stage performer, Brooks plays music that is more tinged with rock and roll than with traditional country style. *People* called Brooks "an electrifying showman who choreographs his act with a unique, kick-ass abandon." *Entertainment Weekly* described his concert performance as "equal parts John Wayne and Mick Jagger." The comparison to John Wayne is an apt reflection of Brooks's love for the legendary star's movies. "I'd like to carry the same messages in song that he did in his movies," Brooks said to Sanderson. "He stood for honesty."

Brooks's road entourage includes close friends and family. His lifelong friend Mick Weber is his road manager, old college roommate and partner Ty Englund his guitarist, and sister Betsy his bass player. Brooks's brother Kelly, who is an accountant, handles tour financing and the star's investments. "I surrounded myself with people who knew me long before I happened," explained Brooks to *People* contributor Jerome. "So if I start acting different, man, they'll square me in a minute. "

Despite Brooks's rocket to superstardom, praise for the performer has not been universal. Nash reported that one critic called the singer "a calculating fake ... a clone of George Strait." And for all his success, Brooks's post-stardom life has not been without its difficulties. During his first six months on the road, in 1989, Brooks found women all around him, and the married man fell prey to temptation—wife Sandy told Jerome that "an informant" confirmed her suspicions. Sandy, who didn't tour with Brooks then, called him the night of November 4, 1989, to confront him and lay down the law. Brooks came home and begged her not to leave. "Garth has said to me a million times that was probably the best thing that ever happened to him," friend Englund said to Jerome. "It took a helluva human being to forgive me," Brooks himself said. "I had to promise I'd make this marriage work. It ain't a bed of roses now, but we [work at it], and it works unbelievably well. For the first time in my life, I feel good about being a husband and a partner."

In the fall of 1991 Brooks gave television a whirl; Brooks appeared on the NBC situation comedy *Empty Nest*—playing himself. "They filmed me, that's about it," he told the *Detroit Free Press*. "There were actors there, but I wasn't one of them. To tell the truth, I feel lucky to be where I'm at in country music. I think I'll just stay here." Though Brooks may not have a second career as an actor, there is talk of his writing an autobiography.

Feeling as fortunate as he does, Brooks insists on keeping his ego in check. "I'm still a bum, I'm no different," he said to Jerome. "I hate to take out the trash and clean my room. Sandy makes me do that stuff. I don't wake up and say, 'I cannot believe I am in the middle of all this.' I just wake up and say, 'You're a bum, go do something worthwhile today.' "

Sources

Country Music, September/October 1991.

Country Song Roundup, December 1991.

Detroit Free Press, October 3, 1991; October 28, 1991.

Entertainment Weekly, September 20, 1991; March 20, 1992; March 27, 1992.

People, September 3, 1990; May 20, 1991; October 7, 1991; October 11, 1993.

Stereo Review, November 1991; December 1993.

Time, September 24, 1990.

Bobby Brown

Born c. 1968
Boston, Massachusetts

"I just want to be Bobby, the Man Who Does Everything."

SINGER AND SONGWRITER

"When Bobby Brown moves, fans swoon," wrote Steve Dougherty in *People.* "And critics shift into hyperpraise. Even the far-from-funky *New York Times* cheered a 'bravado [Brown] performance that harks back to the glory days' of 60s music." Brown is the latest in an impressive string of pop superstars who danced their way to the top of the music world in the 1980s. Such 1980s music phenoms as Michael Jackson, Madonna, Prince, and Paula Abdul all infused their pounding rhythms and up-tempo lyrics with plenty of acrobatic dance steps in their performances. Indeed, in these days of elaborate tour productions and slick music videos, a performer's ability to dance, set new fashion standards, and make a good appearance on camera are nearly as essential as the actual music in determining their success in the increasingly competitive pop market.

And all of this has certainly not been lost on Brown, who has already discovered what he believes to be the key to a lasting show-business career—diversification. "I'm not just a singer, or a dancer, or a performer," Brown told *Rolling Stone*'s Rob Tannenbaum. "I want to be a lot of different things. People don't know what Bobby Brown is. I want to be mysterious. I don't want people to be able to label me." Brown took one large step with his second solo album, *Don't Be Cruel,* a 1988 release that has sold more than six million copies and spawned the Top 5 singles "My Prerogative," "Roni," and "Don't Be Cruel." The album reached Number 1 on the *Billboard* charts in 1989, making Brown, then just 19, the first teenager to attain this goal since Ricky Nelson in 1957 and Stevie Wonder in 1963. The key to Brown's music, says *Rolling Stone*'s Tannenbaum, lies in Brown's ability to adapt "the traditional techniques of soul to the coarser language of rap ... it's obvious that Brown has displaced his elders on the pop charts not just because his songs adapt hip-hop beats but also because he has revived the aggressive sexuality that rap drew from James Brown.

This hybrid sound, which has been called "the new funk," or "new jack swing," was developed simultaneously in the late 1980s by New York producer Teddy Riley and the Los Angeles team of Antonio Reid and Kenny "Babyface" Edmonds. The purpose of the new sound was to make the hard edges of rap a little softer for a wider teen audience. And the smooth, charismatic Brown has proven to be the perfect vehicle for the dawn of the new funk.

When Brown became a bona fide superstar with the success of *Don't Be Cruel,* he was already considered a veteran performer despite his youth. Many music fans would recognize him as a member of the early 1980s teen group New Edition, but Brown's career had its formal debut when he was just three years old. It was then that his mother set him down onstage during a James Brown concert at Boston's Sugar Shack—and his two-minute, impromptu boogie brought down the house. "I just strutted around to the music," Brown told *People.* "Ever since, I liked being onstage."

Grows up in tough neighborhood

Brown grew up in Roxbury, a rough section of Boston, and though he admits his mischief in those days sometimes placed him on the wrong side of the law, he insists that his main weakness was for expensive clothes and jewelry that would set him apart. "There were two kinds of fellas at my school—the stoners and the kind who liked women and wore sharp clothes and put lotion on their hands and said nice things to the ladies," Brown told *People.* "I was the second kind. I lo-o-o-ove women.... They've got so much more to offer emotionally."

But a tragic incident helped transform Brown from a petty thief and pretty-boy to the serious young musician he has become. When he was just 11, Brown watched as his best friend was fatally stabbed in a knife fight. It was then that he made the determination to get out of the life he was leading. Together with several friends, Brown formed a singing group that started out doing harmony covers of Larry Graham and Donny Hathaway records. By 1980, when Brown was just 12, the group became formally known as New Edition, and the boys had their first major break when the producer Maurice Starr heard them performing in a talent competition.

> "People at MCA thought we was into drugs. That wasn't us. We were a bunch of brats, but we wasn't into drugs, we wasn't into liquor. We was into girls."

In 1981 the band signed a recording contract with MCA and, under Starr's direction, began producing singles that sounded strangely similar to such successful teen groups as the Jackson 5 and the Osmonds. Starr has even admitted that New Edition's first hit single, "Candy Girl," was modeled after the Jackson 5 songs "ABC" and "I Want You Back." Regardless, Starr and MCA both knew they had a hot act on their hands, and for the next five years New Edition performed before throngs of screaming teenage girls across America.

The New Edition experience was for Brown, in progression, a dream, an experience, a business, and finally a hassle. He quit the group in 1986 when infighting among the band members had grown intense, and when Brown grew suspicious that he was being swindled by MCA and Starr. There were also rumors that the band was using drugs, rumors which Brown claims were fanned by the rejected managers.

Embarking on his solo career, Brown decided that he wanted to keep closer to home, so he put his affairs into the hands of his brother, Tommy, and his mother. Starr, on the other hand, told *Rolling Stone*, "I was gonna make New Edition the biggest group in the world. When we parted, I said, 'Let me show them how smart I am—I'm coming back with a white teen group.'" Sure enough, Starr did return with the immensely successful, all-white group New Kids on the Block in the late 1980s.

But Brown knows he has moved beyond the teeny-bopper circuit. His heroes have always been the greats—like Michael Jackson, Elvis Presley, and James Brown—and for good measure he would like to develop himself as an actor, a la Madonna, Prince, and Eddie Murphy. When the producers of the film *Ghostbusters II* came knocking on the door of MCA records in search of a distributor for the film's soundtrack album, Brown was MCA's hottest act. MCA was awarded the contract on the stipulation that Brown appear prominently on the album, a project the singer was only too happy to undertake. There was some risk, however, in that the record would have to stand up to comparison with the first *Ghostbusters* soundtrack, which featured Ray Parker's gigantic single "Ghostbusters." Realizing that his participation was the key to the deal, Brown shrewdly agreed to sing on the album on the condition that he be given a role in the film. The result was Brown's surprisingly effective cameo appearance in the film as the obnoxious butler of the mayor of New York. "Acting is just a frame of mind," Brown told *Rolling Stone* with a characteristic shrug. "If you know how to block the camera off from being there, it's easy to act like another person. It's very easy."

In 1992 Brown's long awaited follow-up album, *Bobby,* sold more than 2 million copies. Like *Don't Be Cruel, Bobby*'s sound is "new jack swing." That same year Brown was married to Whitney Houston in a lavish ceremony with over 800 guests, and in 1993 they had a daughter, Bobbi Kristina. Brown credits his daughter with keeping the priorities in their marriage in perspective. In a 1994 interview with *Essence* Brown commented: "When you're building a building, you have to have something strong to hold the building up. Bobbi Kris is the cement that holds our relationship together. When we're going through changes, when we're arguing or whatever, all it takes is for Bobbi Kristina to go waaaahhhhhh. And we crack up."

Sources

Essence, February 1994.

People, November 5, 1984; April 15, 1985.

Rolling Stone, September 7, 1989; June 10, 1993.

Time, April 18, 1977.

Nicolas Cage

Born January 7, 1964
Long Beach, California

ACTOR

With his soulful eyes and offbeat good looks, Nicolas Cage can carry any romantic lead, but he is equally gifted at comedy and is not afraid to play the buffoon. Hard-to-please *New Yorker* critic Pauline Kael called Cage "a wonderful romantic clown" who is "slack-jawed and Neanderthal and passionate." Kael added that Cage "may be the only young actor who can look stupefied while he smolders. And no one can yearn like Cage: his head empties out—there's nothing there but sheepeyed yearning." That ability to "smolder"—to project a heightened sensuality—has made Cage a top draw at the box office. Still, he has resisted typecasting more successfully than any other star of his generation. *American Film* contributor Mark Rowland noted: "There aren't many (any?) ... actors with a resume this solid.... [Cage] is a character actor whose presence is frequently so powerful, it becomes part

"I used to make people laugh, just naturally—that was my means of expression.... Then I discovered Elia Kazan movies ... and I decided that's what I wanted to do, and I didn't want to be funny. I refused to be funny, to make my friends laugh. I started to be serious, and used that many, many years in my work."

of the film's signature. The movies, meanwhile, provide their own clues about Cage." *Los Angeles Times* correspondent Michael Wilmington sees Cage as a "great, elastic, soulful prankster, twisting himself endlessly into outlandish shapes.... He may be the most playful and goofily inventive of young American movie leading men right now."

Related to director Francis Ford Coppola

"Nicolas Cage" is in fact a stage name, chosen to replace a more famous surname. Cage was born Nicolas Coppola in Long Beach, California, and is the nephew of director Francis Ford Coppola. As a youngster Cage lived with his two brothers in a middle-class home in Long Beach. His father was a college professor, so he was raised in an atmosphere of culture and serious study. His own nature occasionally exploded in childhood pranks: once he served egg salad with fried grasshoppers in it to his elementary school class. Cage told the *Los Angeles Times*: "As a child in Long Beach, I spent a lot of time pretending I was other people. I was into the whole concept of trying to disguise myself."

That fascination with fantasy and disguise continued as Cage grew older. When he was 12, his parents divorced and his father moved the family to the outskirts of Beverly Hills. Cage attended high school at Beverly Hills High and remembers being shy with girls because he was not wealthy. His interest in acting was further heightened after seeing the film *East of Eden* in an old revival theater in Los Angeles. "It was the scene with James Dean breaking down in front of his father when he wouldn't accept the money," Cage remembered in *American Film*. "It really devastated me. That's when I thought, 'Yeah, I want to do that.'" At first glance it might seem a stroke of luck for a young would-be actor to have a famous uncle in the movie business. Indeed, Francis Ford Coppola was instrumental in bringing Cage to the screen, first in *Rumble Fish* (1983) and then in *The Cotton Club* (1984). Cage admits that he has learned a great deal from working with his uncle, but he realized that the name Coppola posed limitations for him as well. After giving it careful thought, he changed his name from Nicolas Coppola to Nicolas Cage, taking the surname of two of his heroes—comic book character Luke Cage and avant-garde composer John Cage. The actor explained in the *Los Angeles Times*: "When I first started going to auditions and was still using my real name, it was obvious that people were thinking about 20 years of someone else's history. I wanted to be able to go into an office and just do what I had to do, so I took the name Cage, and the first audition I did under that name was the best audition I'd ever had. That told me I'd done the right thing."

One of the first auditions Cage undertook with his new name was for a low-budget teen film called *Valley Girl*. Cage won the lead in the 1983 movie about a rich suburban girl who falls in love with a punk from Hollywood High. As the rough but tender Randy, Cage managed to pull the film from obscurity—most critics singled out his performance as the saving grace of the otherwise insubstantial movie. *Valley Girl* made Cage a star almost overnight. Offers for other film work came pouring in, and he chose only those that gave him a chance to stretch his talents. To quote Wilmington, "There's been something bracingly nutty about Cage's roles ever since."

Early praise for Birdy

Cage drew strong notices for his work as a psychotic hoodlum in his uncle's film *The Cotton Club* and for his role as a self-centered cad in *Racing with the Moon*. His best-known early performance, however, is his portrayal of a disfigured Vietnam veteran in *Birdy*. The film concerns the reaction of two young men to the horrors of war; Cage had to play many of his scenes with his face swathed in bandages. Although Cage would eventually come to call his performance in the film "emotional vomit," *Birdy* won the Jury prize at the Cannes Film Festival. Cage's deft interpretation of a demanding character proved, in Wilmington's words, that "he could do primal-man roles with the best of them."

At that point it seemed likely that Cage would opt for standard leading-man fare. Instead he took two daring comic roles that made a mockery of his sex appeal. In *Peggy Sue Got Married* (1986), he appeared as Charlie Bodell, a womanizing huckster with few social graces; in *Raising Arizona* (1986) he portrayed a luckless lowlife who steals a baby for his desperate, barren wife to raise. Kael called *Raising Arizona* a "monkeyshines burlesque" that revealed Cage "at his most winning." The critic commented: "Actors have made big reputations as farceurs on less talent than Cage shows here; his slapstick droopiness holds it all together."

In 1987 Cage won a role in the comedy-drama *Moonstruck,* a romantic tale set in Brooklyn. As a finished work, *Moonstruck* is an ensemble performance of high quality, and Cage holds up his end as a romantic and dissatisfied baker who falls for his brother's fiancée. Wilmington wrote: "Cage's romanticism is his most attractive quality. Like the young Jimmy Stewart, he is unafraid of showing desire and passion on screen—and he doesn't mind looking nerdy or grotesque doing it. In *Moonstruck,* when, after a series of outrageous, self-pitying tantrums, he rises to confront his brother's fiancée (Cher) and then sweepingly tosses the table outside, grasps her in a ravenous clinch and carries her off to the bedroom, it's an ultimate [macho] joke—and both Cage and Cher delightedly let us all in on it." Needless to say, his role in *Moonstruck* further endeared Cage to a legion of female fans.

Cage acknowledges that he is still learning his craft and that his earliest work could have been better. But Wilmington has said that the actor has refined his style over time, sweetened it, and opened it up. "Nicolas Cage is not the star we expected, not from his generation, not in this day and age," Rowland concluded. "Somebody forgot to blow-dry his hair, and the cowlick ended up in front. Somebody forgot to tell him that irony is hip, passion passe. Somebody forgot to smooth out that walk and that talk. Kathleen Turner had it right the first time in *Peggy Sue Got Married*—this guy is not the one. She had it right the second time, too. He is the one."

Works with David Lynch on Wild at Heart

Cage's romantic air and rough exterior made him a perfect choice for the lead in the 1990 David Lynch film *Wild at Heart*. A twisted version of the all-American road movie, *Wild at Heart* follows the gothic/romantic adventures of Sailor Ripley and his sweetheart, Lula Pace Fortune. Wilmington called Cage's work in the movie "the latest in his recent string of ingenious, double-jointed performances.... It's a triumph.... And it may signal Cage's emergence as the ace—or, at the very least, joker—of his acting generation."

Wild at Heart garnered numerous honors at Cannes; prior to its American opening, it received a great deal of media attention for its bizarre, violent scenes, much as Lynch's television series *Twin Peaks* did when it was first broadcast in the summer of 1990. The film brought mixed—but by no means uncertain—reviews; those who saw it either loved it or hated it. In any case, *Wild at Heart* did not fare as well as expected at the box office, and the hype that had preceded its debut died down quickly.

Finds success with Honeymoon in Vegas

Cage's next appearance was in the box-office failure *Zandalee* in 1991. With the 1992 *Honeymoon in Vegas,* however, Cage had one of his most successful films. Cage portrayed Jack Singer, a private eye who is torn between his mother's dying wish that he never get married, and his girlfriend's threat that she'll leave him unless they do get married. He reluctantly chooses to wed his girlfriend and the two head for Las Vegas. While there he loses a poker game to a mobster, who asks for a weekend with Singer's fiancée as payment for the gambling debt. A reviewer for the *New York Times* praised Cage for giving "a beautifully disciplined performance."

The 1993 movie *Amos and Andrew* was not a success. Cage played Amos, a kindhearted car thief who befriends a famous black dramatist (Andrew) accused by his wealthy white neighbors of breaking into his own house. While the film did not attract many viewers, Cage was singled out for his performance. David Kehr of the *Chicago Tribune* wrote, "Cage gives Amos an amazingly rich interior life; the character exists with a depth that is rare enough in drama, almost unheard of in a farce."

During its first week of release in the spring of 1994, the comedy *Guarding Tess* grossed an impressive $9 million. In this gentle comedy, Cage plays a secret service agent assigned to guard a moody and hot-tempered former first lady, played by Shirley Maclaine. The relationship between the pair changes through the course of the film from antagonism to friendship.

Most recently Cage has appeared in *It Could Happen to You*, which opened in July 1994. This movie is the last in what Cage calls his "sunshine trilogy." He considers *Weekend in Vegas, Guarding Tess,* and *It Could Happen to You* to be three mainstream, big-budget comedies—a style of film markedly different from the quirky, offbeat work in which Cage usually appears. In *It Could Happen to You* Cage plays a kind New York cop who, when he has no money for a tip, offers to split his lottery ticket winnings with the waitress, should he win. Well, he does win and the comedy begins. Cage described his initial reaction to the script in *Premiere*: "It's like a 40's romantic comedy with a Capra touch. I sat alone and cried when I finished the script and that's rare for me. But it just hit such a nerve."

His film *Red Rock West* (1994) was another oddball film that won a cult following with its setting of evil, violence, and lies. Cage's future films include: *Kiss of Death,* in which he will play a brutal man who kills with his bare hands; *It Happened in Paradise,* a comedy about three brothers who rob a bank on Christmas Eve; and *Leaving Las Vegas.*

Cage regularly makes as many as three feature films each year. He told the *New York Times*, "I've been on the road working nonstop for the last two years. I'm not really comfortable unless I'm working. I'm not very comfortable in life." What little spare time he has is spent primarily in Los Angeles and San Francisco. Cage is unmarried, but has a model girlfriend in L.A. He also has a three-year-old-son by his ex-girlfriend Christina Fulton, with whom he shares custody. "Until I had a child, I was consumed with myself ... it was all about me," Cage revealed in *Harper's Bazaar*. "Now a day doesn't go by that I'm not thinking about my son and worrying. I do think I worry too much."

Sources

American Film, June 1989; June 1990.

Harper's Bazaar, July 1994.

Los Angeles Times, February 21, 1988; August 12, 1990.

Maclean's, May 28, 1990.

New Yorker, April 20, 1987; January 25, 1988.

New York Times, March 23, 1984; December 23, 1984; October 5, 1986; June 2, 1989; July 24, 1994.

People, March 28, 1994.

Playboy, June 1989.

Premiere, June 1994.

Time, May 9, 1994.

John Candy

Born October 31, 1950, Toronto, Ontario, Canada
Died March 4, 1994

ACTOR AND COMEDIAN

J ohn Candy was a comedian with tremen-dous skills, whose untimely death at the age of 42 left the entertainment world stunned and saddened. Formerly a member of the renowned Second City comedy troupe in Chicago and Toronto, Candy gained a world-wide television audience for his daring and memorable characters, such as conceited celebrity Johnny LaRue, eerie 3-D thriller host Dr. Tongue, and clarinet-tooting Yosh Shmenge. In films Candy continued to parody typical American heroes, from idealistic army recruits and Peace Corps volunteers to wise and wisecracking sidekicks.

"We don't realize yet that John will be no more. Feeling his absence will be tremendously hard. Like the air has been sucked out of the world."—Eugene Levy

"He's colossal. He's enormous. He's gargantuan. He's the biggest man in show business and the funniest man, too. He's a giant among comics," *Spin* magazine interviewer Glenn O'Brien said of Candy's talent. In the *New Yorker,* critic Pauline Kael expressed similar enthusiasm for the actor's comic spirit: "John Candy is perfectly named; he's a mountainous lollipop of a man, and preposterously loveable." No one could claim that

Candy lacked initiative; he appeared in more than 40 feature films, starred in the Emmy Award-winning *SCTV* (Second City Television) series, and was seen in three HBO cable presentations, including *Comic Relief*. O'Brien described the 6'3", 300-pound Candy as a performer who "would stand out in any crowd. Perfect timing, facial athleticism, drop-dead delivery, and remarkable versatility made him a great one."

Candy's success in the unpredictable movie industry was up and down. Although he drew critical raves for his supporting roles in such hit productions as *Splash* and *Volunteers*, some of his starring vehicles—among them *Summer Rental* and *Armed and Dangerous*—met with lackluster reviews and poor attendance in the theaters. Candy, who was a more versatile actor than either his appearance or his film work suggested, took great pains to search for films scripts worthy of his talent. Perhaps Candy was a bit too self-critical and susceptible to the critics' barbs. As Mike McGrady noted in the *Detroit News*, even in his lesser offerings, "Candy appears and suddenly you get a feeling of warmth. And before you know it, despite all your taste and higher education, you find yourself smiling, then laughing out loud."

Born on Halloween

John Candy—that was his real name ("Do you think I would change it to that?" he said)—was born on Halloween in 1950. He grew up in Toronto under the care of his mother, aunt, and grandparents, having lost his father to a heart ailment that began during combat in World War II. He attended parochial schools and from an early age he held a number of after-school jobs. "I've been working, Jesus, since I was about ten years old," he told *Spin*. "I used to sell fish and chips. I worked for three drugstores at one time. I was very ambitious. I bought hockey tickets with the money I made. I worked for a grocery store. I was a bag boy." During his high school years, Candy found time for athletics, claiming that he "tried valiantly" at football and hockey without much success. "I got injured real well," he remembered. "I looked good when I got hurt. That was on a fairly regular basis. But I enjoyed sports." He enjoyed watching sporting events, stubbornly maintaining his allegiance to all of Toronto's professional teams. Like many members of the "baby boom" generation, Candy watched hours of television, especially comedy, as a youngster. He told *Playboy*, "I loved watching Jack Benny, Jack Paar, *The Honeymooners*, Burns and Allen, George Gobel, *The Munsters*, *Rocky and His Friends*, *Howdy Doody*, *Rin Tin Tin*, *Lassie*. I wasn't influenced by any one show, I was influenced by the medium."

That influence carried Candy into a theater major at a community college in Toronto. He dropped out after a short time, however, and sought professional acting work. His years as a struggling actor were punctuated by numerous odd jobs—"odd" perhaps summing them up in more ways than one. In his *Spin* interview, he gave a few examples: "I used to sell paper napkins and candles on the road for a company called Perkins Paper in Toronto.... Before that I worked for Eaton's, a department store in Toronto similar to Macy's or Gimbel's. I worked in the sporting goods department, selling skis and guns. I worked in a Glidden's paint factory, mixing large amounts of road paint. Yellow and white. It's pretty strong. I learned my chemistry there." Eventually he got some acting work on Canadian television, in underground theater, and in commercials, one of which featured him as a football player whose helmet would protect him the way Colgate toothpaste protects teeth. Finally he auditioned for the Second City comedy troupe at the prompting of his friend Dan Aykroyd. Candy was astonished when he was accepted and sent to the United States. He told *People*: "The next thing I knew I was in Chicago." There Candy worked with Aykroyd, Gilda Radner, John Belushi, and Bill Murray, a great apprenticeship for what was to become a brilliant career in improvisational comedy.

> Candy's passion was football and when his old high school had to suspend its football program due to a lack of funds, Candy stepped in and offered to finance the team.

Joins cast of Second City

When Toronto opened a branch of Second City, Candy became a pioneering member of the cast. In a short time the Toronto Second City troupe—drawing on the talents of Candy, Eugene Levy, Rick Moranis, and Martin Short—became more recognizable than its Chicago counterpart. Canadian television began to air the shows, and in the wake of the enormous success of *Saturday Night Live*, NBC picked up the series for its late-night time slot. *Maclean's* correspondent Ian Brown has described *SCTV* as "one of the most ambitious television series ever written, acted and produced by Canadians, and quite possibly one of the most successful pieces of television art ever made." The show, purporting to be coming from a broadcast studio in Melonville, Canada, relied on satire and parody, with nothing sacred left untarnished for comic effect. Brown noted: "There are laughs within laughs in every skit. But, within every laugh, there is also a little cry of anguish. There is a subtext, a subliminal message to SCTV Network, and it entails a cultural pain." In their spoofs of talk show hosts, their parodies of commercials, and their racial and ethnic jokes, the group pinpointed both the cultural sterility and the recurrent anxiety of modern life. As Brown put it, "Woven into *SCTV*'s whole cloth, satire chastises all of television's unfulfilled promises." As the popularity of *Saturday Night Live* waned, *SCTV* seemed to gain more viewers. For Candy, it became a calling card to stardom.

Candy's most memorable character for SCTV was that of Yosh Shmenge, a Leutonian folk musician who formed half of the Shmenge Brothers Happy Wanderers polka band. As the Shmenges, Candy and Eugene Levy sought to update their band's image by introducing punk polka, making music videos, and doing an accordion-and-clarinet version of Michael Jackson's hit song "Beat It." The series of Happy Wanderers sketches on *SCTV* were so successful that HBO produced a comedy special—*The Last Polka*—featuring the ever-cheerful, leiderhosen-clad Shmenge brothers. The program, written by Candy and Levy, traces the Shmenges' artistic career from their childhoods in the shadow of the Balkans to their farewell performance. *New York Times* reviewer John J. O'Connor is among the critics who have praised *The Last Polka.* He wrote: "They could have been a one-note gag, bearing a striking resemblance to a Polish joke, but Mr. Candy and Mr. Levy go about their work with such inspired madness that the strange Shmenges have taken on a life of their own. Yosh and Stan live, it seems, and the loony parodies are often inspired." Candy, O'Connor concluded, is "an enormous mountain of a young man and his Yosh is a model of Leutonian affability, spiked occasionally with a suspicious glance at someone who may be trying to put one over on him. His voice is a high-pitched lilt emerging from lips that seem permanently puckered from too many years on the clarinet." Candy and Levy also portrayed the Shmenges on *Comic Relief,* the HBO comedy marathon dedicated to helping homeless people.

Gains recognition with Splash

Splash, the comedy romance about a young man and his mermaid love, brought Candy critical acclaim and, he admits, gave his career a "real shot." In the Ron Howard film, Candy appeared as man-about-town Freddie Bauer, older brother of love-smitten Allen (Tom Hanks). Pauline Kael suggested that in *Splash,* Howard was "the first director who let John Candy loose. This gigantic, chubby Puck has been great in brief appearances, ... but the role of Freddie the playboy is the first role big enough for him to make the kind of impression he made in the SCTV shows.... Candy is the soul of amiability—it's just an awfully large soul. Freddie is the older brother you always wanted to have. He's [Shakespeare's comic character]

Falstaff at fourteen, and the picture probably wouldn't work without him; he doesn't add weight, he adds bounce and imagination." *New York* critic David Denby commented that Hanks and Candy complement one another in their portrayal of brothers: "Hanks ... commands the emotional center of his scenes, holding your sympathy in place, while Candy, ... [an oversexed] blond bull, frightening to behold, frolics madly at the edges." Janet Maslin, in her *New York Times* review, concluded that *Splash* "would not be nearly so successful without the bulldozing presence of John Candy.... The mere sight of the tubby Mr. Candy is funny enough (the spectacle of him playing racquetball really is something to see). But he also gets most of the better lines."

Scott Haller aptly described the downturn in Candy's fortunes after *Splash* when he wrote, "Calling all cars: Be on the lookout for an overweight, underappreciated comedian in search of a vehicle. Although he's one of the funniest performers around, John Candy has had a floundering career in films." Critics often found Candy immensely funny in his movies, but they cited poor scripts and feeble ideas for his motion pictures' failures. In a *Boxoffice* review of *Armed and Dangerous,* for instance, a critic stated: "John Candy turns in his blandest performance and it is distressing to observe. It's not entirely his fault—he didn't write the thing ... it simply doesn't work." *Chicago Tribune* columnist Gene Siskel offered a possible explanation for Candy's lack of quality vehicles: "Whereas his many fans and some critics do not doubt his ability to deliver a performance with a full range of emotion, it may be that the studio executives and directors in Hollywood see Candy only as a jolly fat man, the natural physical comedy successor to John Belushi and his food fights." Candy himself agreed with that assessment, but he added: "I would certainly like to dispel that in upcoming work. I'm certainly looking for projects that have a little more to them.... I'm capable of doing a food fight with the best of them. But I know I can do more. And I'd like to be able to show it."

During the years from 1987 to 1994 there were nearly an even number of hits and misses. Among his more popular characters were the traveling salesman trying to find his way home in *Planes, Trains and Automobiles*; the uncouth hero of *Uncle Buck* (1988); and the persevering Jamaican bobsled coach in the 1993 sleeper hit *Cool Runnings.* He was at work on a new film, *Wagon's East,* when he died. The years of overeating and smoking took their toll and on March 4, 1994, at about 6:00 a.m., Candy suffered a heart attack and died in his sleep. People who witnessed the film's production felt that it was the best performance of Candy's life.

While Candy's off-screen life was not always serene, his wife Rose and their daughter and son offered him great emotional support. He struggled constantly with his weight. Despite diets, exercise programs, and visits to the Pritikin Center for weight control, he never lost his rotund appearance. Yet whatever difficulties he had in his life, of one thing there was no doubt—his immense talent. Writing an obituary for *People*, Brian Johnson spoke of Candy's gifts: "[Candy] could be as funny as anyone. But what set him apart was a tenderness, a gentle emotional candor that made him instantly credible and lovable. Behind the comic mask, the tragic mask was always peeking through, conveying the sense that his character deserved a better fate."

Sources

Boxoffice, May 1986; October 1986; February 1987.

Chicago Tribune, March 30, 1986.

Detroit News, August 27, 1986.

Film Comment, August 1985.

High Fidelity, November 1985.

Life, October 1982.

Maclean's, December 27, 1982; March 19, 1984; June 9, 1986; March 14, 1994.

Newsweek, August 26, 1985.

New York, March 12, 1984; June 10, 1985; September 22, 1986.

New Yorker, November 19, 1984.

New York Times, October 29, 1983; November 24, 1983; March 9, 1984; September 30, 1984; March 10, 1985; March 14, 1985; July 21, 1985; August 2, 1985; August 9, 1985; August 16, 1985.

Penthouse, March 1984.

People, July 13, 1981; September 2, 1983; November 21, 1983; March 12, 1984; June 4, 1984; March 18, 1985; June 10, 1985; July 1, 1985; August 26, 1985; September 2, 1985; January 20, 1986; September 1, 1986; July 19, 1993; October 11, 1993; March, 21, 1994.

Playboy, May 1982; June 1984; November 1985.

Spin, November 1986.

Time, November 22, 1982; June 3, 1985; September 9, 1985; March 14, 1994.

Washington Post, November 22, 1983; June 2, 1984.

Mariah Carey

Born c. 1970

SINGER, SONGWRITER

Pop vocalist and songwriter Mariah Carey set the music world ablaze when her self-titled debut album was released in 1990. Featuring the hit single "Vision of Love," the disc provoked critics to rave over Carey's seven-octave vocal range and gospel-toned voice. The album sold six million copies and won two Grammy awards. She has been compared to the late pop soprano Minnie Riperton, the Peruvian singer Yma Sumac, and, most often, to superstar Whitney Houston. As reviewer Ralph Novak asserted in *People*, Carey "sings with extraordinary control, driving power, lovely pitch, and wide range."

"I'm really fortunate, I'm really happy, and I'm really lucky to be where I am. All I can do now is be the best I can be."

Carey was born to a mother who had sung with the New York City Opera and remained a vocal coach throughout Carey's childhood. Her mother influenced Carey a great deal, the singer revealed in *Seventeen*. "I knew from watching and listening to my mom that singing could and would be my profession." She recounted further that her mother "had to tear me away from the radio each night just to get me to go to sleep." Carey also enjoyed listening to the record collection of her older brother and sister, especially albums by Gladys Knight, Aretha Franklin, and Stevie Wonder.

Signs with Columbia Records

When Carey was 17 she left her family home on Long Island, New York, to live in New York City. Sharing an apartment with another aspiring musician, she waited on tables to earn her living while making demo tapes of original songs to give to music executives. Carey eventually got a job as a back-up singer for a small record label. One of the vocalists she sang for, Brenda K. Starr, was sufficiently impressed with her abilities to introduce her to Tommy Mottola of Columbia Records. At Starr's insistence Carey gave him one of her demo tapes. Mottola listened to it in his car on the way home from the party where the meeting had taken place; he called Carey to sign her the next day.

Carey worked on recording her debut album for the next two years. *Mariah Carey* was released by the time the singer turned 20. Carey cowrote and arranged all of the songs on the album, though critics have not been particularly impressed by her non-vocal efforts. Novak called the tunes "uniformly forgettable, both melodically and lyrically"; Alanna Nash of *Stereo Review* commented that "none of the ten songs sticks in the mind." Nevertheless, the single, "Vision of Love" raced up the pop and adult contemporary charts, eventually reaching number one. She gained further exposure on national television by singing "America, the Beautiful" before the first game of the National Basketball Association finals at Michigan's Palace of Auburn Hills. Carey's debut album also contained the tracks "Someday" and "There's Got to Be a Way," which Nash described as "social-consciousness raising."

"What you remember" about Carey, however, said David Gates in *Newsweek*, "is the voice—all seven octaves or so of it, from purring alto to stratospheric shriek." Likewise, in spite of her criticism of Carey's songwriting, Nash did affirm that *Mariah Carey* "is as exhilarating as a ride on the World's Tallest Roller Coaster." Amusement parks came to the mind of a *Seventeen* reporter as well, who noted that the "lissome diva carries the listener away on a riveting ... roller coaster of sound." Not surprisingly, in light of such comments, Carey's efforts on the album garnered her Grammy awards for best new artist of 1990 and best pop female vocalist.

Releases Emotions in 1991

Due to the overwhelming success of her debut album Carey had greater control over her second release, *Emotions.* As a result, the influence of such Carey favorites as Aretha Franklin and Stevie Wonder is felt on the album. Carey wrote the lyrics for the entire disc and produced six of the songs. The critics were mixed in their reviews of *Emotions,* with the negative reactions alleging that Carey's lyrics were too trite and her delivery too forceful. Among the positive critical reactions were praise for the leaner musical arrangements and the richness of Carey's voice. According to Christian Wright of *New York Newsday:* "Whereas [Carey's] debut was slick and heavily produced, *Emotions* uses simpler arrangements so that the voice is showcased as the most important instrument." The album has sold over three million copies.

In 1992 Carey released the EP *Unplugged,* which sold over two million copies. Her third full-length album, *Music Box,* was released in 1993. As with *Emotions,* many of the critics felt that Carey's work would be better off with more meaningful lyrics to complement her powerful voice. In a review for *People,* Amy Linden wrote that "*Music Box* is a showcase for [Carey's] artistic dilemma: great pipes, lame songs." Critical praise is primarily focused on Carey's vocal control and range. Christopher John Farley commented in *Time:* "[There] are some great moments on *Music Box.* The gospel-flavored "Anytime You Need a Friend" demonstrates Carey's vocal power, although too fleetingly. And the title cut is one of Carey's loveliest songs to date, with her voice humming and hovering above a tinkling, childlike melody."

> Carey has an upstate New York country home, where she drives a jeep, plays with her energetic Jack Russel terrier (Jack), and snuggles with her two Persian cats (Ninja and Tomkins). Carey commented: "I've always had pets—dogs and cats—my whole life."

Launches tour

Until the release of *Music Box* Carey had never undertaken a tour. She told Steven Dougherty of *People,* "I didn't come up doing clubs like most people, so I wasn't ready. Now I am." And so on November 3, 1993, Carey kicked off her first tour in Miami. Some of her audience was underwhelmed and critics panned the performance. Instead of being discouraged, however, Carey listened for the constructive criticism and proceeded to draw raves during her next concert in Boston. In an interview with *Ebony* Carey said, "I took all the anger and put it out there in my next show."

Weds Sony Music president Tommy Mottola

While releasing a successful album and touring for the first time were exciting, the real pinnacle of 1993 was Carey's marriage to Tommy Mottola in an elaborate June wedding. The two were wed at Manhattan's St. Thomas Episcopal Church with such stars as Barbra Streisand, Robert DeNiro, and Bruce Springsteen present. The romance first began when they worked together on her debut album and became public only after Mottola divorced his wife of 20 years in 1990. Carey told Steve Dougherty, "It just sort of happened. Tommy is the greatest person. He knows so much; he's funny. I can't imagine anybody else who would be so supportive and so understanding and so helpful. He lifts me up." Although Mottola is 20 years Carey's senior, she insists that the age difference is not an issue. In an interview with *Ebony* she explained: "I really don't focus on it. We don't look at each other as two people with a big age difference. We are just right for each other, and that is all that matters. If you are really right for each other, that will shine through all the differences, everything—race and age."

Sources

Ebony, April 1994.

Glamour, October 1990.

Newsweek, August 6, 1990.

New York Newsday, March 19, 1991.

People, July 16, 1990; October 4, 1993; November 22, 1993.

Rolling Stone, August 23, 1990.

Seventeen, October 1990.

Stereo Review, October 1990.

Time, September 6, 1993.

Jim Carrey

Born January 17, 1962
Newmarket, Ontario, Canada

ACTOR AND COMEDIAN

A lready famous for his work on the television comedy show *In Living Color,* Jim Carrey became a household name with the back-to-back hits *Ace Ventura: Pet Detective* and *The Mask.* He appeals to young and old alike, with his seemingly elastic face, which shapes itself into an infinite number of expressions. His comedy knows no bounds, as he incorporates physical comedy, facial contortions, impressions, drama, song, and dance into his work. He's truly an original who seems to have a limitless supply of energy and capacity for work. As quoted in *Saturday Night,* Carrey won't find satisfaction until he "turns into light or explodes into a thousand stars" on stage.

"There's really not that much in this world, except the death of a loved one, that should be taken all that seriously—you can even joke about that if you want to. As far as I'm concerned, if God knows where your heart is, you're all right."

Entertains with his distinctive expressions

Carrey was born in a small town just north of Toronto, Ontario, Canada. His first audience was his family, whom he entertained by molding his flexible body into dozens of shapes and poses. But despite his ability to perform for relatives, Carrey was surprisingly shy with new people. It wasn't until the family moved to Toronto that the then-eight-year-old boy learned how to reach total strangers. In a *Saturday Night* article, Carrey recalled an episode on the playground of his new Toronto school: "Well, for some reason I did something where I realized I could get a reaction ... that was when I broke out of my shell at school, because I really didn't have any friends or anything like that and I was just kind of going along, and then finally I did this zany thing and all of a sudden I had a ton of friends."

Carrey's life took a turn for the worse, however, when his father was suddenly laid off from his 35-year job as an accountant. Carrey was forced to quit school at the age of 16 to join his family as they worked at a Toronto truck-rim factory. "We all became so angry," Carrey told *People*. "I was a security guard and a janitor, and I started throwing gigantic tantrums, throwing a bench against a wall or driving a forklift through the bay doors." At one point the family was in such bad financial shape that they were forced to pitch a tent in the backyard of his sister's house. This long, dark period in his life bred both sadness and anger.

Carrey was able to channel some of this anger into a comedy routine. He made his stand-up debut at the Yuk-Yuk comedy club in Toronto. The routine was a disaster, but when he returned a couple of years later his performance was so smooth he brought down the house. He was soon the hottest comic act in Canada, and in 1981 he headed for Los Angeles, California, to try his luck there. He made a name for himself at The Comedy Club, which in turn led to a tour with the comedian Rodney Dangerfield.

Changes act

Up until this point Carrey had centered his act on impressions of famous people. Not wanting to be pigeonholed as an "impressionist," Carrey changed his act almost overnight. Carrey told *Saturday Night*: "I was putting out something that I didn't want to be known for. I wanted to be myself, to create some things that had never been done before, rather than constantly sitting waiting for the next famous person whom I could impersonate. That held nothing for me. It was a slow realization, but at one point I just said 'never again.'"

His first step in this change was to start acting lessons. The lessons led to a starring role in NBC's short-lived series *The Duck Factory,* as well as parts in such feature films as *Peggy Sue Got Married* (1986), *The Dead Pool* (1988), and *Earth Girls Are Easy* (1989). It was this last movie that led to his being cast in the Fox network's *In Living Color.* In *Earth Girls,* Carrey played an odd, sex-starved alien along with Damon Wayans. Wayans is the brother of Keenan Ivory Wayans—the creator of *In Living Color.* When Keenan Wayans began searching for talent for his new show, his brother recommended Carrey. Although initially reluctant to sign on for a weekly series, Carrey finally agreed after he was assured he would have the freedom to play a variety of characters.

After the series debut, it became apparent that Carrey and Damon Wayans were the stars of the show. Carrey was given full reign to create whatever bizarre characters he could imagine. Two of his best-known creations are Fire Marshall Bill and Vera de Milo. The former is a multiple-burn victim, who's more likely to start a fire than put one out, and the latter is a grotesque female bodybuilder who's taken way too many steroids. One time he did a send-up of The Juiceman, who preaches the virtues of making and drinking juices. Carrey chose to juice a rat, drink it with gusto, and proceed to tell the audience that now he could fly.

Makes Ace Ventura

It was with the release in 1994 of *Ace Ventura: Pet Detective* that Carrey achieved widespread fame. Despite some lukewarm reviews, fans arrived in droves to see this zany comedian ham it up on the wide screen. Carrey plays the role of Ace Ventura, a private investigator who finds animals. When the Miami Dolphins mascot, Snowflake, is kidnapped on the eve of the Super Bowl, Ace is called in to find the missing mammal. Soon thereafter, the Dolphins quarterback also turns up missing, and Ace expands his search to look for both parties. The movie was an unexpected hit that remained number one at the box-office for many weeks and eventually pulled in $70 million at a reported cost of only $11 million.

The Mask was released in the summer of 1994, and its immediate success paralleled that of *Ace Ventura.* In the movie Carrey plays a timid bank clerk who becomes a crime-fighting superhero once he dons a magic-filled mask. The film is loaded with special effects. For example, the audience sees Carrey's heart stretch out of his chest and beat in the air. He also appears to plummet to the ground, flatten out like a pancake, then peel himself off the pavement. Unlike the reception for *Ace Ventura,* some critics were favorable in their reaction to *The Mask.* According to Frank Bruni of the *Detroit Free Press,* "[Carrey] proves that he's one of the most imaginative comedians on screen, not to mention one of the most intrepid. He's never afraid to risk making a fool of himself. Happily, *The Mask* makes a fool of no one involved with it. It's great fun."

Since Carrey's sudden entry into the limelight, he has been deluged with scripts. He's recently finished filming *Dumb and Dumber* and he's all set to begin work in the upcoming *Batman Forever*, in which he plays The Riddler. Beyond that he's looking forward to working on a sequel to *Ace Ventura*, and possibly a sequel to *The Mask*. This frenetic pace and obsession with work have taken their toll. He's recently filed for divorce from Melissa Womer, his wife of eight years and the mother of his six-year-old daughter, Jane. According to Shane Peacock of *Saturday Night*, "Carrey keeps searching, working, striving, as though some invisible boss might take everything away in an instant and leave him and his family in a tent in someone's back yard. He prefers to keep his mind, his body, and his career in perpetual motion, unlike his father, who as an aging accountant was turned into a failure because of inflexibility. So Jim Carrey remains flexible, in every possible way."

Sources

Chatelaine, August 1989.

Detroit Free Press, July 29, 1994.

Newsweek, July 25, 1994.

People, November 11, 1991; March 16, 1992; February 21, 1994; February 28, 1994.

Rolling Stone, May 18, 1989.

Saturday Night, June 1993.

TV Guide, June 18, 1994.

Variety, February 7, 1994.

Wall Street Journal, April 14, 1994.

Dana Carvey

Born April 2, 1955
Missoula, Montana

ACTOR AND COMEDIAN

Dana Carvey first gained fame as a regular cast member on NBC's *Saturday Night Live* comedy show. His Church Lady character was a sensation from the moment he introduced her, and his impersonations of such famous people as George Bush, Jimmy Stewart, and Johnny Carson won him a large and loyal following. It is for the film *Wayne's World,* however, that Carvey is best known. A spin-off from *Saturday Night Live, Wayne's World* centers on two guys who basically hang out in a basement as hosts of a cable-access television show. No one was prepared for the film's phenomenal success—it eventually earned more than $170 million worldwide and spawned a sequel, *Wayne's World 2,* which was released in 1993.

"Carvey has this ability to sting, yet you don't feel like he's a bad guy. There's always an innocence and an impishness to the impressions. You can feel like the guy behind them is having a good time. That's Dana's star quality—that he's enjoying himself."—Robert Smigel

Created the "Church Lady" from real-life experiences

Carvey was born in Montana and grew up in San Carlos, California, with three brothers and one sister. Both his parents were schoolteachers who took their children to church on Sundays. According to Carvey, he and his siblings would often pray that their parents would oversleep on Sunday morning, so that the family might be spared attending church. It was his experiences at those Sunday services that would eventually inspire the character of the Church Lady. There were three women in particular, whose extreme self-righteousness and holier-than-thou attitudes helped form the nucleus of one of Carvey's most famous creations. Yet Carvey told *Rolling Stone* that he was sure those women would never recognize themselves in his character: "That's the irony of the character. The people who are like the Church Lady wouldn't get it at all."

Carvey describes himself as a shy and awkward adolescent. In an effort to stave off the loneliness, Carvey would entertain his family by doing impressions of the marine biologist Jacques Cousteau and then president Lyndon B. Johnson. His favorite comedians were those who could create believable, yet funny characters. Carol Burnett, Jackie Gleason, Jonathan Winters, and Rich Little are among those who made him laugh.

After high school, Carvey enrolled at San Francisco State University to study radio and television broadcasting. Still shy, Carvey limited his impersonations and one-liners to his good friends. Then, in 1978, Carvey got up the nerve to appear before a live audience in a club in San Francisco. He did well enough to be invited back and after college Carvey made his living as a stand-up comic.

Heads for Hollywood

In 1981 he headed for Hollywood with high hopes of a movie career. Initially he met with little success, finding only bit parts in such films as *Halloween II, Racing with the Moon,* and *This Is Spinal Tap.* He fared no better in television, being miscast in the 1981 situation comedy *One of the Boys* and the 1983 cop series bomb *Blue Thunder.* One of Carvey's drawbacks was his clean-cut, youthful appearance. He was forever being sent to audition for the-boy-next-door kind of roles and never given a chance to demonstrate his comic talents. He told *Rolling Stone,* "I went through five years of frustration and hell, having this huge secret of all this stuff I could do and never being able to show it."

Things finally changed in 1986 when Carvey was spotted at Igby's Comic Cabaret in Los Angeles by Lorne Michaels, the executive producer of *Saturday Night Live.* Michaels was out searching for new faces for the show and he quickly signed up Carvey to join the ensemble cast. Carvey was an almost instantaneous success and his Church Lady sketches quickly gained fans. The skits had the Church Lady as the host of a Christian talk show, *Church Chat*, who drew laughs by questioning such guest celebrities as Dennis Hopper and Willie Nelson about their love lives. She became famous for commenting, "Well, isn't that *special*?" in a very mocking and preachy tone. Soon people across America were repeating that phrase to one another.

Carvey was so adept at imitating Bush that he was invited to spend a night at the White House, where he slept in the Lincoln bedroom. "He kissed my wife good night right in front of his bedroom," Carvey would recall. "Said: *'Nighty-night. Gonna hit the hay here.'* I go: 'Hey, what are you talking about man? We come all the way out here, and you just *leave?'*"

After a few seasons, Carvey cut back on the Church Lady skits so that he could introduce other characters. Perhaps the most successful of his new "characters" was then-president George Bush, who Carvey imitated to perfection. Other popular characters included Hans, who together with Franz, "pumped themselves up"; Ching Change, an immigrant who becomes attached to the chickens he sells; Derrick ("Choppin' Broccoli") Stevens, a has-been rocker; and Lyle, the effeminate heterosexual.

In 1990 Carvey starred in the film *Opportunity Knocks.* He played Eddie Farrell, a fey con artist, who is reformed after meeting a nice Chicago businessman and falling in love with the man's daughter. The movie was a huge disaster, and even now Carvey cringes when he remembers it. Carvey's wife, Paula, recalled that period in *Rolling Stone*: "[Dana] gets upset only when he's doing something that he'll be embarrassed by. At that point, he'd been doing such great stuff on *SNL,* and suddenly this movie was everything he was afraid of it being. He was just devastated by it."

Wayne's World *is released*

Carvey's reputation was redeemed by the 1992 blockbuster *Wayne's World.* In *Wayne's World,* Wayne (Mike Myers) and Garth (Carvey) trade their freewheeling public-access cable show in Aurora, Illinois, for a chance at the big time at a local Chicago station. They quickly discover that making it big means having to do on-air interviews with their profit-hungry sponsor, which they broadcast from a high-tech studio built to look like Wayne's basement. Wayne also suffers when the show's producer tries to steal his new girlfriend. The duo escape and return to their real basement, where cable is king.

Wayne's World was filmed in 12 weeks on a shoestring budget of $13 million. In the first two months after its release, it earned more than $40 million and made stars of Carvey and Myers. Since they were both still

Carvey as *Wayne's World*'s Garth Algar at the *1992 MTV Video Music Awards*, August 9, 1992.

regular cast members of *Saturday Night Live,* they were required to shoot the movie on a tight schedule so they could be back in time for the season opener in September 1991. The film eventually earned $170 million worldwide. Carvey offered an explanation for the film's popularity in *Rolling Stone*: "In crass technical terms, five-to-ten-year-old boys thought we were cool and needed to see us five to seven times each. We have fun, and we're losers—an equation that's been around forever."

Carvey modeled the character of Garth on his brother Brad, a shy computer genius.

Wayne's World 2 was released in late 1993. In this film, Wayne and Garth have moved out of the basement and now share an apartment they call their "babe lair." After being visited by the ghost of Jim Morrison (the lead singer of the 1960s legendary rock group The Doors), Wayne tries to stage a rock concert. Despite a thin plot and mediocre reviews, this sequel enjoyed moderate success. According to Richard Corliss of *Time*, "On the Please-O-Meter, *WW2* scores high."

Leaves SNL

After seven years as a cast member of *Saturday Night Live*, Carvey left the show. He had received four Emmy nominations during his tenure. He told *Rolling Stone*: "This is an end of an era for me. I know that my time on *Saturday Night Live* is over. Although I'm not closing the door entirely—I may go back and do occasional sketches. But clearly I don't see myself ever being a full-time cast member again. I had my run, and it's time to move on."

In the spring of 1994, the movie *Clean Slate* hit the theaters. In the film, Carvey plays a detective who loses his memory every time he goes to sleep. His next project is *The Road to Wellville*, in which he stars with Anthony Hopkins. And there's currently talk of a full-length feature musical, *Hans and Franz: The Girly Man Dilemma*, based on characters created on *Saturday Night Live*. Carvey hopes that the film will costar famous bodybuilder and actor Arnold Schwarzenegger.

Sources

Entertainment Weekly, July 9, 1994.

Los Angeles Magazine, May 1994.

People, December 20, 1993; May 23, 1994.

Rolling Stone, October 22, 1987; September 3, 1992; May 13, 1993.

Time, December 20, 1993.

Cher

Born May 20, 1946
El Centro, California

*"You're a bimbo; you're a great actress.
Cher to me is just me. There are parts of
my life I have to keep working on. But a lot
of it I'm enjoying. It's real comfortable and
it works for me."*

ACTRESS AND SINGER

Cher has been an integral part of American pop culture for nearly three decades. At times she has been seen as a campy joke and at other times as a serious artist. She first gained fame as a teenager in the mid-1960s as half of the singing duo Sonny and Cher. In the 1970s Sonny Bono and Cher, who were married in 1964, took their act to television, hosting a variety show on and off for six years. After the couple divorced, Cher developed a career as a nightclub entertainer on her own and in the early 1980s concentrated on acting, a lifelong ambition. Earning critical acclaim for several of her film portrayals, she won an Academy Award in 1988 for her starring role in *Moonstruck*. The prominence Cher gained as an actress also helped to rejuvenate her singing career, and she released several successful albums in the late 1980s and early 1990s.

Cher was born Cherilyn Sarkisian on May 20, 1946, in El Centro, California. The daughter of John and Georgia Holt Sarkisian, Cher claims ancestry that is part Armenian and part Cherokee. Her mother, who had worked as a fashion model and a country and blues singer, married eight times, including three separate times to Cher's father. Her mother's other husbands included Gilbert LaPiere, a bank manager who briefly became Cher's stepfather and was the father of her half sister, Georgeanne LaPiere.

Growing up in the San Fernando Valley, Cher was alternately fierce and shy and liked to sing around the house with her mother and sister. She later recalled in the *New York Times* that she "grew up poor," noting as well in *Film Comment* that she "went to school with rubber bands wrapped around my shoes to keep the soles on." The young Cher, who suffered from dyslexia (a disease that impairs the ability to read), also displayed a rebellious streak. Her mother remarked in *Newsweek*, "I was always being called into the principal's office about something she was doing." Her most outrageous move, however, had nothing to do with school.

Meets Sonny

Salvatore "Sonny" Bono was a 27-year-old would-be record promoter when Cher met him. "I was 16 years old ... and he really took care of me," she remembered in *Film Comment*. "I was real sick when I met him; I'd had hepatitis for a long time. I was floundering. I'd moved out; I thought I could take care of myself. I couldn't." Bono cut an exotic figure with his leather pants and pageboy haircut, and Cher's family was horrified when she announced that she had plans to marry him. She dropped out of high school in eleventh grade and began spending time at a record studio where Sonny worked. Both she and Sonny periodically filled in as back-up vocalists on records being made. On October 27, 1964, when Cher was 18 and Sonny was 29, the couple eloped to Tijuana, Mexico.

Cher and Sonny began appearing in small nightclubs, calling their act "Caesar and Cleo." They soon dropped the fake names and landed a job as "Sonny and Cher," opening for the Righteous Brothers and earning $25 a show. In early 1965 the couple borrowed $168 and recorded a song Sonny had written, "Baby Don't Go." When the single enjoyed modest success in Los Angeles, they released a second record titled "Just You." The couple finally hit it big in June 1965 with "I Got You, Babe," a record that eventually sold four million copies. Their careers as pop singers were underway.

Sonny and Cher became famous as icons of the mid-1960s as much as musical artists. Onstage, they wore outrageous unisex fashions that included hip-hugging bell-bottoms, loosely knit tops, and fur vests. They stood for youthful rebellion against authority, playing their music too loud and getting thrown out of restaurants for being inappropriately dressed.

As the youth culture of the 1960s changed, however, this form of defiance soon seemed too tame. After all, Sonny and Cher were married, and they had even made an anti-marijuana film to be shown in high schools. What had previously seemed so hip began to be perceived as almost quaint. A writer for the *New York Times* noted, "There was something at the core of their act that was the kiss of death in the 60's entertainment world: they were essentially harmless."

A film made by Sonny and Cher called *Good Times*, in which they played themselves, bombed in 1967. Two years later, they released *Chastity*; Cher played the title character, a young runaway who searches for her identity. Written and produced by Sonny, the movie failed at the box office, and it was reported that the couple lost half a million dollars on the project. In the age of free love, "chastity" may not have been a ticket to success, but it did become the name of Sonny and Cher's only child, a daughter born in 1969.

Move to nightclub work

Realizing that their younger fans had fallen away, Sonny and Cher changed their focus and began to work as a nightclub act. To appeal to an older audience, the couple changed their look from hippie bohemian to a more upscale, slinky appearance, and Cher began sporting revealing, low-cut dresses. Although they began with a series of one-night engagements, by June 1970 they were playing the Waldorf-Astoria Hotel in New York City.

A new phase in the couple's career began in 1971, when Sonny and Cher gained exposure on television. One such appearance found them acting as guest hosts on the *Merv Griffin Show,* and their performance caught the eye of CBS executive Fred Silverman. Silverman hired the couple to do six one-hour variety shows. *The Sonny and Cher Comedy Hour* went on the air on Sunday, August 1, 1971, in the 8:30 p.m. slot. As it gained popularity, the show was given a permanent spot in the schedule and after December 1971, was slated for 10:00 p.m. on Monday nights.

The Sonny and Cher Comedy Hour featured comedy skits and songs and appealed to a surprisingly wide audience. Viewers young and old tuned in to see what outrageous outfit Cher would appear in that week. Her costumes for a single show, featuring skintight, sequin-covered dresses designed by Bob Mackie, could cost $10,000, and she became notorious for her exotic hairstyles. Improbably enough, Cher became a symbol of glamour. From 1972 to 1973, the show was moved to Friday nights and in its third year was aired on Wednesday nights.

During this time, Sonny and Cher also continued to release records, and Cher developed a solo recording career. Her hit songs during this time included "Half Breed," which dealt with the subject of her Native American heritage, and "Gypsys, Tramps, and Thieves." *This Is Cher, Foxy Lady,* and *Bittersweet White Light* were among the albums she released.

Sonny and Cher divorce

Sonny and Cher's television show came to an end with the 1973-74 season, after their personal relationship began to unravel. Sonny filed for a legal separation from Cher in February 1974, and by 1975 the marriage was over. For Cher, the split from Sonny would eventually provide an opportunity to be more independent. She later referred to Sonny in a *Newsweek* article as "a man who represents a time when I had no power over my life." In the immediate aftermath of the divorce, Cher found herself somewhat adrift, both personally and professionally. "When I left [Sonny]—I was with him from 16 to 27—I didn't have the skills that a person needed, really, to take care of themselves in any fashion, careerwise, any kind of way, you know.... I had to start from scratch and I made lots and lots of mistakes," she later told a *Film Comment* interviewer.

After the divorce, Sonny and Cher's television show was reincarnated without the male half of the duo in 1975. Called *Cher,* it ran for just one season. During that time, Cher became romantically involved with Gregg Allman, a musician who was a member of the Allman Brothers Band and addicted to heroin. In 1975 they got on a plane and eloped. Nine days later, Cher filed for divorce. "I believe it's best to admit one's mistakes as quickly as possible," she remarked in *Ms.*

When the ratings for Cher's solo television show slipped, Sonny and Cher got back together on a professional basis to do the *Sonny and Cher Show* on CBS for the 1976-77 season. Aired at 7:30 p.m. on Sunday nights, opposite the *Wonderful World of Disney,* the show featured its divorced stars holding hands and singing love songs, while Cher was pregnant with Allman's child. The baby, her second, was born in 1976; Cher named him Elijah. The following year she made her final concert appearances with Sonny.

After her television career had finally petered out, Cher turned back to music, forming a rock band in 1979 called Black Rose; they released an album of the same name the following year. She also became romantically involved with record producer David Geffen, who helped her put together a Las Vegas nightclub act—a throwback to her Sonny and Cher days playing lounges—that featured a further refinement of her professional persona. She became "a cartoon of herself ... a Tattoo Queen, Cher as a campy Egyptian Idol, Cher as a Vegas Indian Princess," wrote Stephanie Brush in the *New York Times*.

At the height of her Las Vegas career, Cher was the lead act at Caesar's Palace for 20 weeks a year. In the course of her show she changed costumes 11 times and slid down a 20-foot high slide shaped like a high-heeled shoe. She was paid $350,000 a week. "Staying in Vegas was very easy because there was so much money involved, and you didn't need a brain to do the work.... I made a huge gross," she admitted in *Film Comment*, "but I needed a whole bunch of people around me onstage because I really didn't like what I was doing."

Focuses on acting

Convinced that she would die a lounge singer if she stayed in Las Vegas, never having fulfilled her lifelong ambition to be an actress, Cher gave up her lucrative nightclub career to try acting. This move played havoc with her finances—"she was broke, and at one point I had to loan her money to get her through," reported ex-boyfriend David Geffen in *Newsweek*. Cher, long interested in exercise, began making television commercials for a chain of health clubs, Health and Tennis Corporation of America, to pay the rent. Her risk finally paid off when she landed a role in a play in New York City in 1982. She played Sissy, a small-town siren embarrassed to confess that she's had a mastectomy, in the Broadway production of *Come Back to the Five and Dime, Jimmy Dean, Jimmy Dean*, earning $5,000 a week. She repeated the role in the film version of the play, which was directed by Robert Altman and released that same year.

On the basis of her solid work and respectable reviews in the Broadway production and film, director Mike Nichols tapped Cher to play a supporting role in *Silkwood*, his 1983 movie starring Meryl Streep. Cher portrayed the main character's lovelorn lesbian roommate and won an Oscar nomination for her performance. Despite critical acclaim, she waited two years before finding a starring role she felt enthusiastic about.

Mask, released in 1985, featured Cher as the mother of a boy with a severely disfiguring, ultimately fatal disease. Her character is a tough biker with a substance abuse problem who nonetheless loves her son and demonstrates compassion and strength as a mother. Cher's performance was critically praised and she was disappointed when she failed to receive an Oscar nomination for her work. She graphically displayed her unhappiness at this snub when she showed up for the Academy Awards ceremony that year dressed in a revealing, attention-getting black-widow outfit.

In addition to her acting and singing careers, Cher works on a number of different projects. She has marketed a perfume called Uninhibited and lent her name to a book on exercise and fitness, a collaboration with nutritionist Robert Haas. As a result of her work in the movie *Mask*, Cher has become interested in helping children with craniofacial deformities, and she works as a fundraiser for the Children's Craniofacial Association, serving as honorary chair of the charity's board.

This public statement was followed by a period of intense work, in which Cher appeared in three films released in 1987: an adaptation of a John Updike novel called *The Witches of Eastwick*; *Suspect*, a thriller featuring Cher as a Washington trial attorney; and *Moonstruck*. As a widowed Italian-American accountant in *Moonstruck*, Cher falls in love with the passionate brother of her fiancé. The role brought the actress a long-coveted Oscar for best actress as well as a Golden Globe Award.

Also in 1987 Cher returned to her musical roots with the release of her first record in five years, *Cher*. She was also reunited with ex-husband Sonny for an appearance on a late-night talk show, during which they sang "I Got You, Babe."

Cher released another record album in 1989, *Heart of Stone*, which yielded three gold singles and went multiplatinum, selling more than four million copies. In the last four months of the year, she acted in *Mermaids*, a film about an unorthodox mother and her relationship with her two daughters. The actress reportedly received $4 million for taking the role in the 1990 release, which received mixed reviews.

For the last few years Cher has been markedly absent from the movie industry due to a number of setbacks. She battled the chronic fatigue syndrome associated with the Epstein-Barr virus and her subsequent time off from the gym caused her to gain 25 pounds. In addition she broke up with longtime companion Rob Camilletti and her 1991 album *Love Hurts* was a failure. Much of her time was spent making lucrative hair and skincare infomercials—a practice she recently gave up on the advice of her reps at Creative Artists Agency. "I've sold my soul, in a way," she told Ryan Murphy in *McCall's*. "What I've done is nothing to be ashamed of, but I just don't want to be a businesswoman who does infomercials anymore. It doesn't feel good anymore." She also added that, "It's good to go into hibernation, because the lights are too hot, being in the public eye. I needed to cool down. I needed to come in and get close to myself.... Now I'm learning how to pace myself."

What Cher does want is to get her acting career back on track, and it appears as though she has made great strides. She's scheduled to appear in *Faithful,* a comedy directed by Paul Mazursky that centers on a rich woman who falls in love with the man her husband contracts to kill her. She also has two movies in development: *Tabloid,* which concerns the friendship between a movie actress and a reporter; and *The Enchanted Cottage,* a remake of a 1945 film about two eccentrics who fall in love.

While a four-year absence would be deadly for many in the movie industry, Cher doesn't seem to be worried. According to Lois Smith, Cher's publicist, "The rules that apply to other people simply don't apply to Cher. She makes and breaks her own rules—and always has."

Sources

Film Comment, January/February 1988.

McCall's, May 14, 1994.

Ms., July 1988.

Newsweek, November 30, 1987.

New York Times, March 20, 1988; August 7, 1988; September 4, 1988.

People, March 18, 1985; January 25, 1988; June 19, 1989; January 21, 1991; December 23, 1991; February 14, 1994; May 23, 1994.

Eric Clapton

Born March 30, 1945
Ripley, England

"I'm very much a romanticist musically.
I prefer to be drawn into something by
the way it makes me feel emotionally.
It's not technique I listen for; it's content,
feeling, tone."

GUITARIST, SINGER, AND
SONGWRITER

I think I'm probably the 50th [best guitarist] if anything," Eric Clapton told *Rolling Stone.* If he's not the best, he certainly is the most modest. It would be hard to come up with 5, much less 49, better guitar players than Clapton, especially when dealing with the blues. "Yes, that's what I do best. That is really my personal style," he said in *The Guitar Player Book.* From the Yardbirds to Cream, Blind Faith, Derek and the Dominos, and various back-up bands, Clapton has played styles as diverse as heavy metal, pop, sweet love songs, and even reggae. But, throughout a career that has spanned nearly 25 years, he has always remained true to his blues roots. "If I'm put into another ... kind of situation, I'd have to fly blind," he told Dan Forte in *The Guitar.* "In the blues format I can just almost lose consciousness; it's like seeing in the dark."

Clapton was born in Ripley, England, on March 30, 1945. His mother left him to be raised by his grandparents, Rose and John Clapp, when he was a small child. He was brought up thinking they were his parents until his real mother returned home when he was nine years old. The family pretended that his mother was his sister, but he soon found out the truth from outside sources. "I went into a kind of ... shock which lasted through my teens, really," he said in *Musician*, "and started to turn me into the kind of person I am now ... fairly secretive, and insecure, and madly driven by the ability to impress people or be the best in certain areas."

Discovers blues

Around this time Clapton began hearing American blues musicians like Sonny Terry, Brownie McGhee, Muddy Waters, and Big Bill Broonzy. He was knocked out by the sound and took up the guitar trying to emulate them. Soon he discovered a few friends that were also into this mysterious music from the States and they formed their own clique. "For me, it was very serious, what I heard. And I began to realize that I could only listen to this music with people who were equally serious about it," he told *Rolling Stone's* Robert Palmer. "And, of course, then we had to be purists and seriously dislike other things."

The 17-year-old was soon playing folk blues in coffee houses, and in 1963 he joined his first band, the Roosters. They stayed together for only a few months before Clapton moved on to Casey Jones and the Engineers, which lasted an even shorter period. By then Clapton had begun to hear some of the electric blues that were coming into England, and he switched over from acoustic. "Hearing that Freddie King single ('I Love The Woman') was what started me on my path," he said in *Rolling Stone.*

Word began to spread around town about the hot new guitarist, and in late 1963 the Yardbirds asked Clapton to join their band, replacing Tony "Top" Topham. With the Rolling Stones' popularity verging on worldwide, the Yardbirds took over their spot as house band at the Craw Daddy Club in Richmond. The group specialized in performing rave-ups, driving music that starts low and steady, building to a driving climax before dying down and then repeating again. Clapton was developing his chops on the bluesier numbers and was also gaining a loyal following.

Band manager Giorgio Gomelsky nicknamed him "Slowhand" at this time in reference to his speedy playing and also as a pun on the slow hand clapping Clapton received whenever he broke a string on stage. The band was becoming anxious to cash in on the success of other British bands like the Beatles and decided to record more commercial material which Clapton was totally against. "Single sessions are terrible. I can't take them at all," he told *Rolling Stone*'s Jann Wenner. "No matter what the music is like, it's got to be commercial, it's got to have a hook line, you've got to have this and that and you just fall in a very dark hole."

Clapton's disgust during the "For Your Love" recording session, coupled with an embarrassing session with Sonny Boy Williamson (the bluesman said that Englishmen didn't know how to play authentic blues), prompted him to leave the Yardbirds in 1965. "For Your Love" became a hit for the band, as Clapton figured it would, and he was replaced by Jeff Beck, and later by Jimmy Page, whose style was more compatible with the band's.

Clapton worked with his grandfather for a time, doing construction work. A popular myth has Clapton locking himself in his room with nothing but his guitar for a year, but actually he went and stayed with his friend from the Roosters, Ben Palmer, for a month. "I was all screwed up about my playing," he said in *Rock 100*. "I realized that I wanted to be doing it for the rest of my life, so I'd better start doing it right." Clapton devoted his playing to pure blues, and by the end of 1965 John Mayall recognized the talent and asked him to join his Bluesbreakers. By then Clapton had formed his own style, which borrowed from the traditional masters, yet was easily recognized as something special.

"The boy had it all," Gene Santoro commented in *The Guitar.* " The characteristic hesitations and syncopations, the punching buildups toward chord changes, the lilting phrases punctuated by bent blues notes tumbling into abrupt finishes that accent the power and beauty of the line, the sure-fingered variety of attack, the breathtaking reaches up to the twelfth fret and beyond, the heavy sustain, the flawless timing—it must have been difficult to be a guitarist listening in the audience without being overwhelmed completely."

"Clapton is God"

Clapton was becoming much more than an underground hero. The blues revival of the 1960s was in full swing and the group's album debuting the 21-year-old sensation, *Bluesbreakers*, went all the way to number 6 on the English pop charts. The now-famous slogan "Clapton is God" began appearing on subway walls in England and guitarists everywhere were searching for the key to his magical sound. By 1966 Clapton was growing weary of the strict diet of Chicago-style blues the band was playing and decided to form a new band with former Bluesbreakers bass player Jack Bruce (Clapton was replaced by Peter Green and Mick Taylor, who went on to join Fleetwood Mac and the Rolling Stones, respectively).

Cream, the new band, also included virtuoso drummer Ginger Baker, whom Clapton originally thought "was just too good for me to play with, too jazzy," he said in *Rock 100*. Although the three improvised *a la jazz*, the sound was pure rock and blues, played in a manner which has become synonymous with today's heavy metal. As Charley Walters wrote, "The formula was easy and deceptively limiting: start off simply, explode into a lengthy free-for-all, and end as begun. The brilliant moment occasionally surfaced, but self-indulgence was the general rule." The group released four albums, which contained some live cuts in addition to the studio tracks. Clapton's guitar setup established the sound for future rock and rollers: "Two 100-watt Marshalls. I set them full on everything, full treble, full bass and full presence, same with the controls on the guitar," he said in *Rolling Stone*.

Amidst psychedelia in the arts and turmoil in the youth culture over the Vietnam War, Cream epitomized the times and rode a crest of success. While the fans just couldn't get enough guitar licks, critics like Jon Landau had had more than enough. Landau cited Clapton as the master of the blues cliché in one of his *Rolling Stone* reviews, and it struck home. "The ring of truth just knocked me backward; I was in a restaurant and I fainted," Clapton told Palmer. "And after I woke up, I immediately decided that that was the end of the band." Cream played their final performance at London's Albert Hall in November 1968.

A few months later, Clapton and Baker joined forces with Steve Winwood and Rick Grech to form the first super-group, Blind Faith. Amidst media hype and little rehearsal time, the group played their first gig: a free concert in front of 36,000 fans at Hyde Park in London. Their planned tour of the United States proved to be too much too soon and they broke up in January 1970 with only one album under their belts.

During the tour Clapton converted to Christianity, which was an unusual move at a time when most of his contemporaries were exploring Eastern religions. He was unhappy with the adulation Blind Faith received, feeling that it was unwarranted. He felt the opening act, Delaney and Bonnie & Friends, were playing the type of music he could relate to, so he joined them. Delaney pushed Clapton to develop his singing and writing skills during his stint as a sideman with them. In 1970 he released his first solo album, *Eric Clapton*, with the help of Delaney and Bonnie and their band. Afterwards, Carl Radle and Bobby Whitlock asked Delaney for a raise and he fired them.

Clapton seized the opportunity and picked them up for his own band, Derek and the Dominos, adding Jim Gordon on drums. Clapton befriended Allman Brothers guitarist Duane Allman while recording in Florida and the guitarist was asked to play with Clapton's band. The collaboration had an enormous impact on Clapton's style, and the twin guitars produced some of the finest music in rock and roll. "I think what really got me interested in it (slide guitar) as an electric approach was seeing Duane take it to another place," he told Forte. "No one was opening it up until Duane showed up and played it a completely different way. That sort of made me think about taking it up."

Clapton formed the Dominos and wrote new songs as a way of reaching a certain woman he yearned for, ex-Beatle George Harrison's wife, Patti. The song he wrote for her, "Layla," is "perhaps the most powerful and beautiful song of the Seventies," according to *Rolling Stone*'s Dave Marsh. Patti stuck by her husband, though, causing Clapton to lose his faith and to start on a path of self-destruction. The Dominos were already heavily into drugs, which eventually caused their breakup, but Clapton was now using heroin as a means of easing his emotional pains. "Not Patti herself, as a person, but an image, she was my excuse. That was the catalyst ... a very big part of it," he told Ray Coleman in *Clapton!* "It was a symbol, my perfect reason for embarking on this road which would lead me to the bottom."

The addiction forced Clapton to take a three-year break after his stint with the Dominos, performing only at the 1971 benefit for Bangladesh concert and at the 1973 Rainbow Concert (arranged by Pete Townshend of the Who as a means to get Clapton back into circulation). He eventually underwent electroacupuncture treatment successfully and spent some time on a farm in Wales relaxing and working.

After his recovery, Clapton stated in *Rolling Stone* that "the thing about being a musician is that it's a hard life and I know that the minute I get on the road I'm going to be doing all kinds of crazy stuff. It's just that kind of life." Manager Robert Stigwood booked Clapton into a Miami studio for the recording of his comeback LP, *461 Ocean Blvd.* One of his finest to date, it includes "I Shot the Sheriff" and "Mainline Florida," two tunes that Clapton still performs in concert.

Marries inspiration for "Layla"

Clapton eventually won Patti Boyd-Harrison and the two were married in 1979. He wrote one of his most requested and popular songs, "Wonderful Tonight," for her and it appeared on his *Slowhand* album. Clapton has continued releasing solo albums and playing on other artists' records. His fans still cry out "Clapton is God" at his concerts and they're still waiting for him to cut loose on his guitar like he did with Cream, but he refuses to revert back to that style. Another reason Clapton plays less guitar is fear. "I lost confidence because I thought I'd done it all.... That's why I didn't play as much lead guitar on those albums in the Seventies. I was very, very nervous that I'd said it all," he told *Rolling Stone*.

He has also done work in films, appearing in Ken Russell's *Tommy* and the movie *Water*. He also scored *Lethal Weapon* and the British television series *Edge of Darkness*. In 1983 three former artists from the Yardbirds—Clapton, Beck, and Page—were reunited at the ARMS benefit concert for musician Ronnie Lane. His 1986 tour to promote *August* featured Phil Collins on drums and a four-piece band, his smallest since the 1960s.

Personal tragedy

Clapton and Patti were divorced in 1988 after Clapton fathered a son, Conor, by Italian actress Lori Del Santos. On March 20, 1991, tragedy struck when Conor fell to his death from a 53-story window. "I turned to stone," Clapton recalled in *People*. "And then I just went off the edge of the world for a while." As a way to deal with his grief, Clapton began writing songs for Conor. The culmination of this work, the song "Tears in Heaven," was the greatest critical and popular triumph of Clapton's career. The song became the cornerstone for Clapton's 1992 blockbuster album, *Unplugged*, which won six Grammy awards in 1993.

Continuing his recovery, Clapton next released an all-blues album, *From the Cradle*, a collection of songs written by Freddie King, Willie Dixon, and some of Clapton's other heroes. *From the Cradle* became the first blues album to reach Number One on the Billboard pop chart, and critics liked it as well. "Clapton seems to have an open channel between his guitar and his inner feelings," Neil Strauss wrote of the record's emotion in the *New York Times*. Said Clapton's friend Terry O'Neill, "[Conor's death] would send most people over the edge, but Eric has gathered strength from it. Since Conor's death, he seems a lot more into life."

Sources

Coleman, Ray, *Clapton!*, Warner Books, 1985.

Dalton, David, and Lenny Kaye, *Rock 100*, Grossett & Dunlap, 1977.

Detroit Free Press, April 19, 1987.

Down Beat, March 1987.

Evans, Tom, and Mary Anne Evans, *Guitars: Music, History, Construction, and Players From the Renaissance to Rock,* Facts on File, 1977.

Guitar Player, July 1980; December 1981; January 1984; July 1985; January 1987; December 1987; July 1988; August 1988.

The Guitar Player Book, Grove Press, 1979.

Guitar World, September 1983; March 1985; January 1986; March 1987; April 1987; June 1988; January 1989.

Kozinn, Allan, and Pete Welding, Dan Forte, and Gene Santoro, *The Guitar,* Quill, 1984.

Logan, Nick, and Bob Woffinden, *The Illustrated Encyclopedia of Rock,* Harmony Books, 1977.

Musician, November 1986.

New York Times, October 2, 1994.

People, March 1, 1993.

Rolling Stone, June 20, 1985; August 25, 1988; April 29, 1993.

The Rolling Stone Interviews, St. Martin's Press/*Rolling Stone* Press, 1981.

The Rolling Stone Record Guide, edited by Dave Marsh and Jon Swenson, Random House/*Rolling Stone* Press, 1979.

Shapiro, Harry, *Slowhand,* Proteus, 1984.

What's That Sound?, edited by Ben Fong-Torres, Anchor Press. 1976.

Sean Connery

Born August 24, 1930
Edinburgh, Scotland

Connery is "the closest thing we now have to Clark Gable, an old-time movie star. Everyone knows him and likes him. It's shocking—every age group, men and women. There's something very likable about him on screen."
—*Vincent Patrick*

ACTOR

From humble beginnings as a school dropout, Sean Connery became a major movie star at the age of 32 when he was cast as the sophisticated secret agent James Bond. An unlikely candidate to play Ian Fleming's snobbish 007, Connery became so well known as this character that he nearly didn't break out of the mold. Despite his many years of work on the stage and screen, Connery was still being thought of as "the guy who played James Bond" into the early 1980s. But throughout his career, the stubborn Scot has taken on movie roles that interested him, regardless of how they fit his image. As a result of this shrewd thinking, he now has quite an impressive list of roles in his repertoire and critics talk more about his exceptional acting ability than his inability to break out of a role. With over 50 movies to his credit, Connery has become one of the world's most prominent movie stars.

Born in a tenement

Connery began his life in the humblest of surroundings. He was the eldest of two sons, born in an Edinburgh, Scotland, tenement. During World War II, when he was 13, he dropped out of school to help support his family. "The war was on, so my whole education was a wipeout," Connery reminisced in *Rolling Stone*. "I had no qualifications at all for a job, and unemployment has always been very high in Scotland, anyway, so you take what you get. I was a milkman, laborer, steel bender, cement mixer—virtually anything." After several years of this, Connery decided to better his lot and he joined the British Royal Navy. He received a medical discharge three years later, when he came down with a case of stomach ulcers.

Returning to Edinburgh, Connery began to lift weights and develop his physique. He became a lifeguard and even modeled for an art college. Then in 1953, the toned Connery traveled to London to compete in the Mr. Universe competition. This trip was to mean more to him than the third-place prize he won. While he was there, he heard about auditions for the musical *South Pacific*. He decided he wanted to try out, took a crash course in dancing and singing, and was cast for a role in the chorus.

This small part became a crucial turning point for Connery. At the time, he was teetering between wanting to be an actor and a professional soccer player. But actor Robert Henderson, who was also in *South Pacific*, encouraged him to consider a career in acting. Connery took Henderson's advice: as a soccer player, one is limited by age; a good actor could play challenging roles forever.

The unschooled Connery looked up to Henderson as a mentor. He commented in *Premiere* that "[Henderson] gave me a list of all these books I should read. I spent a year in every library in Britain and Ireland, Scotland and Wales.... I spent my days at the library and the evenings at the theater." He also went to matinees and talked to a lot of other actors, people he met over the year long touring run of *South Pacific*. "That's what opened me to a whole different look at things," said Connery. "It didn't give me any more intellectual qualifications, but it gave me a terrific sense of the importance of a lot of things I certainly would never have gotten in touch with." It is also where he picked up his stage name, Sean Connery. When asked how he wanted to be billed for the musical, he gave his full name, Thomas Sean Connery. After being told that was too long, he opted for Sean Connery, not knowing how long he was going to be an actor. The name stuck.

Begins to work in television and film

After *South Pacific*, Connery began broadening his horizons by working on the stage. He was also notable in his first television role, a British production of Rod Serling's drama *Requiem for a Heavyweight*. After garnering critical acclaim for this role, he received several film offers. In the years from 1955 to 1962, he made a string of B movies, including *Action of the Tiger* (1957). It was there he met Terence Young, who was to be the director of the Bond films. Young recalled in *Rolling Stone* that *Action of the Tiger* "was not a good picture. But Sean was impressive in it, and when it was all over, he came to me and said, in a very strong Scottish accent, 'Sir, am I going to be a success?' I said, 'Not after this picture, you're not. But,' I asked him, 'Can you swim?' He looked rather blank and said, yes, he could swim—what's that got to do with it? I said, 'Well, you'd better keep swimming until I can get you a proper job, and I'll make up for what I did this time.' And four years later, we came up with *Dr. No*." Connery was still doing B movies when he was called in to interview for *Dr. No*, the first James Bond film. But he had matured quite a bit as an actor and exuded a kind of crude animal force, which Young compared to a young Kirk Douglas or Burt Lancaster. Producer Harry Saltzman commented in the *Saturday Evening Post*: "We spoke to him and saw that he had the masculinity the part needed. Whenever he wanted to make a point, he'd bang his fist on the table, the desk, or his thigh, and we knew this guy had something. When he left we watched him from the window as he walked down the street, and we all said, 'He's got it.' We signed him without a screen test."

Dr. No was an instant success, propelling the little-known Connery into fame and sex-symbol status virtually overnight, a situation that the serious-minded and very private Connery did not like. Equally distressing to him was the way the media handled his transition into the role. He commented in *Rolling Stone*: "I'd been an actor since I was twenty-five but the image the press put out was that I just fell into this tuxedo and started mixing vodka martinis. And, of course, it was nothin' like that at all. I'd done television, theater, a whole slew of things. But it was more dramatic to present me as someone who had just stepped in off the street."

Connery also performed many of his own stunts in *Dr. No*. He has continued this practice in many of his movies because it often speeds up the production. One of the stunts in *Dr. No* almost killed him. They had rehearsed a scene where he drives his convertible under a crane. At a slow speed, his head cleared by a few inches. When they actually shot the scene, the car was going 50 m.p.h., bouncing up and down. Luckily for Connery, the car hit the last bounce before he went under the crane and he emerged unhurt.

In 1962 Connery married his first wife, Diane Cilento. She was also an actress, having played the part of Molly in the movie *Tom Jones*. Apparently their relationship was loving, yet stormy. Connery's friend Michael Caine reported in *Rolling Stone*: "I remember once I was with them in Nassau. Diane was cooking lunch, and Sean and I went out. Of course, we got out and one thing led to another, you know, and we got back for lunch two hours later. Well, we opened the door and Sean said, 'Darling, we're home'—and all the food she'd cooked came flying through the air at us. I remember the two of us standin' there, covered in gravy and green beans." The couple divorced in 1974 and their only son, Jason, is now a movie actor.

Between 1962 and 1967, Connery made five James Bond movies—*Dr. No, From Russia with Love, Goldfinger* (which was, at that time, the fastest moneymaker in movie history, netting more than $10 million in its first few months), *Thunderball*, and *You Only Live Twice*. He was tiring of the gruelling pace of producing a new feature every year, and of the constant publicity and invasion of privacy. During the filming of *Thunderball* Connery was working long days and doing press interviews at night. He was also arguing with the Bond movies' producer, Albert (Cubby) Broccoli, because he wanted to slow the pace of the series, completing a feature every 18 months instead of each year. He threatened to cut out of the contract after completing *You Only Live Twice,* and agreed to accept a salary that was lower than normal in exchange for the slower pace.

Says goodbye to Bond films

But the nation was Bond-crazy and the films were a goldmine. Connery agreed to star in *Diamonds Are Forever* in 1971, demanding a salary of $1.25 million, plus a percentage. At that time, it was an unprecedented sum of money for such a role. After completing the film, Connery said "never again" to Bond roles, and donated all of his salary to the Scottish International Education Trust, an organization he'd founded to assist young Scots in obtaining an education. (This is not the only example of Connery's generosity to charities. In 1987 he donated 50,000 British pounds to the National Youth Theatre in England after reading an article on the failing institution.)

After his split with Broccoli, he continued to pursue a variety of movie roles with his main concern being that he find them interesting. He would also do films if he felt his help was needed. He reportedly offered to be in *Time Bandits* for a very modest salary because he heard the producer was running into financial difficulties. With a few exceptions, however, most of the films Connery did in the decade following *Diamonds Are Forever* were not noteworthy.

Reprises the Bond role

Then, in the early 1980s, a strange thing happened. At the age of 53, Connery was asked to reprise the role he had made famous in *Never Say Never Again*. The movie rights to this film had been won in a long court battle by Kevin McClory, an enterprising Irishman whom Connery admired a great deal for being able to beat the system. The movie was also scheduled to go head-to-head with *Octopussy*, a Broccoli Bond epic featuring the new 007, Roger Moore. It seems that twist was too much to resist and Connery signed up. Another possibility is that Connery's second wife, Micheline Roquebrune, whom he had met on the golf course in Morocco in 1970, convinced him to give the role another try.

Connery drew rave reviews as an aging Bond trying to get back in shape for a daring mission. "At fifty-three, he may just be reaching the peak of his career," reported Kurt Loder in *Rolling Stone*. "Connery reminds you anew what star quality is all about. A good deal of that quality is on display in *Never Say Never Again*, a carefully crafted and quite lively addition to the lately listless Bond series." Instead of furthering any Bond typecasting by doing this film, Connery seemed to squash it. In the years since, his performances seem to be getting better and better. In *The Untouchables*, Connery took the supporting role of Malone, a world-weary, but savvy, street cop. "It's a part that gives him ample opportunity to demonstrate his paradoxical acting abilities," wrote Benedict Nightingale in the *New York Times*, "his knack for being simultaneously rugged and gentle, cynical and innocent, hard and soft, tough and almost tender." For his portrayal of Malone, Connery won an Academy Award.

Connery was also very strong in *Indiana Jones and the Temple of Doom*, where he played the scholarly father of the ever-adventurous Jones, entangling himself in danger and intrigue. Peter Travers commented in *Rolling Stone* that "Connery, now fifty-eight, has been movie-star virility incarnate. Here in his scholar's tweeds, with an undisguised horror of creepy-crawly things ... and armed only with an umbrella and a fountain pen, Connery plays gloriously against type."

Similarly, in his most recent roles—a monk in *The Name of the Rose*, a deranged Russian submarine commander in *The Hunt for Red October*, a research scientist working in the rain forest in *Medicine Man,* the knowledgeable police detective in *Rising Sun*—Connery continues to prove his versatility and maturity as an actor.

Connery has worked hard throughout his career and taken professional risks with his roles. For these efforts, he has become a greatly respected actor, almost a legend in the screen world. Vincent Patrick commented that "You suddenly realize [Connery is] the closest thing we now have to Clark Gable, an old-time movie star. Everyone knows him and likes him. It's shocking—every age group, men and women. There's something very likable about him on screen." Yet, in spite of this, he remains a very conscientious worker, always trying to improve the movie he's in rather than sabotage others' performances to make himself look better. When asked whether he can now write his own ticket when he decides to star in a movie, he replied in *Premiere*: "I have enough power in terms of casting approval and director approval. But I don't think it's something someone can brandish like a sword. I sense myself as much more a responsible filmmaker in terms of what's good for the overall picture, and for the actors as well, because I have had all this experience, and I've seen a lot of waste."

Sources

American Film, May 1989.

Newsweek, June 8, 1987; May 29, 1989.

New York Times, November 12, 1965; June 7, 1987.

People, October 17, 1983.

Premiere, April 1990; August 1993.

Rolling Stone, October 27, 1983; June 15, 1989.

Time, November 1, 1982; August 2, 1993.

Vanity Fair, June 1993.

Bill Cosby

Born July 12, 1937
Philadelphia, Pennsylvania

"I'm trying to reach all the people. I want to play John Q. Public."

ACTOR, COMEDIAN, DIRECTOR, AND PRODUCER

When Bill Cosby made his television debut in 1965, he was the first black actor ever to play a lead role in an American television series. The television program was *I Spy*, in which Cosby and Robert Culp costarred as American secret agents. The civil rights movement of the 1960s was in full force, and Cosby's role in some ways legitimized the new role for blacks in America. Although his *I Spy* character was essentially serious, Cosby was a comedian by trade, and following the cancellation of the series he went back to comedy. In the late 1960s and 1970s, Cosby tried several comedy and variety television series with little success, although he did host a popular Saturday morning children's program entitled *Fat Albert and the Cosby Kids*, beginning in 1972. In 1984 Cosby appeared in yet another comedy series, but unlike his previous efforts, this one became highly successful. Entitled simply *The Cosby Show*, the program became the television ratings leader for the season, and remained the number one program for many years. Part of the huge appeal of Bill

Cosby can be traced to his de-emphasis of race. He did not tell racial jokes as a comedian, and his television program addressed real people and real problems, not racially stereotyped situations. Rising from a childhood of poverty in a Philadelphia ghetto, Cosby has risen above the imaginary boundaries of race to entertain millions of Americans in a humane and inevitably funny way.

Bill Cosby was born in an all-black ghetto area of north Philadelphia in 1937. He was the eldest of three sons. His father was a mess steward for the U.S. Navy, and his mother was a domestic worker. Cosby's mother read to her boys often, favoring passages from the works of Mark Twain. As a child, Cosby was an excellent athlete and a would-be comedian. He was also fascinated by salesmanship, and paid close attention to the way television advertising salesmen hawked products. In school he always did well on standardized tests which purported to measure intelligence, but his grades were poor. He was always trying to make people laugh, and neglected his studies. As a student at Germantown High School in Philadelphia, he was captain of both the track team and the football team. Unfortunately, Cosby's grades were so poor that he failed the tenth grade and, rather than repeat the grade, he dropped out of school and joined the navy.

During his four years in the navy, Cosby was assigned to both land and sea duty at various times, and earned a high school diploma through correspondence courses. After he left the navy, he entered Temple University in Philadelphia on a track scholarship. While at Temple, he majored in physical education and played on the track and football teams. To earn money, Cosby substituted as a comedian at nightclubs and cafes. After his junior year at Temple he quit college to pursue a full-time career as a comedian.

Cast in I Spy

Cosby's early career as a comedian was similar to the careers of many other young comics, except in the types of jokes he told. He performed in clubs around the country, sharing the stage with the likes of Woody Allen, but his humor was a gentle middle-class American humor. He did not tell racial or sexual jokes, but rather concentrated on everyday situations in familiar family contexts. In 1965 he got his big break during an appearance on the *Tonight Show*. He was spotted by producer Sheldon Leonard, and offered a part in Leonard's new television series *I Spy*, which would involve the adventures of two globetrotting American secret agents travelling under the guise of a tennis pro and his trainer. Although the program was a drama the scripts allowed the humor of both Cosby and his costar, Robert Culp, to come through. The dry humor accounted for much of the program's popularity.

Cosby's casting in *I Spy* was the first time a black person had been cast in a starring role in a television series. Although Cosby offered a positive image of a black man defending America's interests, rather than a stereotypical cartoon-like caricature, he was criticized by some of the more militant members of the black movement of the 1960s as portraying a character who was too bland and unrepresentative of American blacks. Cosby's response was that *I Spy* was not a series about the problems of blacks in America, and that the portrayal of a black as a human being without regard to race was what made the program effective. For his role, Cosby received three consecutive Emmy awards as the outstanding actor in a dramatic series. In fact, the show was so popular that in 1994 Cosby reprised his role in the TV movie *I Spy Returns*.

After the cancellation of *I Spy* in 1968, Cosby tried another series beginning in 1969. Entitled *The Bill Cosby Show,* the program was about a physical education teacher at a Los Angeles high school. The high school was in a lower-middle-class neighborhood, and the program concerned the relationships of Cosby's character with students, family, and fellow teachers. Although it achieved high ratings during its first season, it went downhill during its second season and was canceled.

At the same time that he was starring on television, Cosby was performing live at Las Vegas clubs and making comedy records. *Life* magazine reported in 1969 that Cosby had sold more records than any other entertainer except Herb Alpert, and that his comedy concerts netted Cosby about $50,000 per show. By the time he was in his early thirties, Cosby was a millionaire several times over.

In 1972 Cosby began another television series, a Saturday morning program for children. Entitled *Fat Albert and the Cosby Kids,* the cartoon show featured characters based on real-life people from Cosby's childhood. In 1984 the program was still a Saturday morning staple on NBC television. Cosby also began to make a few feature films during the 1970s. His first, in 1972, was *Hickey and Boggs,* in which Cosby was reunited with his old companion from *I Spy,* Robert Culp. Other films followed through the years, including *Uptown Saturday Night, Mother, Jugs, and Speed* and *Leonard Part VI.* Cosby also stayed in the public eye with a seemingly endless number of commercials. Many of his commercials for products such as Jell-O pudding, Coca-Cola, and Kodak film are classics, and his long-running contracts promoting the same products attest to his mastery of salesmanship.

Earns Ph.D. in education

During this time, Cosby also became interested in pursuing higher education, so he enrolled in a part-time doctoral program in education at the University of Massachusetts at Amherst. Despite the fact that he did not even have a bachelor's degree, in 1977 he received a doctoral degree in education. He was later criticized by at least one member of his doctoral committee, however, who said that Cosby attended no classes to receive the degree and received credit for life experiences, including his guest appearances on television programs such as *Sesame Street* and *The Electric Company*. Another professor, however, later defended Cosby's performance.

Cosby appeared in two other television series during the 1970s, but they were unsuccessful. Both were variety programs featuring Cosby and guests and lasted only one season. In 1984 Cosby approached the major television networks about yet another series. This one was to take place in New York City, and was to be about a family similar to Cosby's real-life family. Only NBC, the perennially third-rated network, was willing to take a chance on the new program.

Entitled *The Cosby Show,* the program premiered in September 1984. It was about the Huxtable family, and was centered in a townhouse in New York City. Cliff Huxtable (Cosby), an obstetrician, and his wife Claire (Phylicia Rashad), an attorney, had five children, four girls and one boy (just like the real-life Cosby family). The program became the television ratings surprise of the season. It not only was the most watched program among all the networks, it achieved audience levels not reached by network programming for many years. An estimated 60 million Americans tuned in for *The Cosby Show* each week. The program remained extremely popular for several years, proving that it had the substance to be more than just a passing fad. The show was the number one rated program every year through 1989, and maintained a solid audience share until it ended in 1992.

The success of *The Cosby Show* was a reflection of the gentle, humane humor of Bill Cosby. The program avoided sexual and racial humor at all costs, and tried simply to present the trials and joys of a family in America. Some critics complained that the program was a very unrealistic model for American blacks in general, but Cosby responded with his usual reply: he was trying to reach all the people of the world, not just blacks. The values reflected in the program were human values, and were intended to speak to human beings without regard to race.

Reaps Large Profits from *The Cosby Show*

The huge success of *The Cosby Show* provided even greater financial rewards for Bill Cosby. Syndication rights for the program set monetary records in the initial sale to local stations (for reruns), and may eventually reach one billion dollars. Cosby owns one-third of those rights.

The success of Bill Cosby can be traced not only to hard work and dedication, but to his unique vision of the values of humor and of what is funny. Rather than play to people's insecurities and fears, Cosby has always joked about the joys of life. His emphasis on family values and everyday situations which are encountered by everyone have made Cosby unusual, if not unique, among American comedians. His grand successes in books, records, concerts, and television have shown that his humor does indeed reach all the people.

Sources

Cosby, Bill, *Fatherhood,* Doubleday, 1986.

Cosby, Bill, *Time Flies,* Doubleday, 1987.

Ebony, May 1964.

Haskins, James, *Bill Cosby: America's Most Famous Father,* Walker & Co., 1988.

Jet, May 4, 1992; February 7, 1994.

Life, April 11, 1969.

Newsweek, June 17, 1963; May 20, 1968; September 2, 1985.

Saturday Evening Post, April 1968.

Time, September 28, 1987.

Kevin Costner

Born January 18, 1955
Compton, California

ACTOR AND DIRECTOR

S trong, silent, and sexy, actor Kevin Costner emerged as one of Hollywood's most
sought-after actors in the late 1980s. After his
success playing the lead in *The Untouchables,*
No Way Out, and *Bull Durham,* Costner was
described as a throwback to actors of an earlier era, "the heir to the legacy of Gary Cooper
and Henry Fonda," wrote the *New York Times.*
"Hollywood's new romantic leading man,"
wrote *Time* magazine. "The new James Stewart," wrote the *Chicago Tribune*'s Gene Siskel,
"an Eagle scout with umpteen merit badges."
Costner himself is bemused by all the compar-
isons. Although Cooper and Stewart are his
acting heroes, he does not see himself as a star.
"You want to see a movie star, go talk to Sean
Connery or Robert De Niro or Gene Hackman," he told the *Los Angeles Times.* "I'm not a
movie star. I'm an actor."

Costner is "as all-American as Jimmy Stewart and Henry Fonda, and he's the first star in many years to be compared to Gary Cooper. Like Cooper, Costner radiates a lethal combination of sensitivity and masculine resolve most women find impossible to resist."—Leo Janos

Decides to become actor

The decision to be an actor came relatively late to Costner. He grew up planning to become a professional athlete. Later, he went to college with the idea of becoming a businessman. Only after trying out for a few community theater productions did Costner realize his true ambition. "I was trying to sort out what acting meant to me," he told the *New York Times*. "I come from a pretty practical background, so I kept asking myself, "Is this just a way of getting out of being something?" I didn't know if I was running from my own shadow. But there was something very real going on. With acting, I was on fire."

Costner grew up in middle-class southern California. His family moved frequently, making him the perennial new kid who attended four high schools. "I was always on the outside," he told *Time*. "I didn't feel 'there' until the end of the year, and then we'd move again." Although he was just 5'2" in high school (he is now 6'1"), Costner found his niche in sports, lettering in football, basketball, and baseball. He sang in the church choir, participated in musicals, and wrote poetry. He later majored in marketing at California State University at Fullerton, but spent his first three years, he admitted, basically drinking beer and partying. While at school, he met his future wife, Cindy Silva, a former Disneyland Snow White. (The couple divorced in 1994.)

In his senior year, Costner decided that pushing other people's products wasn't for him. He auditioned for college plays, landed a few roles, and changed his perspective. "I always knew I was performance-oriented, I just never listened to who I was," Costner told the *New York Daily News*. "This was the first time I made a real decision about anything. And I thank God it happened." The tug between acting and a business career lasted until after he graduated from college and took a job in marketing. He lasted 30 days before telling off the company's biggest account and quitting the job. Then he discovered the South Coast Actor's Co-Op and began appearing in community theater productions such as *Waiting for Lefty* and *A View From the Bridge*.

Pays his dues

Costner was not an overnight sensation. He appeared in a forgettable flick, *Sizzle Beach*, and then spent years learning the ropes while being rejected for parts. When he was rebuffed by casting directors, he told the Fort Lauderdale *News and Sun-Sentinel*, "I'd walk out of their offices with my fingers in my ears so I wouldn't have to hear someone who didn't know as much as I did telling me what to do." Costner had a three-year shift as stage manager of the Raleigh Studios, where he would wait for everyone to go home so he could experiment with the equipment. He worked at another studio sweeping trash. "I made a promise to myself that I wasn't going to be a bartender and I wasn't going to sell shoes while seeking acting jobs," he told the *News and Sun-Sentinel.* "I was going to work close to the industry, where the action was. If I was going to push trash, it was going to be movie trash."

Among Costner's hobbies are basketball, running, skiing, fishing, canoeing, hunting, swimming, volleyball, golf, and baseball.

His movie debut in *Frances* was supposed to be a significant part. In the end, however, all but one line got cut out. He then had bit parts in *Night Shift* and *Table for Five* before delivering an impressive performance, as a young father whose baby daughter dies, in the PBS movie *Testament.* Costner won his first leading role in the 1984 film *Fandango,* playing a fraternity hell-raiser in crumpled tuxedo and shades. But his big break was expected to come later that year, when he was cast as the suicidal Alex in Lawrence Kasdan's *The Big Chill.* Indeed, Costner turned down the lead in John Badham's *War Games* to appear in Kasdan's movie. In the end, however, all of Costner's scenes were cut from *The Big Chill.* He appeared only as a corpse in the opening scene. "It doesn't matter [that the part was cut]," he told the *Atlanta Constitution.* "I knew I was with the right circle of people. I had a pretty healthy idea of why I was in acting, and it wasn't for the reviews or the fact that I was in a $100 million hit. It bothered me a little bit because when the film was going around, you had this feeling, 'Hey, I was there—really I was there!' But now it's in my soul, and I know why it happened to me."

Kasdan made amends by casting Costner as the rip-roaring gunslinger Jake in the so-called yuppie western *Silverado.* It was not a big role, but Costner nearly stole the show from stars Kevin Kline and Scott Glenn. He says he took great joy in the role and improvised a good deal. "I played that role for every boy or girl who ever wanted to get on a horse and play cowboys," he told the *Washington Post.* The performance opened new doors for Costner. But while he appeared as a bicycle racer in the box-office flop *American Flyers* in 1985, he gained more fame turning down several roles in promising films. Costner said he did not want to be involved in movies that reminded him of those he had seen before during his career. He turned down the leads in *Big, Jagged Edge, Midnight Run,* and *Mississippi Burning.* "I'd like the kind of movies I do to be benchmarks for their genre," he told the *New York Daily News.* "That's my goal for the next ten years. What's the point of doing something if it's not original? I have a very strong point of view about films. I don't think there is a point I can't make in movies." That kind of attitude is rare in Hollywood. Producer Anson Mount told the *Atlanta Constitution* that Costner "is a man with some values. He's a man who doesn't act like a movie star. We haven't seen that around these parts since Gary Cooper. He's a real guy."

Discusses on-screen heroes

Cooper, Spencer Tracy, and Henry Fonda remain Costner's on-screen heroes. "Those early movie stars taught me what it was like to be a man," he told the *New York Times*. "They taught me the kind of man I'd really like to be. You learn a lot from watching heroes act. Henry Fonda once said, 'I've played enough great men in my life that I felt like I learned something from them.'" In his next role, Costner got to play one of the strong, silent heroes that Fonda and Cooper made famous. In *The Untouchables*, a stylish 1987 remake of Robert Stack's old television series, Costner was cast as supercop Eliot Ness. This Ness was a teetotaler who saved babies in runaway carriages with one hand and tossed gangsters from buildings with the other. And Costner played Ness as a tender father who gives his daughter an Eskimo bedtime kiss.

He received mixed reviews for the role. Some critics commended his restrained performance while others faulted him for a hollow, colorless portrayal of the famed Chicago fed. "I knew going in what people's problems would be with my character," Costner told the *Los Angeles Times*. "The reason I did *Untouchables* was that I thought the movie had a chance to be a fresh, original movie. The notion that a traditional American hero doesn't have all the answers and asks for help confuses us. We'd rather have Rambo who kills a hundred people for us and does all our thinking for us. It bothers us to watch a movie where the guy who is supposed to be in charge doesn't know what's going on. It wasn't the most charismatic role, and that's unusual for a lead in a movie."

The Untouchables established Costner as a solid leading man, a role he called "just a description," in the *Atlanta Constitution*. "I realize that just my physical features are going to dictate that I'm the guy in the middle going down the movie. So, I'm the lead. It's not as if they're looking for me to play the Elephant Man. I'm going to play kind of a circle of characters that aren't going to be too far removed from each other." In his next movie, the 1987 political thriller *No Way Out*, Costner played a Soviet double agent. It was his first romantic lead. Wrote *Los Angeles Times* critic Sheila Benson, "*No Way Out*'s greatest prize is Costner, a leading man at last: fiercely good, intelligent, appreciatively sensual in a performance balanced perfectly between action and introspection."

Viewed as a sex symbol

Costner's steamy love scenes with actress Sean Young in *No Way Out* had women in the audience looking at him in a different light. "My sex symbol status is not an easy thing for my wife to look at objectively," Costner told the *Houston Post.* "We hadn't orchestrated a sex symbol kind of thing. I'm not surprised I get paired with women, although for a long time I resisted it. But I don't want to hide from it now. My physical specifications dictate that I'm going to play that kind of role." His character of Commander Tom Farrell in *No Way Out* was "an easier guy to relate to than Eliot Ness," Costner told the *Philadelphia Daily News.* "Eliot was a harder role for me because I knew the problems that would come after the movie and people's interpretation of that role. Tom Farrell was a more complicated role for me to play because of the things he hid as a character in terms of his personal life. Always during a scene, I usually had mountains of notes to make sure I was concealing those things at all times."

Works on developing characters

Taking notes to develop his character is one of Costner's techniques. Another is to develop his character through dreams. "I dream all the time when I'm working," he told the *Chicago Tribune.* "It's not a technique or anything. It's just that I know actors are always thinking at the end of the day what they might have done in a given scene. And to my mind if you can think of it after you've been shooting, you can also think of it before. It's all concentration. I can't control what I dream about, but instead of thinking about what's going to be served for lunch tomorrow, I try to think about certain things pertaining to the day's scenes."

Costner's next film gave him his third consecutive box-office hit. *Bull Durham,* co-starring Susan Sarandon, featured Costner as Crash Davis, a minor-league catcher nearing the end of his career." For once, Costner has a role that he can sink into, that fits his skills, and he shows enormous authority and charm," wrote a *Washington Post* reviewer. "Physically, it's a marvelous incarnation: He swings well (from both sides of the plate) and even has a good home run trot. He's totally in his jock character's body, and with this one performance, he emerges as a true star presence." Costner said his own strong background in athletics helped make *Bull Durham* a success. "I think a problem in sports movies in certain instances is that the people portraying the athletes don't really look like athletes," he told the *Atlanta Constitution.* "I knew I would be able to fulfill that obligation."

His next film, 1989's *Field of Dreams,* was also about baseball—the tale of a young farmer obsessed by the legend of Chicago White Sox center-fielder Shoeless Joe Jackson, based on W. P. Kinsella's novel *Shoeless Joe.* Wrote the *Boston Globe*'s Jay Carr: "The movie succeeds. One reason is that it isn't afraid to take a few big swings. Another is Costner, in every facial expression and every flicker of body language. This one moves with a measured tread into a realm of enchantment and renewal, its warm energies anchored by Costner's rootedness and convincing ability to project in a dozen subtle ways the reactions of a man who loves his wife and kids deeply." Costner told the *Chicago Tribune*: "I think movies that can be great always run the risk of being bad movies. This is a very [heartwarming] film, which means it can be schmaltzy or, if you pull it off right, it will endure. It could be our generation's *It's a Wonderful Life.*"

While Costner broke his string of box-offices smashes with *Revenge* (1990), he more than made up for it with his directorial debut, *Dances with Wolves* (1990). The movie concerns an Army officer (Costner) who befriends the Sioux Indians—and is ultimately adopted by them. Praised for its historical accuracy, the movie marked the first time that Native Americans were portrayed as fully realized human beings who were essentially swindled out of their land. The movie was an overwhelming success and won seven Academy awards.

It appears that Costner's success will follow him well into the 1990s. In his most recent roles—the legendary title character in *Robin Hood: Prince of Thieves,* the controversial New Orleans district attorney Jim Garrison in *JFK,* the security officer who falls in love with a superstar in *The Bodyguard,* the escaped criminal in *A Perfect World*—Costner continues to prove his flexibility and capability as an actor.

In the summer of 1994 Costner returned to the Western format with *Wyatt Earp.* Directed by Lawrence Kasdan, the movie focuses on the human side of Wyatt Earp as he maintains law and order in Tombstone, Arizona, during the late 1800s. "In retrospect, everything I've done looks like good career moves," Costner told the *New York Daily News.* "But the moves I make are simply about what I like in movies. My agenda is nothing but the movie. When I'm acting I leave a window open for creativity, but I still like to be very open about what I'm thinking about. I try to get so in control that then I get out of control when I act."

Sources

Atlanta Constitution, June 24, 1988.

Boston Globe, April 21, 1989.

Charlotte Observer, April 29, 1988.

Chicago Tribune, April 16, 1989.

Cosmopolitan, March 1992.

Houston Post, June 12, 1988.

Los Angeles Times, August 19, 1987; April 21, 1989.

Mademoiselle, May 1994.

Morning Call (Allentown, Pa.), August 16, 1987; June 17, 1988.

News and Sun-Sentinel (Fort Lauderdale, Fla.), June 12, 1987.

New York Daily News, April 20, 1989.

New York Times, April 23, 1989.

Orlando Sentinel, August 21, 1987.

People, December 26, 1988; December 6, 1993.

Philadelphia Daily News, August 18, 1987.

Rolling Stone, July 14, 1988.

Teen, January 1992.

Time, September 7, 1987; April 24, 1989; November 29, 1993.

Washington Post, August 14, 1987; June 15, 1988.

Tom Cruise

Born July 3, 1962
Syracuse, New York

Cruise has "a straight-ahead, clean-cut sexiness, a presence both modest and strong."—David Ansen

ACTOR

Tom Cruise began his screen career as just another pretty face among the so-called "brat pack" of aspiring young actors in the 1980s. However, while fellow brat pack actors have sometimes been forgotten, Cruise's reputation as an actor has substantially increased throughout his career.

Discovers acting after pulling some muscles

According to Cruise, the decision to become an actor came by accident in his senior year of high school. In order to lose weight for an upcoming wrestling tournament, he was running up and down stairs in his home when he slipped on some homework papers one of his sisters had left behind. He fell, pulled several muscles, and was sidelined for the season. "It was a mess," Cruise told *Seventeen* magazine. "I had to be on crutches, and I was crushed because I couldn't wrestle that season. To cheer me up, a teacher suggested, 'Look, go out for *Guys and Dolls,* the school musical.' That's when I discovered acting." Cruise sensed immediately that performing could satisfy a long-buried need for self-expression. "It just felt right," he told *People* of his first experience on the stage. "It felt like I had a way to express myself." He also told *Cosmopolitan* magazine, "I just remember feeling so at home on stage, so relaxed." Wrestling and the many other sports at which Cruise excelled were forgotten as he embarked on a more satisfying undertaking.

The only son in a family of four, Cruise was born in Syracuse, New York. His father was an electrical engineer, whose work necessitated moving frequently. Before he was 11, Cruise had lived in Kentucky, Missouri, Ohio, Canada, New Jersey, and New York. Cruise told *Seventeen* that the constant mobility caused him to feel "kind of scattered" growing up. He tried to ensure popularity by excelling in athletics, explaining in *People*: "I would pick up a new sport as a way to make friends. I'd go up and say, 'Do you play tennis? Do you want to play sometime?'"

Cruise's childhood was further complicated by dyslexia, a reading disability he shares with his mother and sisters. He first became aware of the problem, he told *Seventeen,* when he was in kindergarten. "I didn't know whether letters like "C" or "D" curved to the right or left. That affects everything you do." That difficulty compounded his struggle for acceptance at each new school. "I was put in remedial reading classes," he recalled to *People*. "When you're a new kid, all you want to do is blend in with everything and make friends. It was a drag. It separated you and singled you out." Patient tutoring by his mother, however, helped him to surmount the problem, and his achievement has helped him to form a philosophy that has carried over into his acting career. He told *Seventeen*: "Right now my dyslexia no longer affects me, but it did influence my life, because growing up, I've always had to overcome something. It's as if God has given you this great mind and then holds you back, saying, 'Ah, but you're going to have to work for this.' I'm a very driven person in that I set goals for myself—goals to prevent myself from quitting."

Cruise's parents divorced when he was 11, but the family continued to move frequently until he was in high school. Finally settling in Glen Ridge, New Jersey, Cruise completed his schooling there and began to learn not to stereotype himself and others. "I was a jock, and I sang in the chorus," he told *Seventeen*. "Jocks don't do that, so I always felt challenged. I always tried not to fall into the mold, not to judge people by where they came from or what they were."

Looks for work in New York

After graduating, Cruise had no desire to go to college. Instead, he moved to New York and supported himself by doing odd jobs—including busing tables and loading trucks—while attending open calls for stage and film roles. His first part was a small one, a few lines in the movie *Endless Love,* starring Brooke Shields and Martin Hewitt. The scene took one day to film, but Cruise made an impression on director Franco Zeffirelli, leading to three years of virtually nonstop work.

The next role Cruise received was more substantial. He was cast as an unstable cadet in the film *Taps,* starring Timothy Hutton. The movie concerns a group of students at a military academy who decide to "defend" their school when it is scheduled to be razed in favor of a condominium development. The cadets commandeer weapons and produce a dangerous standoff with the real military troops just beyond the academy walls. As part of his preparation for the role, Cruise gained 15 pounds by swigging milkshakes. "The character had to make a visual impact," he explained in *Seventeen,* "because he wasn't in that many scenes." Though still new in the acting business, Cruise was able to persuade director Harold Becker to add a scene that showed his gung-ho character lifting weights. Though small, the role Cruise created was intense and memorable, and offers for more films followed.

Afraid of being typecast as a "crazy," Cruise took a starring role in the comedy *Losin' It.* The film, described in *Seventeen* as "tasteless," was a box-office failure. The story concerns a group of California teenagers who journey to the Mexican border for an evening of revelry. En route to Tijuana, the boys pick up a hitchhiker (played by Shelley Long) who eventually forms a romantic relationship with Cruise's character. *Losin' It* has run numerous times on cable television, to Cruise's embarrassment. Filming the comedy, he recalled in *Seventeen,* was "the most depressing experience of my life. I won't take any more films like that. But it was an eye-opener. It made me understand how you really have to be careful about what you do. You may feel you can make a script into something good, but you've got to examine all the elements of a project. Who's directing? Who's producing? I've learned to evaluate what everyone has to say before making up my own mind."

Cruise next signed on for a supporting role in the *The Outsiders,* an artful film based on an S. E. Hinton novel of the same title. Once again determined to sculpt himself properly for the part, Cruise had a cap removed from one of his front teeth and refused to shower for most of the nine weeks of shooting. Cruise, who has few lines in the *The Outsiders,* appears in the film as one of a gang of "greasers" who inhabit an Oklahoma town where class lines are drawn with violent force. The combined effect of this gang is described by Richard Corliss in a review for *Time* magazine: "The greasers, with their sleek muscles and androgynous faces, display a leonine athleticism as they move through dusty lots or do graceful, two-handed vaults over a chain-link fence. Their camaraderie is familial, embracing, unselfconsciously homoerotic." Cruise recalled the experience of filming *The Outsiders* in *Seventeen*: "I was nineteen and had an opportunity to work with [director] Francis Ford Coppola, and to act with guys like Matt Dillon and Rob Lowe and Emilio Estevez and have a good time."

Catapulted to stardom with Risky Business

Following *The Outsiders* was the 1983 summer release *Risky Business*, starring Cruise and Rebecca De Mornay. Called "this summer's one genuine sleeper" by *Newsweek's* David Ansen, the film was an immediate success, earning $56 million in its first 11 weeks. *Risky Business* catapulted both Cruise and De Mornay into stardom and earned Cruise his first serious critical attention. "Here he is, Superman in miniature," praised Richard Corliss of *Time,* comparing Cruise to *Superman* star Christopher Reeve: "the hooded eyes, the sculpted body, the offbeat comic timing, the self-deprecating manner, the winning smile, Cruise [is] a surprise package of 1983."

Risky Business charts the adventures of a high school senior (Cruise) who literally capitalizes on his parents' absence by turning their home into a one-night brothel for his friends. With the help of a shrewd prostitute, Lana (De Mornay), Joel, the young "Future Enterpriser," pairs his friends with those of the prostitute for fun and profit. Critics viewed Cruise's performance in *Risky Business* with mixed reactions. In her *New Yorker* review, Pauline Kael noted: "Imagining himself a rock star dancing, [Cruise] is a charmingly clunky dynamo. (At times, he's like a shorter Christopher Reeve, and the film seems to be raising the question 'Can nice boys be sexy?').... [But later in the film] Joel becomes an Example, and he loses whatever likability he had as a goofball kid; Cruise isn't allowed enough emotions to sustain the performance." The *National Review* critic said simply, "Tom Cruise is unremarkable as Joel." On the other hand, praise for Cruise's portrayal came from Lawrence O'Toole in *Maclean's*: "As the gullible, slightly dopey Joel, Tom Cruise gives a sunny performance, beaming with good nature." David Ansen echoed that sentiment in *Newsweek*, writing, "Joel, smartly and attractively played by Cruise, is very much a success-obsessed child of the '80s." And Paul Brickman, the director of *Risky Business,* described his satisfaction with Cruise's performance in *Seventeen*: "Tom had a good instinct for the truth of the character. To a certain extent, Tom is a spokesman for his generation."

Follows with All the Right Moves

If Cruise indeed served as a "spokesman for his generation" in a film that satirized wealth and get-rich-quick ideals, he must also have served as a spokesman for another segment of modern youth in *All the Right Moves,* his second starring role in 1983. In *All the Right Moves,* the principal character, Stef Djordjevic (Cruise), strives for a football scholarship that will allow him to escape the hopeless future in a Pennsylvania steel town. Stef's dreams appear about to be thwarted when he alienates his high school coach, who then tells recruiters Stef has a "bad attitude." Lawrence O'Toole praised the film in *Maclean's* as "a decent, modest movie, ... one of the first films to take a long, hard look at North America's current economic malaise."

Cruise again had a megahit with *Top Gun* in 1986. In the film Cruise plays an air force ace who is eager to serve his country with high-tech weaponry. Full of macho and military spectacle, the film was criticized as being a shallow examination of a U.S. military flight school. Cruise was required to do little beyond looking good in the sleek weaponry as he whizzes through the skies. Still, *Top Gun* became one of the most successful films of the decade, and established him as a top box-office draw.

Seeks respect as an actor

In subsequent years, Cruise has made a determined and successful effort to establish himself as a respected actor. He has continued to play in coming-of-age stories, usually as a young man in search of success who is taken in hand by a father figure. Coincidentally, in these films the actor has worked with a number of noted directors and critically validated older actors, whose presence have lifted his own professional standing. Paul Newman teaches him how to be successful in Martin Scorsese's *The Color of Money* (1986); Bryon Brown is the seasoned bartender Cruise emulates in *Cocktail* (1988); while Dustin Hoffman plays the autistic older brother who softens Cruise's hard-edged character in *Rain Man* (1988). (In the publicity for the Oscar-winning *Rain Man,* much was made of Hoffman's professional respect for his young counterpart.)

Cruise's transformation from a cocky, grinning 1980s pretty boy into a mature actor for the 1990s was completed in Oliver Stone's *Born on the Fourth of July* (1989). The film tells the true story of Ron Kovic, who goes off to Vietnam as an idealistic young patriot and returns as a physically paralyzed, emotionally embittered antiwar protester. Tom Cruise as an actor also underwent a transformation with this character. He was able to shed his all-American boyish charm and prove himself in an "unattractive" and difficult role, winning critical acclaim and his first Oscar nomination in the process. Interestingly, though, after the praise he returned to the familiar territory of the action film in *Days of Thunder* (1990), a racing-car drama that critics derided as "*Top Gun* on wheels." In *Chatelaine*, the reviewer noted: "In *Top Gun*, Tom flew for his country and exuded winsome loyalty. In *Thunder*, he's just racing for cash and looks like a commercial."

Marries Nicole Kidman

There was an added benefit to filming *Days of Thunder* for Cruise—that's where he first met and worked with his future wife, Nicole Kidman. It made headlines in 1987 when Cruise married actress Mimi Rogers, and headlines again when the two were divorced in January 1990. Apparently Cruise's fame was too much for Rogers to handle. She explained in *People* about the burden of being "Mrs. Tom Cruise": "You cease to become a singular individual. You're never again mentioned without that name. And that's hard." Apparently Kidman was willing to shoulder that responsibility, as she told *People:* "I knew it would be difficult for my career when we decided to get married. But I figured, God, you fall in love with somebody and get married once, properly. I want to be happy, and that's a big part of being happy." The two were married on Christmas Eve 1990. In August 1993, the couple adopted a baby girl whom they named Isabella Jane.

The couple's second film together, *Far and Away* (1992), was a box-office disappointment. The epic follows the lives of two Irish characters (Cruise and Kidman) who flee Ireland and attempt to make their way in late-nineteenth-century America. The two, who initially dislike each other, eventually realize they're in love. Despite the negative reviews and lower-than-expected attendance, the movie still made more than $100 million.

Back on top in 1993

Cruise quickly climbed back to the top in 1993 with the films *A Few Good Men* and *The Firm*. The former has Cruise playing Lieutenant Daniel Kaf-

When at home, both Tom and Nicole like to hang out in jeans and T-shirts and go to the movies. "I couldn't tell you the name of one posh restaurant," Kidman has said. "We don't have an entourage. My husband is my best pal. His company is enough for me."

fee, a young marine lawyer who is assigned to defend two marines accused of killing their platoon mate. Peter Travers of *Rolling Stone* praised Cruise's performance: "The part is a great fit for Cruise. He's a fireball, ... and unexpectedly touching when he lets Kaffee's insecurities shine through." In the latter film, Cruise plays a recent law school grad who accepts an offer from a Memphis law firm that is, indeed, too good to be true. After a few months on the job the young lawyer realizes his firm is in bed with the mob, and his attempt to get out from under provides this thriller with plenty of suspense. The movie was adapted from John Grisham's best-selling novel of the same name.

Controversy has surrounded Cruise's newest project, *Interview with the Vampire,* in which he plays the vampire Lestat. The movie is based on a series of books written by Ann Rice that have developed an almost cult-like following, and Rice's fans have been extremely vocal about the all-American Cruise playing the thin, sensuous vampire. Rice herself even joined in the outcry, calling the choice of Cruise "almost unimaginable" (though she changed her tune once she'd seen advance footage of the film). Critics liked it as well, praising Cruise's performance as the evil vampire. Cruise had told *People* that he was" terribly excited about playing Lestat. I have a lot to contribute to this character." Cruise's fans should agree

Sources

Chatelaine, September 1990.

Cosmopolitan, January 1984.

Esquire, March 1994.

Los Angeles Magazine, October 1993.

Maclean's, August 15, 1983, November 7, 1983.

Mademoiselle, April 1985.

Moviegoer, December 1985.

National Review, October 14, 1983.

New Republic, September 19-26, 1983.

Newsweek, August 15, 1983; November 7, 1983.

New Yorker, September 5, 1983; June 1, 1992.

People, September 5, 1983; March 5, 1984; June 8, 1992; December 14, 1992; July 12, 1993; November 8, 1993; May 9, 1994.

Rolling Stone, August 9, 1990; June 25, 1992; January 7, 1993.

Seventeen, February 1984; April 1985.

Sports Illustrated, November 14, 1983.

Teen, November 1982; December 1983.

Time, December 14, 1981; April 4, 1983; November 7, 1983; July 5, 1993; August 2, 1993.

Billy Crystal

Born March 14, 1947
Long Beach, New York

ACTOR AND COMEDIAN

"Billy's the single most gifted person I've ever worked with. He's a great actor, a writer of frightening ability, a talented filmmaker. What's remarkable is that at the core of all this is an enormous decency."
—Peter Hymans

Billy Crystal has won the hearts of movie-goers across the nation by combining sensitivity with humor when playing in such successful movies as *When Harry Met Sally* and *City Slickers*. His astonishing ability to improvise and play a wide array of unlikely characters helped make Crystal one of America's most popular comedic actors. Crystal, who always said he would rather play shortstop than Shakespeare, built a loyal following as the star of two network shows: ABC's *Soap*, from 1977 to 1981, and NBC's *Saturday Night Live*, from 1984 to 1985. It was on *SNL* that Crystal first gained widespread acclaim as a versatile mimic. His cast of characters included Sammy Davis, Jr., Herve Villechaize, and Fernando Lamas (whose oft-repeated line, "You look maaaaaavelous" was once an American catch-phrase).

Was babysat by Billie Holiday

Crystal was born into a show business family in 1947. His father, Jack Crystal, managed the famous Commodore Record Store on 42nd Street in New York City and started the Commodore jazz record label. By the time Billy was five years old, he knew some of the nation's top jazz artists, whom he described to *Playboy* as "great characters and funny.... I loved the fact that they made people feel good. I would run up on stage and tap dance with them. That's when I started performing." One of his friends was singer Billie Holiday, who frequently babysat for the young boy. "But it's not like my folks said, 'Billie, it's $3 an hour, there's food in the fridge and stay off the phone,'" he told *Sunday's People* magazine. "It's more like I hung out with her sometimes." Holiday and other musicians nicknamed the young boy "Face." Three decades later, Crystal's nightclub act would feature an aging trumpet player talking wistfully to a young boy named "Face."

From the start, Crystal was fascinated with show business. Growing up on Long Island, he recalls, he would watch the *Jack Paar* show, pulling his chair next to the television to play the sixth guest. His two boyhood heroes were comedian Ernie Kovacs and New York Yankee second baseman Bobby Richardson. Crystal's father died when he was 15. "That got me angry," he told *Playboy*. "It still does. You come to a point in life when you want to say, 'I'm doing good.' ... I miss being able to say that to my dad."

Crystal was captain of his high school baseball team and attended Marshall University on a baseball scholarship. He told *People* magazine that after one year at the school he decided, "Huntington, West Virginia was a little too-off Broadway," so he transferred to Nassau (Long Island) Community College. The transfer also marked the end of his dream of playing shortstop for a major league ball club. Crystal says his diminutive size (five-foot-six), rather than a lack of skills, prevented him from going further in the game. One year later, Crystal switched to New York University, where he studied directing with Martin Scorsese. He graduated in 1970 with a degree in television and film direction. That same year he married his wife, Janice, whom he had met at school. Her income as a guidance counselor, along with the small amount he brought in as a substitute teacher, kept the couple going as Crystal pursued an acting career. "I never made more than $4,200 a year back then," he later told *People*.

Crystal was house manager of an off-Broadway theater and then toured with an improvisational group, 3's Company. After several unsuccessful years, he met talent manager Jack Rollins, who convinced Crystal to try working on his own. "With 3's Company I was hiding from being by myself," he told the *New York Times*. "I wanted to be out there by myself. But I was frightened." Later, Crystal was performing solo at Los Angeles's Comedy Store nightclub in front of television producer Norman Lear and several ABC executives. It was "one of those strange Hollywood nights when everything clicked," Crystal told *People*. Lear hired him to appear on several episodes of the hit series *All in the Family,* and ABC gave him a guest spot on Howard Cosell's short-lived variety show.

Stars in Soap

In 1977 Lear chose Crystal to star in the comedy *Soap* as Jodie Dallas, the first openly homosexual character in the history of television. The role was assailed both by conservatives and the National Gay Task Force, which put Crystal on its enemies list, saying he advanced gay stereotypes. Eventually the character was toned down, and the gay-rights organization called him "the one sane, sensitive person on the whole show." *Soap* and Crystal proved extremely popular. The actor received "very graphic letters from fans. Women find Jodie very sexy. They think they could cure him in one night," he told *People*.

Crystal appreciated his newfound fame but considered his role limited and confining. "One character. Boring," he later told the *Detroit Free Press*. Among those watching *Soap* was comedienne Joan Rivers, who liked what she saw. Rivers cast Crystal in her film *Rabbit Test,* about the first man to become pregnant. The film was neither a critical nor financial success. On the first day of filming for *Rabbit Test,* Crystal's wife's own pregnancy test proved positive. The day of the film's screening, she delivered a baby. The couple now has two daughters, Jennifer and Lindsay.

In the early 1980s, Crystal starred briefly in his own comedy hour for NBC, made several cable television specials, and appeared as a guest on situation comedies, such as *Love Boat.* He also appeared in several television dramas, including NBC's critically acclaimed *Enola Gay: The Men, the Mission, the Atomic Bomb.* At that point, Crystal later told the *Columbus Dispatch,* he "felt the need to get back to live comedy before live audiences." He then started touring nightclubs and college campuses.

Creates Fernando Lamas character

One of Crystal's tours had him opening for entertainer Sammy Davis, Jr. "I used to talk with him and I would relate to people, things that Sammy said," he told the *Detroit Free Press*. Unconsciously, Crystal began to take on Davis's characteristics and the imitation became a popular part of his act. But his most famous imitation was of the late actor Fernando Lamas. "The whole thing got started when I was watching *The Tonight Show*, and Fernando Lamas was on," Crystal told *Playboy*. "I used to love him because he would say, 'You look marvelous, John.' ... He would just say it and that seemed to be the thrust of his in-depth conversation. And then one night ... Fernando said, 'I'd rather look good than feel good.' I got hysterical. I was running for a pad." Crystal's imitation of Lamas became part of his nightclub act. The character would star in a make-believe talk show, *Fernando's Hideaway*, where he pandered to guests as Crystal improvised. "Making it up as we go along is the key to its success," he told the *Washington Post*. "You can't put those things in a script. Improvisation is what makes it work."

Crystal and his characters joined the cast of NBC's long-running *Saturday Night Live* in 1984. In 1976 Crystal was to have been part of the show's original cast. But his only skit got bumped from the first show, and his role became limited to a few guest appearances. He decided to pursue other opportunities. Seven years later, Crystal guest-hosted an episode of *Saturday Night Live* that proved to be the most popular one of the season. Producer Dick Ebersol asked him to join the cast of *SNL* for the 1984-85 season. Crystal agreed, which proved to be a wise career move. Writing "99 percent of my own material," as he told *The Albany Capital Dispatch*, he emerged as the most popular performer on the show. His impersonations became regular skits, as did his portrayals of other zany characters: Willie, a masochist who frets about the pain of "stapling bologna to my face"; Rabbit, an old veteran of the Negro Baseball League; and an unnamed elderly, punch-drunk boxer, who once boasted of breaking his nose 77 times in one fight.

Crystal's character comedy is often compared to that of Lily Tomlin or Richard Pryor, two of his favorite performers. Said the *Los Angeles Times*, "Crystal, perhaps only like Tomlin and Pryor, can comedically move an audience." *Washington Post* critic Joe Sasfy said of a Crystal performance, "He impressively employed a range of surreal vocal effects, as well as some superb physical mimicry, ... an entertaining and fast-paced blend of topical humor, character sketches and ethnic impressions." Crystal considers his own work "bittersweet. Nobody else will take a chance on doing anything with poignancy," he told *People*. "I'm not that concerned with getting laughs. If I can move the audience, that's more important to me." His comedic model is Bill Cosby. "Like Cosby, I try to be honest out there," he told the *Albany Capital Dispatch*. "I just rap, just talk. It's real stuff. The jokes are there, but they don't scream 'joke, joke, here comes a joke.'"

Doing *Saturday Night Live* "helped eliminate ghosts in my own mind and of how people perceived me. It has taken the anvil of *Soap* off my chest," Crystal told the *Columbus Dispatch*. And, he said, the show gave him the opportunity to display his versatility. "This show for me has relieved great frustrations that I felt in that I've never had, week in and week out, the place to show people everything I can do.... It's been a wonderful year in many ways," he told the *Detroit Free Press*. But the show proved to be a grind. "Every show I go 15 rounds," he said to the *Detroit Free Press*. "It's 18-hour days." And, he told *Sunday's People* magazine, "It's 3 in the morning and I'm writing jokes.... No one else in the whole country is up doing this but us." In August 1985, Crystal was nominated for an Emmy Award for best individual performance in a variety or music program for his work on *Saturday Night Live*.

Leaves Saturday Night Live *for career in films*

In August 1985, Crystal left the *Saturday Night Live* cast. MGM chose him to costar with Gregory Hines in the movie *Running Scared,* a comedy about a pair of undercover Chicago policemen. Crystal refers to this film as his big break in the movies because it paved the way for the 1988 movies *Throw Momma from the Train* and *Memories of Me.* The former cast Crystal as a standard comic character, but the latter surprised critics and viewers alike by revealing Crystal's ability to captivate an audience with his portrayal of a bitter son. But Crystal's true breakthrough came with the 1989 movie *When Harry Met Sally.* Directed by his old friend Rob Reiner, *Harry* tells the story of two friends who stumble through a series of relationships with other people before they realize it is each other they love.

Crystal's next movie, the 1991 *Cityslickers,* was also a box-office smash. Crystal cowrote the script, which follows three middle-aged men who search for an answer to their respective mid-life crises on the western plains. As a fortieth birthday present for Mitch (Crystal), his two best friends take him on a fantasy trip where they can be "real" cowboys herding cattle. Along the way there is some male bonding, some comedy, some pathos, and an uplifting moral—love and family make life worthwhile. The film eventually grossed $130 million worldwide.

The 1992 *Mr. Saturday Night* was a terrible disappointment to Crystal. It was the first picture he wrote, directed, produced, and in which he starred. The title refers to the movie's main character, Buddy Young, Jr. (Crystal). Young is a Jewish comedian who found fame in the 1950s and 1960s, but then basically self-destructed by becoming so difficult and ornery that others refused to work with him. According to Margaret Carlson of *Los Angeles Magazine,* "Crystal set out to portray someone who embodied the idols of his youth—[the comedians] Milton Berle, Jack E. Leonard, Alan King—yet exuded the fear of failure that makes some comics do themselves in, onstage and personally, instead of waiting for life to do it for them." Neither critics nor fans found the premise appealing and the movie flopped; Crystal's acting, however, could not be faulted.

The 1994 sequel to *Cityslickers, Cityslickers II: The Legend of Curly's Gold,* was also something of a disappointment. Mitch was once again looking for adventure, only this time he and his two sidekicks were searching for lost treasure. The film was faulted for its lack of invention and tired story line. David Ansen of *Newsweek* wrote, "Crystal was more appealing in the first go-round; now that he's a born-again cowboy, a hint of smugness takes some of the fun out of him."

Crystal's next project will be the romantic comedy *Forget Paris.* In addition to his work in the movies, Crystal had an extremely successful run as host of the Academy Awards shows. From 1987 to 1993, Crystal infused impromptu humor and good will into the annual telecasts. When he is not working, Crystal likes to play tennis and baseball, cook Japanese food, and "collect miniature furniture. It gives me a great feeling of height," he told *People.*

Sources

Albany Capital Dispatch, May 9, 1985.

Christian Science Monitor, April 2, 1985.

Columbus Dispatch, July 8, 1985.

Cosmopolitan, October 1992.

Detroit Free Press, April 26, 1985; June 26, 1985; August 2, 1985.

Entertainment Weekly, June 17, 1994.

Los Angeles Magazine, September 1991.

Los Angeles Times, August 11, 1985.

Newsweek, June 27, 1994.

New York Times, August 1, 1976; September 5, 1979; February 5, 1982; April 7, 1985; June 9, 1985; August 6, 1985.

People, April 8, 1978; October 15, 1979; September 30, 1985; January 17, 1994.

Playboy, September 1985.

Sunday's People, June 30, 1985.

Washington Post, October 8, 1984; June 18, 1985; June 24, 1985.

Macaulay Culkin

Born in 1980

Macaulay Culkin "has captured a big youth audience along with an adult audience—a child star hasn't done that in many years, if not decades."
—Brian D. Johnson

ACTOR

M acaulay Culkin is one of the most well-known child actors in America. His blonde-banged, mischievous grin has beamed brightly from billboards, magazine covers, newspaper pages, and television screens. And he had good reason to smile, as the young star recently made an $8 million dollar deal with MGM Studios.

Big break with Home Alone

Being cast as Kevin McCallister in *Home Alone,* the youngster whose frazzled family forgets to take him along on a Christmas trip to Paris, was a lucky and timely break for Culkin. Baby Boomer movie fans who had searched for suitable family viewing found a gem in *Home Alone.* The 1990 sleeper hit outdid considerable holiday competition and earned more than $246 million at the box office. Many believe that Macaulay's talent and charm were responsible for luring fans back for second and third viewings.

As Kevin, Macaulay acts out every child's worst fear and biggest thrill: left alone in his family's spacious suburban home, he revels in the absence of parents and annoying siblings, ignores bedtime, watches TV all night, eats mountains of junk food, and freely explores previously off-limits areas. Comic reality sets in, however, when two bumbling burglars—played by Joe Pesci and Daniel Stern—target the McCallister home for a break-in. Feisty Kevin overcomes his fears in time to outwit the thieves in hilarious slapstick style; through a series of ingenious tricks employing toys and common household appliances, Kevin booby-traps his home. Then, satisfying sentimental audiences, he gives in to a bout of lonesome holiday blues just in time to welcome back his frantic family.

Writer-producer John Hughes wanted to do a movie that would appeal to all ages and received his inspiration while preparing to take his own family on a vacation. While making lists of things not to forget, he was struck by the funny thought that he'd better not forget his kids. He interrupted his packing to write pages of notes that later turned into *Home Alone*. Hughes suggested Culkin for the lead after watching the boy's standout performance as John Candy's precocious nephew in *Uncle Buck*. Director Chris Columbus auditioned more than 100 children before choosing Culkin. "Mack was very real and very honest. He seemed to be a real kid, one that you wouldn't be annoyed with if you had to spend two hours with," Columbus told *Time*. Still, the director was concerned that the then-nine-year-old would have trouble learning so much dialogue. Macaulay convinced Columbus by memorizing two scenes for his callback interview.

Hughes shared Columbus's anxiety over a youngster handling the lead in a $15-million film. In an interview with *Entertainment Weekly* he said, "The question was, could I get a 9-year-old to carry a whole film? The key is to get the real kid and not the actor kid who has a dialogue coach and parents reading him lines.... We really found that as a little kid, Mack's terrific. When he's jumping on a bed, he's not Kevin, he's Mack. He was having a great time in that scene. When we said, 'Okay, you have to stop now,' he said, 'Why?'" Hughes added, "Chris [Columbus] worked with him so well. He's sort of like a kid too." That may have been the reason Columbus and Culkin worked so well together; Culkin was impressed by Chris's habit of rocketing around the soundstage on roller skates, and since Columbus often directed scenes with his baby daughter in his arms, he tended to be sensitive to the behavior and needs of children.

Culkin admitted to *Entertainment Weekly* that he felt the pressure at times: "I had to do so many things at one time and I was like, 'Okay, what do I have to do first?' And I had to keep on doing lines over and over because I would keep on forgetting." Columbus countered with a system of rewards. "During rehearsals, we had a deal," he told *Entertainment Weekly*. "Mack could play Nintendo if he'd memorized his lines. He'd show up and go through the entire script in about 15 minutes.... Mack is such an intelligent kid and so far advanced, it's like working with an adult." David Friendly, producer of *My Girl*, Culkin's follow-up to *Home Alone*, told *People*: "He had more presence than any child actor I can remember since Shirley Temple." In the same interview Friendly did concede, however, that "he does have a mischievous streak. Every time [director] Howard Zieff would ask him to do something, he'd say, 'Director, may I?' But then at the end he went around and thanked everybody—a real professional."

Began career in The Nutcracker

Macaulay began his career at the age of four, appearing in off-Broadway shows. He danced the part of Fritz in *The Nutcracker* at New York City's Lincoln Center, was Burt Lancaster's favorite grandson in *Rocket Gibraltar*, and played Jeff Bridges and Farrah Fawcett's son in *See You in the Morning*. He learned to ride a two-wheeler for his role as Tim Robbins's son in *Jacob's Ladder*. His performance in *AfterSchool Special* at the Ensemble Studio Theatre was touted by the *New Yorker*, and he delighted audiences with his kitchen-table interrogation of John Candy in *Uncle Buck*.

It was the success of *Home Alone*, however, that set the stage for higher earnings and a more prominent public profile for Culkin. His next role was in the 1991 movie *My Girl*, in which he costarred with Dan Aykroyd and Jamie Lee Curtis. In this bittersweet film, Culkin befriends the motherless daughter of a small-town mortician. Despite her crush on her creative-writing teacher, the girl eventually finds a little romance with Culkin's character—and Culkin receives his first on-screen kiss. While the film begins as a gentle comedy, the death of Culkin's character turns it into a tear-jerker. Many parents felt deceived by the lighthearted coming attractions for the movie and vocalized their unhappiness at such a somber ending for a family film. Even with this controversy, *My Girl* performed remarkably well at the box office.

The long-awaited sequel to *Home Alone*, *Home Alone 2: Lost in New York*, was released in late 1992. The movie follows the same premise as the original, but instead of Culkin being left alone at home, he is lost in New York City where he is chased by the same two bumbling burglars who chased him in the first movie. While the critical reaction was lukewarm, families with children flocked to see Culkin perform the same antics that won him fame in the first *Home Alone*.

Culkin's next films were *The Good Son, Getting Even With Dad,* and *The Pagemaster.* Culkin abandoned his wholesome persona and played against type in the 1993 psychological thriller *The Good Son.* In the film, Culkin plays a violent and death-obsessed youth who torments and frightens his visiting cousin. In the 1994 *Getting Even With Dad,* Culkin plays a

Although Culkin has been getting up to $8 million per film, he generously donated his services to the Pierpont Morgan Library in New York City for free. The library had an exhibit about Antoine de Saint-Exupery—the author/aviator who wrote the children's classic *The Little Prince*—and Culkin narrated a 20-minute video to accompany the exhibit.

boy who traps his negligent father into being a Superdad for a week. Along the way the two form a genuine bond and realize their love for one another. *The Pagemaster* is a live action/animation adventure story about a ten-year-old who's afraid of everything. During a thunderstorm, Richard Tyler (Culkin) takes shelter in a library, where a painting filled with characters from classic novels and fantasies comes to life. When a fiery dragon chases Richard into another world, Richard must overcome his fears. All three films were met with mixed reviews.

Although it is difficult to predict the future of a child actor, industry observers believe Culkin has the ability to continue along the star track. "He could certainly continue acting if he doesn't get bored with it," Columbus told *Premiere.* "He was always really interested in the cameras and storyboards, so, who knows, maybe he'll be a director one day." Macaulay's reaction to all the fuss over whether he's enjoying his luminary status enough to continue to act is a matter-of-fact "pretty much so." While he considers his options, his bank account and legions of fans continue to grow.

Sources

Detroit Free Press, February 11, 1991; March 4, 1991; March 9, 1991.

Entertainment Weekly, December 7, 1990.

Maclean's, December 9, 1991.

Newsweek, September 4, 1989; December 3, 1990.

New York, November 30, 1992.

New Yorker, June 1, 1987.

·*New York Times,* November 16, 1990; December 10, 1990; January 7, 1991.

People, September 12, 1988; December 17, 1990; October 11, 1993.

Premiere, December 1990; April 1991.

Time, December 10, 1990; June 27, 1994.

USA Weekend, April 5-7, 1991.

Jacques d'Amboise

Born c. 1935

"When I was young, I was very much involved in the arts, and the teachers I had were the best people in the world. They influenced my whole life. I would like to introduce children to the arts the way I was introduced—by performing them, and performing them under the direction of the best people."

DANCER AND CHOREOGRAPHER

A principal dancer with the world-famous New York City Ballet for 32 years, Jacques d'Amboise considers his greatest achievement to be the creation of the National Dance Institute. Established in 1976, the Institute reaches over 1,000 students in 30 schools and teaches them to dance. All the students are drawn from the New York City area and many of the students are underprivileged, come from various ethnic backgrounds, and some even fight visual and hearing impairments. By challenging these kids to discover the art of dance, d'Amboise succeeds in reaching those who might otherwise have never had the opportunity to understand the pleasure and fulfillment of performing.

Grew up in tough neighborhood

D'Amboise grew up in Washington Heights—a part of Manhattan that borders Harlem and boasts zip guns, gangs, and crime. Most of his childhood friends became either policemen or criminals. Yet at his home, d'Amboise was exposed to high culture and the arts by his French-Canadian mother.

D'Amboise demonstrates a jump to his young students backstage at New York's Lincoln Center, October 30, 1965. D'Amboise at the time was a principal dancer of the New York City Ballet.

When Jacques was seven he accompanied his sister Ninette to her ballet class. Because he used to interrupt class by making noises, the ballet teacher challenged d'Amboise to perform a series of dance steps. Appar-

Both d'Amboise's parents were Catholic, his mother French-Canadian and his father an Irish-American native of Boston. Although his father's last name was Ahearn, his mother convinced her husband that her surname, d'Amboise, would sound more fitting for the children she was determined to see become professionals in the arts.

ently he had some talent and when he turned 12 he won a scholarship to the School of American Ballet. He began performing with the Ballet Society, which later evolved into the New York City Ballet. At 17 he was awarded major roles, and at 21 he had already performed in a number of Broadway and film productions including *Carousel, Seven Brides for Seven Brothers*, and *The Best Things in Life Are Free.*

Establishes the National Dance Institute

D'Amboise married a dancer who worked with him at NYCB and they have four children. It was when their son George was two and recently diagnosed with cancer of the nose that d'Amboise was initially inspired to work with children. The doctors told d'Amboise that George's illness would probably be fatal. D'Amboise recalled this painful episode in *Smithsonian:* "There was nothing they could do. I couldn't deal with him, seeing him in the crib with his nose all bloody in the hospital, so I went in the other room and started doing little games and telling [the children there] stories and dancing for them." His reception was enthusiastic and he realized then and there that he had a gift for working with children. D'Amboise's greatest discovery, however, came when his son made a complete recovery from the cancer.

In 1976 d'Amboise went to the head of his children's school and asked for space and a piano so that he might teach some students to dance. His initial objective was to help his sons and their friends understand that dance was far more than an activity in which only "sissies" would participate. From there the Institute was born and then continued to grow by leaps and bounds. His first performance was at the New York State Theater and showcased 80 children from four New York City public schools. The following year he hired additional teachers so that he could reach more students, in more schools, and the number of participants grew to 200. Soon thereafter d'Amboise coordinated 1,000 dancers from almost 30 schools and began the annual "Event of the Year"—a lavish production that is staged at Madison Square Garden and attracts both the publicity and revenues the Institute needs.

D'Amboise told *Publishers Weekly* that his aim is not necessarily to create performers, but rather to expose young people to the arts and "to open up their minds and hearts to possibilities of excellence." According to d'Amboise, children must learn that they can control their destiny. He

D'Amboise leads a Saturday morning rehearsal of dancers selected from classes he teaches at various New York City public schools, November 6, 1993. The children will participate in d'Amboise's "Event of the Year."

explains: "They discover that they can do their best by using their mind and their energy. They're not out of control, at the whim of fate. They can direct the story of their life.... [Children can learn to] make the best of the

David Fong, a school principal in the section of New York called Chinatown, has credited the National Dance Institute with encouraging kids to learn while keeping them out of gangs and away from drugs. As quoted in *Smithsonian*, Fong said that the Institute "allows the kids to express themselves physically and emotionally in a different way, and I think this extends to the classroom."

way things turn out—even adversity. That's what this program does. That's what the arts do."

The "Event of the Year"

Every September d'Amboise holds auditions and 30 students, aged 8 to 15, are chosen from nearly 30 schools. The children are picked not by virtue of their talent, but by their willingness to work. A sometimes clumsy child who sweats with determination will always be chosen over the graceful athlete who scoffs at or makes fun of the proceedings. Classes are held weekly in whatever space is available—auditoriums, gyms, cafeterias. D'Amboise visits all the schools and teaches ten classes each week. Individual instructors oversee each school's program and teach their students the part they'll dance in the "Event of the Year."

Each "Event" has its own theme, which d'Amboise chooses at the beginning of the year. He then creates a separate part for each school and, like the pieces of a puzzle, fits them all together before the annual performance. One year the theme was "China Dig," in which the dancers tunneled their way to China. Another time the dancers dressed as seagulls, fish, and rollercoasters for "A Day in the Life of Coney Island." Many of the performances have used international themes, with young people from China, Russia, Australia, and India traveling to New York to participate.

For his work with children and in education, d'Amboise has received a number of awards. In 1990 he won the MacArthur Foundation "genius" award and in 1991 he won the "As They Grow" award given by *Parents* magazine. In 1992 the children's book *I Feel Like Dancing* was published. Written by Stephan Barbosa, the book features the story of the National Dance Institute and Jacques d'Amboise. It also features photographs taken by d'Amboise's wife, Carolyn George d'Amboise. D'Amboise's enthusiasm and dedication to both his students and the arts is astounding. Each year witnesses greater shows and more student involvement. As quoted in *Smithsonian*, Governor Mario Cuomo of New York once said, "I think Mr. d'Amboise's secret ambition is to someday stage and direct a five-continent extravaganza starring the world's entire population with only the heavens for an audience."

Sources

d'Amboise, Jacques, Hope Cook, and Carolyn George, *Teaching the Magic of Dance*, New York, 1983.

Bremser, Martha. *International Dictionary of Ballet,* St. James Press, 1993.

Dance Magazine, May 1991.

Parents, March 1991.

Publishers Weekly, May 25, 1992.

Smithsonian, March 1990.

Bette Davis

Born April 5, 1908, Lowell, Massachusetts
Died October 6, 1989, Neuilly-sur Seine, France

Davis "lived her life ... with ferocious will and flamboyant originality."
—Brad Darrach

ACTRESS

Bette Davis was a legendary film actress best known for her portrayal of strong and often scheming characters. Her large and expressive round eyes, exaggerated mannerisms, distinctive voice and diction, and ever-present cigarette became her trademarks. She is credited with broadening the range of roles available to women and redefining the concept of beauty in Hollywood.

Born in a thunderstorm

Davis was born in 1908, in Lowell, Massachusetts, "between a clap of thunder and a streak of lightning," as her mother, Ruth Davis, liked to tell her. She spent the first eight years of her life in Lowell, until her parents divorce in 1916. According to Davis, her parents were constantly fighting throughout their marriage. Apparently Davis's father, Harlow Morrell, was only recently beginning his law practice when his wife became pregnant with Bette. Not wanting the financial burden of a baby, Morrell insisted that Ruth give young Bette away. When she refused, Morrell withdrew into himself and by the time a second daughter, Barbara, was born, he was resentful and cool toward his entire family.

After the inevitable divorce, Morrell was stingy with alimony and Ruth found herself financially strapped. She moved her family around New England as she searched for work as a cleaning lady. For a while she was able to enroll her daughters in a boarding school in the Berkshires, in New York. While there, young Bette played Santa Claus in the Christmas pageant, and when her beard caught on fire doctors were forced to remove the very top layer of her skin, thus giving her the celebrated Bette Davis paleness. Ruth eventually became successful as a photographer, and settled her family in Newton, Massachusetts. Davis studied for a time at the Newton High School and completed her education at Cushing Academy, in Ashburnham, Massachusetts.

While Davis had shown some interest in dramatics during her high school years, it was not until she graduated from Cushing that she began to pursue the theater in earnest. At 17 she auditioned for the famous actress and teacher Eva LeGallienne. But LeGallienne thought Davis frivolous, and advised her to choose another career. With Ruth's help, however, Davis ignored LeGallienne's advice and won a scholarship to the John Murray Anderson Dramatic school in New York City.

Makes professional debut

Davis made her professional debut as Hedvig in Henrik Ibsen's *The Wild Duck*. She received excellent reviews, and soon won roles in the Broadway productions of *Broken Dishes* and *Solid South*. Armed with these Broadway successes, Davis went to Hollywood to film some screen tests. Because of her unconventional looks, which included huge eyes, a sharp nose, and a scrawny frame, her tests were met with dismay by studio executives. Sam Goldwyn of the MGM studio was said to have gasped, "Who did this to me?"

Nevertheless, Davis signed a contract with Warner Bros., where she worked for 17 years. While there she became America's most influential female star. Because of Davis, the working-class heroine became not an occasional feature of American film, but the role model by which the women of the 1930s could measure themselves. Above all Davis exhibited resilience and resourcefulness, taking nothing for granted and accepting no statement without its due degree of skepticism. She typified the kind of woman we now think of as a mid-century standard: tough, ambitious, competent, yet vulnerable, retaining her femininity even as she competed with men. Both in films and in her dealings with the studios she controlled her environment and the people in it to achieve her ends, always demonstrating her strength and independence.

During the 1930s Davis made a dozen minor pictures which established her as a fighter and a survivor, a distinct contrast to the other female stars then at Warner Bros: in *Three on a Match* Ann Dovark is the socialite who comes to a bad end, Joan Blondell is the showgirl who rises in her place, and Davis plays the stenographer who is simply lucky to be alive at the end. Davis would always survive. She may suffer as Spencer Tracy's self-sacrificing mistress in *20,000 Years in Sing Sing,* but it is Tracy who goes gallantly to the electric chair for the crime she committed in an attempt to save him. And in *Dangerous,* the melodrama for which Davis won her first Oscar, Franchot Tone willingly toys with destruction to rescue her, however embittered and suicidal she might be.

Dramatic range increases

The Davis technique of those days—brave lifts of the chin, a measured seductiveness in the use of forearms and hands—conformed exactly to the calculation and vulnerability that were her identifying traits. As her range of roles expanded, her technique and style also developed until by 1939 she could play with conviction a queen in *The Private Lives of Elizabeth and Essex.* Davis made three films with William Wyler, a director with a painstakingly precise style who changed what had become mere mannerisms into new and adaptable techniques. According to *People,* "Wyler sculpted her style, taught her to moderate her excesses and vary her intensity."

In *Jezebel,* Warner Bros. hurried answer to the threatening success of *Gone with the Wind,* Davis schemed and sacrificed with a potent sensuality. As an emotionally cold murderess in *The Letter,* she captures husband Herbert Marshall in a net as intricate as the lace she wears around her face. And in *The Little Foxes,* as ruthless, self-regarding Regina Giddens, she shows a precisely perfected seductive skill. The final confession of *The Letter,* "I still love the man I killed," and the moment in *The Little Foxes* where she withholds from her husband the medicine that will prevent his heart attack, are insights into a type of character almost unknown in American movies of the time.

The 1940s sharpened Davis's film instinct for survival. Warner typecast her as the woman who was always abandoned or betrayed, nobly swallowing her medicine. Since her type of character usually lived on inherited money, or relied on someone stronger for support, she was usually driven to spite. Her female friends in *Old Acquaintance,* a twin sister in *A Stolen Life,* an ingratiating protégé in *All About Eve*—all of these women let her down. Nor

did men understand her; or, if they did, their wives did not. Lovers or employers exploited her in *The Man Who Came to Dinner,* in *Beyond the Forest,* and in *Now Voyager.*

Davis entered her forties with *All About Eve* and began a new career in character roles. These roles were usually sensational. The grotesques she played in *The Anniversary* and *Whatever Happened to Baby Jane?* exploited the physical decline of a woman who did not age well. She turned, then, to television and made a series of made-for-TV movies and guest-starred on nighttime series.

Troubled marriages

Davis's personal life was as stormy as her professional life. She was first married in 1932 to Harmon (Ham) Oscar Nelson, Jr. The two had met while at school. Although Nelson worked as a club musician, he brought home far less in salary than Davis. This frustrated him to the point where he became abusive to her. Davis, in turn, sought comfort in a number of extramarital affairs. Her paramours included the director William Wyler and multimillionaire Howard Hughes. After her divorce from Nelson in 1938, Davis married Arthur Farnsworth—an aircraft engineer who died in 1943. In 1945 Davis met and married an ex-Marine and landscape artist named William Grant Sherry. With him she had a daughter, Barbara (B.D.). In her 1982 memoir, *This n' That,* Davis described her marriage to Sherry as being filled with physical abuse. The two were divorced in 1950, and that same year she married her costar from *All About Eve,* Gary Merrill. The couple adopted two children, Margot and Michael, and Davis attempted to settle down into domestic life. All was not well, however. Merrill turned cruel when he drank, and Davis was once again a battered wife. She stayed in the marriage for ten years because she saw Merrill as "her last chance at love." In 1960 they divorced.

In her mid-seventies, Davis suffered a series of setbacks. She was diagnosed with breast cancer and underwent a mastectomy. Nine days after the operation she suffered a stroke. Only three months later she broke her hip and had to undergo surgery. Remarkably, by 1987, Davis

Davis in *Whatever Happened to Baby Jane?*, 1962.

was able to star in *The Whales of August* with the silent-screen star Lillian Gish. Many praised this performance as one of her finest.

During her last years Davis was able to attend tributes with the help of her secretary and constant companion, Kathryn Sermak. In fact, riddled with cancer and weak, Davis was able to fly 6,000 miles from Los Angeles to San Sebastian, Spain, in order to attend a film festival during the fall of 1989. They had an award for her and she was determined to accept it. While there she became even weaker and was flown to a hospital in France. Brad Darrach of *People* paid her this final tribute: "The pain was stronger than any medicine could control, but she stood up to it, lucid to the end. She lived her death as she had lived her life, with ferocious will and flamboyant originality."

Sources

Leaming, Barbara, *Bette Davis: A Biography,* New York, 1992.

Newsweek, October 16, 1989.

New York Times, October 8, 1989.

People, October 16, 1989.

Quirk, Lawrence J., *Fasten Your Seat Belts: The Passionate Life of Bette Davis,* New York, 1990.

Time, October 16, 1989.

Daniel Day-Lewis

Born April 29, 1957
London, England

"I love to sit and watch people. I love to sit and listen to people. And I do bitterly resent that it's not always possible now, because I'm an object of scrutiny. When the cloak which allows you to observe is stripped from you, then the most useful and indeed fascinating tool of your work is taken with it."

ACTOR

Actor Daniel Day-Lewis has been compared to Laurence Olivier, Montgomery Clift, and Cary Grant. He has played such diverse characters as a moody, homosexual street punk in *My Beautiful Laundrette,* a prudish Victorian in *A Room with a View,* and a frontier warrior in *The Last of the Mohicans.* His versatility and range have propelled him to the forefront of today's screen actors. "I'm in danger," he told David Hutchings of *People,* "of being typecast as a chameleon."

Began acting while still in school

Day-Lewis is the son of the late Cecil Day-Lewis, Britain's poet laureate, and actress Jill Balcon, whose father produced Alfred Hitchcock's early films. Day-Lewis began acting at the Bedales Progressive School. Even at this early stage Day-Lewis was a heartthrob. As quoted in *People,* one former schoolmate recalled: "Every girl was hopelessly in love with him." His early acting led to roles with the National Youth Theatre and to his first film, *Sunday, Bloody Sunday,* in 1971. He studied drama at the Bristol Old Vic Theatre School, then joined the Bristol Old Vic and Royal Shakespeare companies. Day-Lewis made his stage debut in *Another Country* in London's West End. He later toured in Royal Shakespeare productions of *Romeo and Juliet* and *A Midsummer Night's Dream.* He also appeared in the 1982 film *Gandhi* and in 1984's *The Bounty.*

> Among Day-Lewis's avocations are soccer and motorcycling. In fact, in 1993 he pleaded guilty to driving his motorcycle over 100 m.p.h. while near his residence in County Wicklow, Ireland.

In 1985 Day-Lewis was cast as Johnny, a gay, tough London punk, in *My Beautiful Laundrette.* The next year, he played Cecil Vyse, a repressed upper-class Victorian, in *A Room with a View.* The actor's performances in these films were widely praised, and he was soon offered leading roles. In 1988 he starred in both *The Unbearable Lightness of Being,* portraying a womanizing Czech neurosurgeon, and in *Stars and Bars,* where he was Henderson Dores, a bewildered English art dealer. Critics, noting the variety of these roles, lauded Day-Lewis's talent and range. In a *Newsweek* review of *A Room with a View,* Jack Kroll commented: "The metamorphosis of Daniel Day-Lewis from the punk street kid in *My Beautiful Laundrette* into Cecil Vyse is astonishing. [He] makes a figure both appalling and poignant out of Cecil." *Interview*'s Christina de Liagre described Day-Lewis's film work as a series of "virtuoso screen performances," adding that he "has the uncanny ability to transform himself beyond recognition."

After *Stars and Bars*'s negative critical reaction, Day-Lewis decided to "do everyone a favor and just stop for a while," as he told Graham Fuller in *American Film.* When he came back to the screen, he came back with a vengeance. Day-Lewis won an Oscar for his portrayal of Christy Brown, the Irish writer and painter crippled by cerebral palsy, in the 1989 film *My Left Foot,* directed by Jim Sheridan. What next to play? Why not a virile and adventurous frontiersman, in the 1992 film adaptation of James Fenimore Cooper's classic American tale *The Last of the Mohicans.* As Hawkeye, a young man raised by Native Americans, Day-Lewis stole the hearts of women all over the country with his very masculine, down-to-earth performance. As *Mohicans* director Michael Mann suggested in *People,* Day-Lewis had become the "secret fantasy of [women] across the world."

In Day-Lewis's next two films, he again portrays characters at the opposite ends of the spectrum. In director Martin Scorsese's 1993 film adaptation of Edith Wharton's novel *The Age of Innocence,* he plays a sensitive lawyer bound by the "civilized" conventions of New York City society in the 1870s. Aristocratic Newland Archer (Day-Lewis) is torn between passion and duty, for while he is committed to his fiancee, May (Winona Ryder), he finds himself drawn closer and closer to May's scandalous cousin the Countess Olenska (Michelle Pfieffer). The restrictions of that society, however, prevent him from exploring his feelings for the Countess. In fact, society demands that a gentleman keep his thoughts and emotions in check. By failing to act, Archer allows young May to triumph—she will become the rigidly conformist society matron that is her fate, and both Archer and the Countess will be denied the joy they might have known with each other. At the end, Archer is left with only his bittersweet memories of what might have been. Critical response to *The Age of Innocence* was very positive. According to Richard Corliss of *Time*: "[Scorsese's] faithful adaptation of the *Age of Innocence* ... is a gravely beautiful fairy tale of longing and loss." And of Day-Lewis's performance, Corliss stated: "Newland represents perhaps the most pristine, focused work of Day-Lewis' career."

The following year, Day-Lewis went on to play the very antithesis of restraint as the Irishman Gerry Conlon in Jim Sheridan's *In the Name of the Father*. Based on a true story, the film follows Conlon as he is convicted and jailed for a terrorist bombing he didn't commit. Also wrongly imprisoned on the same charge is Conlon's working-class father, and the two end up sharing the same British cell. The film traces Conlon's development from a petty thief in Dublin, Ireland, to a man fervently committed to clearing his name. After spending 15 years behind bars and watching his innocent father die in prison, Conlon finally succeeds in proving that his "confession" had been obtained through the physical and psychological brutality of the British police. Day-Lewis's angry and gritty performance earned him an Academy Award nomination for best actor.

Prepares for roles

Day-Lewis's preparation for each film is usually extreme and intense. For *My Left Foot*, he confined himself to a wheelchair and learned to eat, paint, and type using only his left foot. While making *The Last of the Mohicans*, Day-Lewis learned how to shoot muskets and skin animals. During the filming of *The Age of Innocence*, he walked around New York City in Victorian clothes. In order to prepare for the scene in *In the Name of the Father* where Conlon is interrogated, Day-Lewis spent a week in a closed-down Belfast, Ireland, prison. Day-Lewis explained in *People*: "I did place myself in a prison cell and had a crew member wake me up every few hours to make sure I understood how mad one becomes when deprived of sleep. I also ate very little. It was a way to plunge myself into the despair of my character. And I didn't want to just pretend—I wanted to live the experience."

Currently Day-Lewis has no movie projects in the works. He likes to take time to relax when not filming, often reading and visiting friends. As far as his personal life is concerned, Day-Lewis has been linked romantically with Juliette Binoche, who starred with him in *The Unbearable Lightness of Being,* and French actress Isabelle Adjani, with whom he has lived on and off for a number of years.

Sources

American Film, January-February 1988.

Film Comment, February 1988.

Interview, April 1988.

New Statesman, November 15, 1985.

Newsweek, March 10, 1986.

New Yorker, February 8, 1988.

New York Times, June 21, 1989.

People, February 22, 1988; September 20, 1993; January 10, 1994; January 24, 1994; May 9, 1994.

Time, September 20, 1993; March 21, 1994.

Johnny Depp

Born in 1963
Owensboro, Kentucky

"You want to be as honest as possible in your work. Looking at yourself, you are reminded of everything you could have done to make it better."

ACTOR

Johnny Depp's leading role in the television series *21 Jump Street* whisked him from obscurity to teen idol status in a remarkably short time. Within weeks of his first appearance on the show, he had become a staple of fan magazines such as *Sixteen* and *Tiger Beat*, despite his refusal to grant them interviews. Depp undoubtedly welcomed the opportunities that came with the excessive media exposure, but from the start he was disturbed by the superficial nature of his fame. As soon as he could, he left *Jump Street* behind to search for roles that would challenge both his acting ability and his fans' two-dimensional image of him. "If Depp is anything, he is interesting," asserted *Rolling Stone* contributor Bill Zehme. "He takes the big risks."

Depp's rebellion against the commonplace began early. He was a troublemaker in school, fighting, smoking, drinking, and earning at least one suspension for dropping his pants in front of a teacher. Ironically, one of the most important influences in his young life came from an uncle who was a fundamentalist preacher. The influence was not of a religious nature, however. One of his services, featuring a gospel group, marked the first time Depp ever saw an electric guitar. "I got obsessed with the electric guitar," he told John Waters in *Interview*. "My mom bought me one from them for about twenty-five bucks.... Then I locked myself in a room for a year and taught myself how to play."

His dedication to music did nothing to improve his academic performance. He told Waters that after three years in high school, he had earned "no credits.... I didn't want to be there, and I was bored out of my mind, and I hated it." Not surprisingly, he dropped out when he was 16. For the next five years, he played guitar in rock clubs around Florida, first in a group called Flame and then in the Kids. The Kids eventually became a regional success; besides drawing large crowds at clubs, they also opened shows for the B-52's, Talking Heads, Iggy Pop, and others. Eventually they attracted the attention of Don Ray, a booking agent from Hollywood. He encouraged them to move to the West Coast and offered to manage them. The Kids saved some money, bought a car, and drove across the United States to what they hoped would be a new level of success.

The music scene in L.A.

The Kids were just one of many hungry bands in Los Angeles, however. Competition was fiercer than anything they'd experienced in Florida, and at first they found it impossible to make money. Depp endured a period of working miserable side jobs, struggling to find gigs, and watching his year-old marriage crumble. Eventually the Kids did attain a measure of success in Los Angeles, playing on bills with the Bus Boys and Billy Idol, but Depp's life was about to take a turn that would spell the end of the band. He had made the acquaintance of actor Nicolas Cage, whose agent felt that Depp might be right for a part in the film *Nightmare on Elm Street*. Depp told Waters that the part had been designed for "a big, blond, beach-jock, football-player guy. And I was sort of emaciated, with old hairspray and spiky hair, earrings.... Five hours later that agent called me and said, 'You're an actor.'"

The part was small—Depp played a boy who was eaten by a bed— but it was enough to let him know that he liked acting. The Kids were forced to disband because their guitarist was now spending most of his time studying drama at the Loft Studio and reading for parts. He played an interpreter in the Vietnam drama *Platoon,* and although he didn't have a lot of time on-screen in the completed film, the ten weeks spent in the jungle with director Oliver Stone were an important learning experience.

Platoon sat unreleased for a few months and Depp went for some time without landing another acting job—long enough for him to begin playing guitar in another group, the Rock City Angels.

Hard up as he was for work, Depp still reacted negatively when his agent asked him to read for a television show about undercover high school cops. "I said, 'No, no, no, no, no,'" he told Waters. "I didn't want to sign some big contract that would bind me for years. So they hired somebody else to do it, and they fired him after about a month, and then they called me and said, 'Would you please come in and do it?'" Depp relented, and was immediately cast as Tom Hanson in the Fox television series *21 Jump Street*. The show was one of the fledgling network's first big successes, running for four years, but Depp hated the whole project and claims to have seen only a half-dozen episodes. The hysterical hero-worship he now inspired in his fans was, to him, both embarrassing and frightening.

Makes Cry Baby

Filmmaker John Waters saw something more than a pinup boy when he looked at Johnny Depp—he saw something sinister as well. The combination of those qualities was exactly what he wanted for his work-in-progress, *Cry Baby*. Waters, known for his offbeat films, was putting together his own interpretation of the story behind Shakespeare's *Romeo and Juliet*, the 1970s musical *Grease*, and the 1960s musical *West Side Story*: young lovers from different social levels struggle with society's disapproval. He wanted Depp to play Cry Baby, the juvenile delinquent who falls in love with a high-society girl.

Depp was delighted with the casting and the tone of the whole venture. "There were a lot of scripts where I would carry a gun, kiss a girl, and walk around corners and pose, and things like that," he observed in *Interview*. *Cry Baby* "makes fun of all the stuff I sort of hate. It makes fun of all the teen-idol stuff. It makes fun of all the screaming girls.... It gave me a chance not only to make fun of the whole situation but to do something really different. To be able to work with someone like [Waters], who's an outlaw in filmmaking and has always done his own thing." It also gave him an opportunity to work with an unusual array of fellow cast members, including rock star Iggy Pop. *Cry Baby* drew mixed reviews, with some critics praising Waters's bizarre, original vision and others dismissing the story as one told too often. But Depp's performance was well received; *Time*'s reviewer wrote that "the winsome tough from TV's *21 Jump Street* ... radiates big-screen grace and swagger."

Depp as the title character of *Edward Scissorhands*, 1990.

Breaks away from pretty-boy image with
Edward Scissorhands

His next film took him even farther from the pretty-boy image perpetuated

Depp's own life has similarities to that of Gilbert Grape. Before the age of seven his family moved all over Kentucky. When they finally settled in Mirimar, Florida, they lived in over 30 houses before Depp left at the age of 20. Depp recalled his "weird upbringing" in *Gentlemen's Quarterly:* "We'd go from neighborhood to neighborhood, sometimes from one house to the house next door. I don't know why. My mom would get ants somehow. There's a huge history of my family out there: Furniture, my toys, schoolwork, everything, was abandoned, left in attics or garages—all gone."

by *21 Jump Street.* As the title character in Tim Burton's *Edward Scissorhands* he played a sort of modern-day Frankenstein's monster—a spectral, somber being created by a lonely inventor (Vincent Price) who dies before completing his work. Edward sports an unwieldy pair of blades in place of each finger, and his face is covered with small scars caused by his awkwardness with his own "hands." Taken in by the neighborhood Avon lady (Diane Weist), Edward struggles with society, his own creative and destructive powers, and his feelings for the Avon lady's pretty cheerleader daughter.

Edward was played "with touching gravity," according to Peter Travers, a reviewer for *Rolling Stone.* Depp had intense feelings for the Scissorhands character that came through in his performance. When making the film, he purposely remained in his uncomfortable costume all day, and even learned to smoke his cigarettes while wearing his sharp-edged prostheses. Although his dialogue was minimal, he used his eyes and body language eloquently. He confided to *Rolling Stone's* Bill Zehme that he based his performance on a dog he once owned. "He had this unconditional love," Depp explained. Edward "was this totally pure, completely open character, the sweetest thing in the world, whose appearance is incredibly dangerous—until you get a look at his eyes. I missed Edward when I was done. I really miss him." Director Tim Burton drew parallels between Edward Scissorhands and the actor who portrayed him, telling Zehme: "Like Edward, Johnny really is perceived as something he is not. Before we met, I'd certainly read about him as the Difficult Heartthrob. But you look at him and you get a feeling. There is a lot of pain and humor and darkness and light."

In 1993 Depp continued to play slightly offbeat, quirky characters in the movies *Benny and Joon* and *What's Eating Gilbert Grape?* In *Benny and Joon* Depp plays an endearing drifter who falls in love with a mentally ill woman. The movie was a box-office success. In *What's Eating Gilbert Grape?* Depp plays the title character—a small-town grocery clerk enmeshed in complex relationships with his retarded brother and 500-pound mother. When a free-spirited teenager comes to town, she sparks a desire in Grape to break away from his role as the family caretaker and instead explore the world. According to Richard Corliss of *Time,* "Depp is, as always, a most effacing star. Here, as in *Edward Scissorhands* and *Benny and Joon*, he behaves wonderfully on screen."

The following year saw Depp in the title role of *Ed Wood*, which reunited him with Burton. As the 1950s cross-dressing writer-director-actor, Depp brought a sincerity and sweetness to the part, capturing the oddball enthusiasm of the man responsible for *Plan 9 from Outer Space* and other such B films of the era. *Ed Wood* opened to glowing reviews and, despite its decidedly unconventional nature, seemed poised to become a hit. Once again, Depp's risk had paid off.

Sources

The Advocate, May 1993.

Cosmopolitan, May 1993.

Detroit Free Press, October 7, 1994.

Detroit News, October 1, 1994.

Entertainment, December 7, 1990.

Gentlemen's Quarterly, October 1993.

Harper's Bazaar, May 1993.

Interview, April 1990.

Mademoiselle, May 1990.

People, April 16, 1990; January 10, 1994.

Premiere, October 1990.

Rolling Stone, December 1, 1988; April 19, 1990; January 10, 1991.

Time, April 23, 1990; January 10, 1994.

Snoop Doggy Dogg

Born in 1972

"Listen to my music—it's a conversation rather than rap."

RAPPER

E ven before the release of his debut album, *Doggystyle,* Snoop Doggy Dogg had been featured on the covers of such popular magazines as *Rolling Stone, Vibe,* and *The Source.* His performance on several tracks of rapper Dr. Dre's 1992 hit album, *The Chronic,* drew such a following that *Doggystyle* debuted at the top of the pop charts in the fall of 1993. At the same time as the album's release, Snoop was also making headlines for his alleged role in a murder that occurred in west Los Angeles in August 1993.

Troubled youth

Snoop Doggy Dogg—who was born Calvin Broadus according to most sources, though one cites his given name as Cordavar Varnado—grew up amid drug deals and violence in Long Beach, California, and his music reflects the ugly reality of a life exposed to brutality and poverty. Snoop's mother raised her family alone. In order to protect her son from the negative influences of the street, she was very strict. If Snoop wasn't in his house by nine o'clock at night, he was locked out and he had to face his mother's wrath the following morning. When asked in *Time* how his mother reacts to the explicit language of his songs, Snoop replied: "My mama and my grandma—these are religious people I'm talking about—they respect me for my music. I'm not out there gang banging, shooting [people] up. I'm trying to do something positive with my life."

Snoop performs a kind of music known as "gangsta rap," which chronicles often violent and squalid urban conditions. This kind of rap has many critics who maintain that its lyrics glorify brutality and encourage violence. "That's a lie," Snoop told *Time*. "Before rap came out, there was violence. When I was nine years old, one of my homeboys got shot in some gang violence. And wasn't no rap music being played then. So you tell me the music we make now made him die?" Those who defend gangsta rap maintain that rappers are merely reflecting their environment. Fab 5 Freddy, who directed a music video for one of the cuts on *Doggystyle*, told *Interview* that "rappers are just taking all this stuff they see around them and twisting it and throwing it right back out there, like a spear."

The "Long Beach Sound"

Within gangsta rap there has recently emerged a newer sound, the "Long Beach Sound," and Snoop Doggy Dogg deserves most of the credit for spreading this distinctive musical style to people around the globe. According to a correspondent for the *Detroit Free Press*, the sounds coming from Long Beach are "a mix of singing, laid-back rapping, sampling and instrumental tracks." In addition to Snoop, the newcomers Domino, Warren G, and Nate Dogg hail from Long Beach and their sounds are currently climbing the rap charts. The Long Beach Sound originated at such hangouts as V.I.P. Records on Pacific Beach Highway, where in 1988 owner Kelvin Anderson put a drum machine in a back room so that aspiring rappers could practice. While in high school, Snoop, Nate Dogg, and Warren G were known locally as the group 213. "Snoop was one of the promising acts," Anderson told the *Detroit Free Press*. "We put together a demo tape and actually shopped it around to major labels. Those that responded to it said he wasn't what they were looking for or he didn't have any talent."

Snoop's luck changed, however, when he got in touch with Dr. Dre of the rap group N.W.A. Dr. Dre liked what he heard and Snoop appeared on Dre's best–selling album *The Chronic*. Snoop's delivery so excited rap fans that when his debut album, *Doggystyle*, was released in the fall of

1993 it hit the charts at Number One. The album was produced by Dr. Dre and it sold 800,000 copies in the first week of its release. Christopher John Farley of *Time* praised the album: "[Snoop's] relaxed vocal style is a perfect match for Dr. Dre's bass-heavy producing. The songs on this album are built around '70s-style funk grooves; Snoop's voice is lithe enough to snake its way around the big beats.... Snoop makes great party music and that's the key to the album's appeal." The songs on the album are rife with four-letter words and many describe the pleasures of casual sex and drugs. Some even detail gunning down enemies. Critics have singled out the song "Murder Was the Case (Death After Visualizing Eternity)" for extending beyond the limits of typical gangsta rap. In the song, Snoop has been shot and is near death. After hearing a supernatural voice promise that his life will be better, Snoop recovers filled with hope and love.

Faces murder charges

At the same time *Doggystyle* was being prepared for release, Snoop was gaining notoriety for his alleged involvement in a murder. On August 25, 1993, Philip Waldemariam was gunned down from a car by Snoop's bodyguard, McKinnley Lee. Police have accused Snoop of being in the car's driver seat, and charged him with being an accomplice to murder. According to police, Snoop, Lee, and a third man, Shawn Abrams, went looking for Waldemariam after an encounter at the apartment building where Snoop and Lee lived. Snoop has pleaded not guilty, asserting that the shooting was in self-defense because Waldemariam reached for a gun. In April 1994, a judge refused to dismiss the charges, contending that there was "sufficient evidence" for the case to be heard by a jury. Because he was convicted in 1990 for drug possession, Snoop has also been charged with being a convicted felon in possession of a firearm. He denies this charge as well.

Snoop is currently awaiting trial and is free on a $1 million bond. Whatever troubles have plagued his personal life, his album continues to sell well. *Doggystyle* sold over three million copies in the U.S. and has also hit the charts in the United Kingdom, Canada, Australia, and New Zealand. According to Fab 5 Freddy, "Snoop is a truly creative artist. Snoop is not a gun-brandishing, braggadocios type of fella. The sensibility he has is more like that of a blues musician. He has a southern accent, and the music he listens to when he drives around in his car is like old-school rap, old blues, and heavy, heavy soul: things that you wouldn't expect your average urban youth to be that into. It's amazing how humble and meek he still is."

Sources

Detroit Free Press, April, 6, 1994; July 15, 1994,

Entertainment Weekly, November 26, 1993.

Interview, December 13, 1993; February 1994.

Spin, October 1993.

Time, November 29, 1993; December 13, 1993.

Clint Eastwood

Born May 31, 1930
San Francisco, California

"I'm meditative and contemplative. I guess I'm shy. I don't really like drawing attention to myself."

ACTOR AND DIRECTOR

He seems chiseled out of stone: a cold, intimidating squint above high cheekbones and square jaw, a lanky, no-nonsense frame, and a mouth tailor-made to sneer at bad guys. He is Academy Award-winner Clint Eastwood, one of the most popular film actors in the world. Eastwood has been starring in movies since 1964 and has been producing and directing since 1970. Other filmmakers might have made more money here and there, but over the long run—with blockbuster after blockbuster to his credit—Eastwood has out-worked and overshadowed most competitors. As a *Vogue* magazine contributor put it: "Eastwood has reworked and reinvented America's two most popular movie genres, cowboy and cop, into personal formulas and made himself a rumored $2 billion along the way." The actor-director has also overcome critical barbs to earn the industry's highest honors in America and abroad.

Eastwood forged his extraordinary career by portraying a series of antisocial heroes who pursue personal vendettas with little respect for the letter of the law. *Commentary* correspondent Richard Grenier noted that in a typical Eastwood vehicle, the star "kills a lot of people and never flinches once. They are all very bad people, of course, so there is no need to feel sorry for them. But [his] hand never trembles."

For years the actor offered variations on this ever-popular character, sometimes in westerns, sometimes in detective dramas. "His wince is an instrument of understatement," wrote the *Vogue* reporter. "Poor saps come at him six or 10 at a time, trying to brain him with meat hooks and crowbars. He's cornered into a chivalrous position: reluctantly he takes charge. He gits mad, plumb mad-dog mad, and the body count multiplies. Through clenched teeth he invites his victims to 'sit there and bleed awhile afore you git to taste real pain.' Then he says, 'I bin here way too long,' and rides back into the sunset, women running after him."

Yet after looking at the evolution of his films, it appears that Eastwood never was a straightforward hero. Indeed, his recent movies paint vivid portraits of men who pay a steep emotional price for their supposed invulnerability. "I like playing people with a little bit of a chink in the armor," he told *Vogue.* "It's like they have some problems they're trying to overcome, other than the antagonist."

Moved often while growing up

Clinton Eastwood, Jr., was born in Depression-era California on May 31, 1930. His family moved from town to town throughout the state while his father pursued various temporary jobs. The Eastwoods were not poverty-stricken like many of the Dust Bowl immigrants to California. Their unsteady prosperity rested on Clinton, Sr.'s strong work ethic, which was passed on to Eastwood and his sister. The family relocated more than ten times while Eastwood was a youngster. "Since I was almost always the new boy on the block, I often played alone and in that situation your imagination becomes very active," the actor told *McCall's.* "You create little mythologies in your own mind."

Finally, the elder Eastwood obtained a permanent position with the Container Corporation of America in Oakland. Clint settled into Oakland Technical High School, where he played varsity basketball. "Nobody ever told him he was smart or promising," noted John Vinocur in the *New York Times Magazine.* Certainly, Eastwood had little inkling what lay in store for him career-wise. After graduating from high school, he went straight to work. He pumped gas, cut lumber, fought fires in Oregon, and even worked in a Texas blast furnace. In 1950 he was drafted. The army sent him to Fort Ord in Monterey, California, where he taught other recruits how to swim. While at Fort Ord he became friends with a number of aspiring actors, including the late David Janssen. They encouraged him to try to break into the film business.

Following his discharge from the service, Eastwood moved to Los Angeles and took courses at Los Angeles City College. Once again he was rarely idle, pumping gas, digging swimming pool foundations, and even picking up garbage in order to make ends meet. In 1955 he was hired by Universal Studios as a contract player. His salary was $75 a week, and his assignments included bit parts in "B" pictures such as *Revenge of the Creature, Francis in the Navy,* and *Ambush at Cimarron Pass.* Eastwood told *Show* magazine: "I'd always play the young lieutenant or the lab technician who came in and said, 'He went that way' or 'This happened' or 'Doctor, here are the X-rays' and he'd say, 'Get lost, kid,' I'd go out and that would be the end of it." After 18 months, Universal let Eastwood go.

He persevered, however, supplementing his meager wages as a bit player by serving as a lifeguard. Occasionally he drew unemployment. The lean years might have dragged on indefinitely, but one day in 1959 he was visiting a friend in the CBS studio cafeteria and was spotted by a producer who was casting for a new television western. The producer offered Eastwood a screen test, and he won the role of Rowdy Yates on the popular series *Rawhide.* The show—centered on a cattle drive to Missouri—ran for seven years, garnering top ratings through 1962. Although Eastwood was never fond of his Rowdy Yates character, he did find the weekly television schedule a good training ground, both in terms of acting experimentation and nuts-and-bolts production.

Gains popularity with "spaghetti westerns"

During the 1964 hiatus in *Rawhide,* Eastwood accepted a $15,000 offer to make a feature film in Spain for Italian director Sergio Leone. Eastwood later said he only took the assignment because it gave him a chance to visit Europe. Whatever his motivation, he found himself involved in a project that would catapult him from a dead-end television career to stardom in the movies.

The film was called *A Fistful of Dollars.* Eastwood portrayed a hired gun, a nameless man who successfully manipulates—and ruthlessly kills—rival gangs of bandits. The script was wordy. Eastwood slashed pages of dialogue and convinced the director that audiences would root for a terse hero. He was right. While he was back in America filming a

Eastwood in *High Plains Drifter*, 1973.

new season of *Rawhide*, *A Fistful of Dollars* was causing a sensation in Europe. Over the next two years, Eastwood returned to Europe to film *For a Few Dollars More* and *The Good, the Bad, and the Ugly*, both also featuring the "Man with No Name." Even Eastwood thought the Italian trilogy—first of the so-called "spaghetti westerns"—was too violent for American audiences. Nevertheless, United Artists bought the rights to the films and released them in the United States.

The success of the Leone westerns enabled Eastwood to secure similar roles in American films. By 1970 he had become a top box-office draw with leads in movies such as *Hang 'em High, Coogan's Bluff, Kelly's Heroes,* and *Two Mules for Sister Sara.* Eastwood's superstardom was written in stone in 1971, when his own fledgling production company released *Dirty Harry.* An action movie set in San Francisco, *Dirty Harry* introduced Eastwood as Harry Callahan, a dedicated policeman whose search-and-destroy mission against a psychotic killer is frustrated by legal bureaucracy. "The film caused an uproar," wrote Grenier. "Eastwood was called a brute, a fascist, and worse. But he had his defenders, too, and it was curious how those sympathetic with the film in general tended to like Eastwood's acting, while those who hated the film thought he was the worst performer who had ever stepped in front of a movie camera." No matter what the critics thought, the American public flocked to see *Dirty Harry.* The movie grossed three times more than any other Eastwood vehicle up to that time, and it set the stage for a series of popular sequels, including *Magnum Force, The Enforcer, Sudden Impact,* and *The Dead Pool.*

Begins directing

Eastwood made a career out of standing up to extreme violence. He evinced the same kind of cool determination in such westerns as *The Outlaw Josey Wales, High Plains Drifter,* and *Pale Rider.* He offered similar characters in other action movies, such as *The Gauntlet, Firefox,* and *Tightrope.* At the same time, however, Eastwood showed an experimental flair—a willingness to produce, direct, and star in movies that provided an alternative to his ever-cool killer hero. In *Honkytonk Man,* for instance, he portrayed a Depression-era singer in need of a lucky break, and in *Play Misty for Me* he appeared as a disc jockey pursued by an overzealous fan. Biskind contended that Warner Bros., Eastwood's distributor, "is not going to lose much on an Eastwood picture, no matter what it's about."

Only Clint Eastwood could have convinced Warner Bros. to finance and distribute a comedy in which he starred with a sassy orangutan. The studio executives were aghast at the idea, but allowed Eastwood to proceed with *Every Which Way but Loose.* The film was released in 1978 and quickly became one of the year's biggest hits. It cost about $8 million to make and grossed about $85 million, despite the critics' almost unanimous disdain for the picture. A sequel, *Any Which Way You Can,* performed almost as well in 1980.

As early as 1980, the critical community began to reassess Eastwood's contribution to cinema. Open hostility turned to grudging acceptance and then to admiration as the decade progressed. The critical about-face had two main causes. First, more and more people began to appreciate Eastwood's contribution as producer and director of a number of his films, especially the smaller, more personal offerings, including *Play Misty for Me* and *Honkytonk Man.* Second, a swing toward conservative politics gave heightened credibility to Eastwood's heroes and their justified vigilantism. While Eastwood told the *New York Times Magazine* that he "never begged for respectability," he nonetheless flew to Paris to accept the honor of Chevalier des Arts et Lettres, a national award, in 1985.

Since then Eastwood has often opted for the more personal, character-driven projects. Known in the business as a director who brings movies in ahead of schedule and under budget, he is rarely thwarted on a potential project. This freedom to pursue offbeat work has produced *Bird,* a critically acclaimed feature about jazz musician Charlie Parker, and *Unforgiven,* a western that significantly alters the perception of violence in that particular genre. Eastwood did not think that *Unforgiven* would find a large audience, because the film seeks to de-glorify violence. On the contrary, critics paved the way with rave reviews, and the grim western earned more than $100 million nationwide by the end of 1992.

In *Unforgiven* Eastwood has come full circle. A *Vogue* critic contended: "In this surprising movie there is no superhuman figure and no obvious moral line. It's a western that debunks the western and explodes the myth of the cowboy hero." *Unforgiven* earned Eastwood his first Academy awards, for best picture of the year and best director, as well as a shelf full of other trophies.

In 1993 Eastwood starred in *In the Line of Fire.* The movie examines an aging Secret Service agent (Eastwood) who was unable to save President John F. Kennedy from being fatally shot in 1963 and who now, 20 years later, sees a chance to redeem himself by stopping another assassination attempt on the president. Eastwood is again cast in his new image of the flawed hero. Richard Grenier of *Commentary* called the part "the perfect role for the new Clint Eastwood. He could carry a gun, be strong and brave, but demonstrate his valor in a purely defensive role, protecting the life of the President of the United States."

Became mayor of Carmel in 1986

For more than 25 years Eastwood has made his home in Carmel, California, a quaint coastal village in the northern part of the state. The town has always been a tourist attraction, but it made national news in 1986 when its most famous citizen ran for mayor and won. Eastwood sought the $200-per-month position because he disapproved of zoning laws in the village. After serving one term—and changing the laws—he stepped down with no regrets. He says he has no interest in running for national office.

Not surprisingly, the popular star is often the target of tabloid journalism, especially since he is very reluctant to talk about his private life. Eastwood was married for 25 years to the former Maggie Johnson. After they separated in the late 1970s, he spent more than a decade living with actress Sondra Locke, his costar in numerous films. That relationship ended bitterly in 1989; Locke sued for palimony. More recently Eastwood has been linked with another costar, Frances Fisher. In August 1993 the two had a baby girl that they named Francesca Ruth. The child is Eastwood's third and Fisher's third. The actor prefers to live outside Hollywood and to spend time with friends who are not involved in the entertainment industry. And he is known as a loyal employer whose production crew includes people who have worked for him for 15 years.

By 1993 Eastwood had made 41 major motion pictures and directed 17 of them himself. Early in that year the actor told *Premiere:* "I figure that by the time I'm really old, somebody at the Academy Awards will get the bright idea to give me some sort of plaque. I'll be so old, they'll have to carry me up there." But Eastwood did not have to wait that long. At a remarkably fit 62 he won his first two golden statuettes for a film that reflects his personal hatred of violence. After the March 1992 Academy Award ceremony, Eastwood told reporters that the wait for the award had been worth it. "I think it means more to me now," he was quoted as saying in the *Philadelphia Inquirer.* "If you win it when you're 20 or 30 years old you're wondering, 'Where do I go from here?' ... You learn to take your work seriously and not yourself seriously, and that comes with time."

Sources

Commentary, April 1984; March 1994.

Cosmopolitan, August 1993.

McCall's, June 1987.

Newsweek, July 22, 1985; April 7, 1986; April 24, 1986.

New York Times, June 17, 1979; January 11, 1981.

New York Times Magazine, February 24, 1985.

People, December 24-31, 1984; August 7, 1989.

Philadelphia Inquirer, March 31, 1993.

Premiere, April 1993.

Show, February 1970.

Time, January 9, 1978; April 6, 1987; August 30, 1993.

Vogue, February 1993.

Gloria Estefan

Born in 1958
Cuba

SINGER

"To know so many people care about me on a personal level is something I'll have for the rest of my life. It's the most any human being can hope for, to be loved."

Through her talent and determination, Gloria Estefan has achieved worldwide acclaim and popularity as a singularly exciting pop singer. Estefan and the Miami Sound Machine grew from a Latin-inspired band whose primary audience was in Spanish-speaking countries, to a group that enjoys international fame and success. Yet, perhaps Estefan's greatest success lies in her courageous comeback from the devastating spinal injury she suffered in a car accident. Although the prognosis for complete recovery was doubtful, Estefan overcame her pain and injury and returned to singing and songwriting.

Estefan was born Gloria Fajardo in Cuba in 1958. While only a toddler, Estefan and her family fled Cuba when Communist dictator Fidel Castro rose to power. Her father, Jose Manual Fajardo, had been a Cuban soldier and bodyguard of President Fulgencio Batista. After coming to the United States, Fajardo was recruited for the 2506 Brigade. The Brigade was funded by the Central Intelligence Agency (CIA) and composed of

Cuban refugees whose goal was to invade Cuba and overthrow Castro. Their efforts resulted in failure, however, and nearly brought Russian-backed Cuba into a war with the United States in 1961. This episode is referred to as the Bay of Pigs invasion—named after the bay off the Cuban coastline where the mission was centered. After President John F. Kennedy negotiated the release of the captured soldiers, Fajardo rejoined his family. He eventually joined the U.S. Army and served for two years in Vietnam.

As a child Estefan liked to write poetry, and though she took classical guitar lessons, she found them tedious. As a teenager, music grew to play an important role in her life. After her father's return from Vietnam he was diagnosed as having multiple sclerosis. His condition was a possible result of having been exposed to the chemical Agent Orange, which the United States military used to burn the leaves off trees and bushes during the Vietnam war. Estefan's mother, who had been a teacher in Cuba, worked to support the family during the day and attended school at night. Young Gloria was therefore left to take care of her younger sister and her father. She had little social life, and because she felt the weight of such responsibilities she turned to music as a release. "When my father was ill, music was my escape," Estefan revealed in an interview with the *Washington Post*. "I would lock myself in my room for hours and just sing. I wouldn't cry—I refused to cry.... Music was the only way I had to just let go, so I sang for fun and for emotional catharsis."

Joins future husband's band

In 1975 Gloria met keyboardist Emilio Estefan, a sales manager for the rum company Bacardi who also led a band called the Miami Latin Boys. The group played popular Latin music, and because there was no lead singer, each member of the quartet took turns singing. A mutual friend asked Emilio to advise Gloria and some friends about organizing a band for a special event. Emilio heard Gloria sing, and when he met her again at a wedding at which the Miami Latin Boys were entertaining, he asked her to sit in with the band. A few weeks later Emilio asked Gloria to perform as a lead singer with the band, and she accepted. At first Gloria sang only on weekends, because she was still attending the University of Miami. A year and a half after Gloria joined the group, by then renamed the Miami Sound Machine, the band recorded its first album for a local label. *Renacer* was a collection of disco pop and original ballads sung in Spanish.

Although Estefan was somewhat plump and very quiet when she joined the band, she lost weight with an extensive exercise program and worked to overcome her shyness. After several months on a professional level, Emilio and Gloria's relationship turned personal, and on September 1, 1978, they were married. Their son Nayib was born two years later, about the time that Emilio quit his job at Bacardi to work full time with the band, then made up of bassist Marcos Avila, drummer Kiki Garcia, keyboardist, arranger, and saxophonist Raul Murciano, keyboardist Emilio, and vocalist Gloria.

By 1980, the group had signed a contract with Discos CBS International, the Miami-based Hispanic division of CBS records. Between 1981 and 1983 the Miami Sound Machine recorded four Spanish-language albums made up of ballads, disco, pop and sambas. The group had dozens of hit songs around the world—particularly in Venezuela, Peru, Panama, and Honduras—but enjoyed little recognition in the United States.

Finds success in North America with first English songs

With the recording of their first album with some English content, *Eyes of Innocence,* the Miami Sound Machine found success in North America. The disco single "Dr. Beat" went to the top of the European dance charts. Because of the song's popularity, CBS moved the group to its parent label, Epic, and encouraged the group to start writing songs in English. They began with a few English songs on the otherwise Spanish album *Conga.* The title song from the album, a rousing dance number, became the first single to crack *Billboard*'s pop, dance, black, and Latin charts all at once. In an interview with the *New York Tribune* Estefan remembers: "I'll never forget when we first did 'Conga.' A producer told us that the song was too Latin for the Americans and too American for the Latins. 'Well, thank you,' I said, 'because that's exactly what we are!'" Estefan and the group, whose members have changed over the years, pride themselves on the combination of Latin rhythms, rhythm and blues, and mainstream pop that makes up their original sound.

In 1986 the album *Primitive Love,* the band's first recording entirely in English, set off a string of hit singles. "Bad Boys" and "Words Get in the Way" made their way into the Top 10 of *Billboard*'s singles chart. Behind the scenes was the work of a trio known as the "Three Jerks"—producer-drummer Joe Galdo and his partners Rafael Vigil and Lawrence Dermer—who wrote, arranged, and performed the majority of the music on *Primitive Love* and the following album, *Let It Loose.* In the studio the "Three Jerks" and session players made records, while the road band, which included Garcia and Avila, continued to perform during concerts. Only Estefan performed both in the studio and on-stage. Extensive tours, concerts in 40,000-seat stadiums, and music videos made the Miami Sound Machine a top band in the United States. Estefan gradually became the star attraction, and the act came to be billed as Gloria Estefan and the Miami Sound Machine or sometimes simply Gloria Estefan.

After the *Let It Loose* album, Galdo and friends quit working with the Miami Sound Machine, so the band was on its own creatively. Early on the band's biggest hits were dance numbers, but by the end of the 1980s it was Estefan's ballads that sustained the group. "Ballads are basically what I'm about," Estefan explained in an interview with the *Boston Herald*. "I just feel you can express yourself more completely and eloquently in a ballad. It's easier to identify with someone else and form a closer bond with the audience." From the *Let It Loose* album the songs "Rhythm Is Gonna Get You," "Betcha Say That," and "1-2-3" made it to *Billboard*'s Top 10, but it was the ballad "Anything For You" that topped the charts.

Despite the group's popularity with English-speaking listeners, the Estefans have not forgotten their roots. There are always Spanish language projects in the works, and the title of their 1989 album *Cuts Both Ways* indicates their dedication to their international audience. Estefan contributed to *Cuts Both Ways* in more ways than just being the lead singer; she was also involved in its planning and production, composed some of the music, and wrote lyrics to most of the songs.

Fractures spine in traffic accident

Emilio Estefan gave up his position as keyboardist with the Miami Sound Machine after the birth of their son Nayib. He then devoted his time and energy to managing the band. His sound business sense eventually made the Estefans producers of their own and others' records. While Estefan toured with the band, her husband would stay home with Nayib. A close family, the Estefans would arrange to meet as often as possible during tours. While traveling together on March 20, 1990, the band's bus was involved in an accident with a tractor trailer on snowy Interstate 380 near the Pocono Mountains of Pennsylvania. While Nayib's shoulder was fractured and Emilio received minor head and hand injuries, Gloria suffered a broken vertebra in her back. In a four-hour operation several days later, surgeons realigned Estefan's spine and implanted steel rods to support the fracture. The outlook was not promising, and Estefan retired to her home on Star Island, near Miami, to begin her long recovery.

Thanks to extensive physical therapy, intense determination, and the support of her family and fans, Estefan made what many consider a miraculous recovery. She marked her return to performing with an appearance on television's American Music Awards in January 1991. Two months later she began a year-long tour to publicize her comeback album, *Into the Light*. The tour was one of her most physically demanding. She continued the whirlwind with the smash record *Mi Tierra*, which marked Estefan's return to singing in Spanish and earned her her first Grammy for a Spanish-language album. Then in the fall of 1994 Estefan released a critically acclaimed collection of her favorite songs, *Hold Me, Kiss Me, Thrill Me*.

In August 1992, Hurricane Andrew wreaked destruction and havoc throughout Miami and Estefan was once again faced with recuperating from a crisis. In an interview with *TV Guide,* Estefan explained her feelings of *deja vu:* "In some respects I had gone through personally what we were going through in the city. It was a traumatic experience that was going to take a long time to recover from." Yet, Estefan drew upon the same strength and determination that saw her through her recovery and organized the Hurricane Relief concert during the fall of 1992. The concert boasted many well-known musicians and the three million dollars it raised caused the press to call Estefan "Miami's Mother Teresa."

The impact of Estefan's accident will no doubt continue to affect her attitudes and outlook on life. According to *People,* her "long, sometimes uncertain recovery" gave the singer-songwriter "a renewed feeling about life," as she told writer Steve Dougherty. "It's very hard to stress me out now. It's hard to get me in an uproar about anything because most things have little significance compared with what I almost lost." She added that "so many people got behind me and gave me a reason to want to come back fast and made me feel strong. Knowing how caring people can be, how much they gave me—that has changed me forever."

Sources

Boston Herald, March 7, 1990; March 14, 1990.

Miami Herald, September 30, 1988; May 7, 1989; July 9, 1989; May 29, 1990.

New York Tribune, September 14, 1988; December 13, 1989.

People, October 27, 1986; February 18, 1991.

Rolling Stone, June 14, 1990.

USA Weekend, April 1-3, 1994.

Washington Post, July 17, 1988.

Emilio Estevez

Born May 12, 1962
New York, New York

ACTOR

E milio Estevez burst onto the movie scene as one of a group of young film stars who became known as Hollywood's "whiz kids" or "brat pack." His earliest hits were the movies *Repo Man, The Breakfast Club,* and *St. Elmo's Fire,* and he soon extended himself beyond acting into screenwriting and directing. Of the "brat pack" actors, Estevez distinguished himself by his ambition and work ethic. "Starmakers have their eyes and their money on Emilio Estevez, who at 23 is one of the most productive young actors in Hollywood," declared the *Chicago Tribune*'s Robert Blau. "His promise as an actor, his glaring intensity and his slicked-back hair recall James Dean and [Marlon] Brando, whose careers were launched by the kind of teen-age road-and-romance movies Estevez has been starring in for the last five years."

"Longevity is in the stars for me. I'm not the kind of guy who's going to be in there for a couple of shots; I don't ever want to be on one of those shows, 'Whatever Happened to ...?'"

"I knew I had an ability to perform from an early age," Estevez told *Teen* magazine. Although he didn't begin acting professionally until after high school, Estevez grew up performing in neighborhood dramatic productions and in school plays. He also began writing at an early age. One effort was a science-fiction story he wrote as a second grader and submitted to the producers of television's *Night Gallery* series. The story was rejected, but Estevez continued to write, turning out, for example, a play about Vietnam veterans entitled *Echoes of an Era.* Under the direction of his boyhood friend Sean Penn, Estevez starred in his high school's production of that play. He landed his first professional acting job—a part in an after-school television special entitled *Seventeen Going on Nowhere*— immediately after graduating from high school. Subsequent television dramas in which he appeared include *To Climb a Mountain, Making the Grade,* and *In the Custody of Strangers.*

Finds audience with Repo Man

Estevez made his motion picture debut in *Tex,* a film based on a novel by best-selling author S. E. Hinton. He next appeared in *The Outsiders,* another screen adaptation of a Hinton novel. Following *The Outsiders,* he earned a starring role in the 1984 film *Repo Man,* in which he portrayed a young punk working as an apprentice to a group of Los Angeles automobile repossessors who steal back the cars of people who don't make their payments. According to Thomas Wiener in *American Film, Repo Man* was "a flop in its initial theatrical release, [but it] found a second life on videocassette and was then miraculously revived in theaters like New York's Eighth Street Playhouse, where it ran for months."

When Estevez first read the script for *Repo Man,* he was immediately drawn to the film's leading character, he told Wiener. However, he was unfamiliar with the punk rock scene and felt he needed to understand it better in order to prepare for the role. "So I started listening to the music and going to the clubs, and I began to understand what the punk movement is all about," he explained to Wiener. He also went out on a couple of occasions with a real repo man. Asked by Wiener if he had feared being typecast as a rebel kid, Estevez answered: "Not at that point in my career. I didn't think I was perceived by the public as being a punk or a type. And I didn't feel that it would be detrimental in any way for me to be seen as such."

Plays jock in The Breakfast Club

In his next film, *The Breakfast Club,* Estevez portrayed a high school varsity letterman, a role quite unlike the one he played in *Repo Man.* The action in *The Breakfast Club* occurs in a suburban high school library during a daylong detention that the film's five leading characters have been sentenced to serve. The movie focuses on the interaction among the characters, each of whom represents a different teen stereotype. There's a prom queen, a rebel, a kooky artist, a brain, and Estevez's champion wrestler Andy. As the film opens, the five are strangers to one another. But "in the course of the day, under the prodding of the rebel and mellowing effect of the marijuana he provides, they peel off layers of self-protection, confess their problems with their parents, and, after much shedding of tears, are stripped down to their true selves," summarized Pauline Kael in her *New Yorker* review of the movie.

Critics who were impressed with Estevez's performance in *The Breakfast Club* include Janet Maslin, who wrote in her *New York Times* review that "Emilio Estevez has an edgy physical intensity," and Kael, who especially enjoyed Andy's "long monologue about his father's always telling him to 'win, win." Describing his character for *Teen* magazine, Estevez said: "Andy has a lot of turmoil. Everyone rides him. It's an intolerable burden. He really wants to break out, but he's conditioned not to. If a wrestler lets down his defenses, he loses. So he can't and won't be vulnerable."

St. Elmo's Fire, released just a few months after *The Breakfast Club*, again featured Estevez as one of several young actors in an ensemble cast. *St. Elmo's Fire* explores the relationships among its seven leading characters—a group of close friends who've recently graduated from college and are trying to adjust to post-college life. Estevez's character, a law student named Kirbo, is infatuated with a medical student several years his senior. She, in turn, "thinks he's cute but bananas," observed Jack Kroll in *Newsweek*.

Writes screenplay for That Was Then ... This Is Now

Late in 1985, Estevez appeared in *That Was Then ... This Is Now,* a film for which he also wrote the screenplay. The movie is based on a novel by S. E. Hinton that Estevez had first read in 1981 during the filming of *Tex*. After reading *That Was Then ... This Is Now,* Estevez contacted the author, and she agreed to his offer to adapt it for the screen. "I don't necessarily want to be a screenwriter," Estevez told *Teen*. "But I came across a project that I became passionate about. I wanted to bring it to the screen because it's a film about young people that's honest. Hopefully, my vision will be captured."

Unlike the novel, which is set in the sixties, Estevez's film version is set in contemporary Minneapolis-St. Paul. It concerns the relationship between two teenage boys whose longtime friendship is threatened when one of them falls in love. "No pals could be more dissimilar, and that's part of the key to their bond," wrote Peter Rose in the *Detroit News*. "Mark [Estevez] is impetuous, with a hearty dash of the criminal. Byron [played by Craig Sheffer] is the proverbial good kid." Discussing his *That Was Then* character with the *Chicago Tribune*'s Robert Blau, Estevez reflected: "There's probably a lot of him in me, the alter ego screaming to get out every once in a while. Fortunately, I was able to vent it in a film and not in real life."

Estevez admits that he enjoys writing. He told *American Film*'s Thomas Wiener that if he weren't an actor, he'd probably be interested in journalism or some other writing-related field. As it is, he's done a significant amount of writing in the movie industry. In addition to *That Was Then*, he wrote an original screenplay for the movie *Wisdom*—which he also starred in (with his then-fiancée, Demi Moore) and directed. The movie, released in 1986, centers on a man who is unable to get a job because of a felony conviction he received for joyriding in a stolen car when he was only a teenager. Estevez explained the character's predicament in *Nuestro* magazine: "[John Wisdom] is someone who got a raw deal, because of that black mark by his name which prevents him from getting a job. He had great expectations of himself, and his parents had certain expectations of him, and life isn't going like he planned. So he reaches a point where he says, 'Society's left me no choice but to become the one thing I've really resisted becoming—a criminal.' But his conscience is too strong to be a criminal against the people, so he decides to be a criminal *for* the people." Despite Estevez's conviction, *Wisdom* was a disappointment both critically and commercially.

Estevez continued his writing/directing/starring role in the 1990 comedy *Men at Work*. The film, about California garbagemen who become involved with a murder and an ocean-polluting chemical company, also starred Estevez's brother Charlie Sheen. Again, critics were unkind in their view of Estevez's work. Ralph Novak, writing in *People,* believed that "finding things to like in this film resembles—what else?—garbage picking. You have to poke through the junk to get to the good stuff."

Estevez's work in two films that both spawned sequels, however, was immensely popular. In 1988 he starred in *Young Guns*. The hit film, which follows the exploits of Billy the Kid (Estevez) and his gang, also features Kiefer Sutherland and Lou Diamond Phillips. All three actors, along with others, reprised their roles in the 1990 sequel, *Young Guns 2*.

In 1987 Estevez had starred with Richard Dreyfuss and Madeleine Stowe in the comedy/thriller *Stakeout*. The film, about a pair of police detectives who stake out a woman's apartment hoping to find her

boyfriend who broke out of prison, was a success. Six years later, Estevez and Dreyfuss
teamed up again in *Stakeout 2*. This time they
had to keep an eye on a woman who was
going to testify against the Mob.

> When asked about changing his name, Estevez told *Teen:* "Emilio Sheen sounds stupid anyway. Emilio Estevez sounds more romantic."

Estevez enjoys acting because it "gives you a license to be crazy," he
told *Teen*. "I can be a doctor, a hoodlum, an athlete or whatever. The possibilities are endless." Sometime in the future he hopes to costar with his
father, actor Martin Sheen, in *The Subject Was Roses*. Father and son have
worked together in the past—they costarred in the television movie *In the
Custody of Strangers* in 1982 and onstage in a Burt Reynolds Dinner Theatre production of *Mr. Roberts*. But Estevez is reluctant to align himself
professionally with his famous father; he's eager to make his own way in
the industry, thus his decision to retain the family name, rather than use
Sheen, his father's stage name. "I'm not ashamed of him in any way,"
Estevez said when discussing that decision with Wiener. "But a lot of
times ... it's not Emilio Estevez on the street, it's Martin Sheen's son, and I
think the more I disassociate myself, the more the public sees Emilio
Estevez without that identification following him."

Being the son of an actor has its advantages, Estevez admits. "I've
been around sets my whole life," he told *Teen*. "As a kid, I thought they
were boring, but I didn't realize how much information I was absorbing.
It was like being in school." His father wanted him to be a doctor or a
lawyer, Estevez revealed to *Teen*. "He thought becoming an actor was the
dumbest thing I could do because he knew what I was getting myself
into." Nonetheless, Estevez reports that his father has been "extremely
supportive" of his career decisions. Sheen also helps his son keep his
growing fame in perspective: "The most significant thing my father
taught me is that my job is no more or less important than someone
else's," Estevez told *Teen*. "When I realize there are a billion people in
China that don't know I exist, any flightiness is swept away."

In 1992 Estevez married Paula Abdul, the equally famous dancer/
singer. With the media and their fans following their every move, the couple found it hard to lead a private life. The pressures of a Hollywood marriage soon proved to be too great, and the couple divorced in 1994.

Sources

American Film, March 1985.

Boxoffice, February 1986.

Cosmopolitan, June 1983.

Detroit Free Press, June 28, 1985; November 8, 1985; November 11, 1985.

Detroit News, October 29, 1985; November 12, 1985.

Films in Review, May 1985.

Hispanic, May 1994.

Hollywood Reporter, October 16, 1985.

Maclean's, February 18, 1985.

Nation, December 15, 1984.

Newsweek, August 2, 1982; February 25, 1985; July 1, 1985.

New York, February 18, 1985.

New Yorker, August 6, 1984; April 8, 1985.

New York Times, September 28, 1982; July 6, 1984; February 15, 1985.

Nuestro, April 1987.

People, February 18, 1985; September 16, 1985; November 25, 1985; September 17, 1990.

Rolling Stone, March 14, 1985.

Teen, September 1982; March 1985; July 1985; February 1991.

Time, February 22, 1993.

TV Guide, April, 24, 1993.

Washington Post, February 15, 1985.

Laurence Fishburne

Born in 1962
Augusta, Georgia

ACTOR

Since his stage debut at age ten, Laurence Fishburne has spent his life acting. "He's the kind of actor you can't wait to say action on—because you can't wait to see how he's gonna take it and deal with it," director Abel Ferrara said of Fishburne in a *Film Comment* interview. The roles Fishburne has chosen have been equally unpredictable, from psychopaths to activist lawyers, from the solid, hands-on father he played in *Boyz N The Hood* to the troubled cop of *Deep Cover*. "For every thug, for every nut, I try and do somebody who's a reasonable person, who's an educated person," the actor told Tom Perew of *Black Elegance*. Perew quoted a casting agent who praised Fishburne's selectivity and dedication: "I get the feeling he's more interested in the quality behind the work than the money."

"I don't think of this as people gambling on me because I'm a sure thing. I'm not going to get in front of the camera and choke. I've been doing this too long."

Fishburne was born in 1962, in Augusta, Georgia. His father, a corrections officer, frequently took him to the movies, but it was his mother, a schoolteacher, who introduced him to the stage. The family moved to a

> "My father took all the guys at this juvenile correction facility in the Bronx to see [*Cornbread*]. Afterward, we got together and they told me that I was doing good, that I had something really fine going for myself and that if I ever [messed] up, they'd be waiting. That kept me in line."

middle-class neighborhood in Brooklyn, New York, when Laurence was young, and soon he was auditioning for parts in local plays. "I've always been an actor," he remarked to James Ryan of *Premiere;* he informed *New York* magazine that his first role was in the second grade: "I was Peter Pan, the boy who never grows up. I still am—I play make-believe for a living." At age ten he appeared in the play *In My Many Names and Days* at the New Federal Theater. "I played a little 10-year-old baseball freak from Brooklyn who used to dig going to Ebbitts Field and watching Jackie Robinson," Fishburne recalled to *Washington Post* correspondent David Mills.

Fishburne next landed a role in the 1972 television film *If You Give a Dance, You Got to Pay the Band,* which led to a part on the soap opera *One Life to Live* when he was 11 years old that lasted three years. After joining the daytime series, he appeared in the dramatic film *Cornbread, Earl and Me.* The actor then earned a part in a Negro Ensemble Theater production and was accepted into the prestigious High School of Performing Arts in New York City. At 15, Fishburne embarked on the acting experience that would utterly transform him: a role as a member of the boat crew in Francis Ford Coppola's Vietnam epic *Apocalypse Now.*

Grew up on Apocalypse *set*

The *Los Angeles Times* quoted Fishburne as saying that shooting *Apocalypse* was "the most formative event" of his life. He had a chance to observe several luminaries of American film acting—Marlon Brando, Robert Duvall, Martin Sheen, and others—and to consult them for advice. Coppola taught Fishburne that acting "could be taken seriously, as art, with potential for educating, entertaining and touching people." And in the drenching rain and chaos of the filming in the Philippines, Fishburne lived a sporadically unsupervised fantasy of adolescence: "I was smoking reefer like everybody else," he told Patrick Pacheco of the *Los Angeles Times.* "My mother was there with me, but she couldn't control me so she called in the big guns, my father. Everybody in the company referred to him as 'the jailer,' but all he had to do was say, 'OK, that's enough of that,' and I'd come around."

Fishburne made the second of what would be a series of appearances in Coppola films, portraying Midget in *Rumble Fish,* after playing a heavy in *Death Wish II.* "I was only getting work playing bad guys, and I wanted to be an actor and didn't want to wait tables," he told Perew in *Black Ele-*

gance. "But I would have [done so, if necessary]." In what Mills called Fishburne's "least dignified professional moment," the actor's *Death Wish* character "shielded his head with a boom box while fleeing vigilante Charles Bronson."

Fishburne was concerned with balancing the roles he portrayed and combating Hollywood stereotypes. He succeeded by appearing in two more Coppola films, *The Cotton Club* and *Gardens of Stone,* as well as in Steven Spielberg's *The Color Purple.* He also participated in the PBS drama *For Us the Living,* based on the story of Medgar Evers, a crucial figure in the American school desegregation movement of the late 1950s and early 1960s. Fishburne explained in the *Los Angeles Times* that "this is a gig where I had to put myself up and pay my own transportation, but to be involved with Roscoe Lee Browne, Howard Rollins, Dick Anthony Williams, Irene Cara. Well, that was my ancestors saying to me, 'OK, here's some work we can do.'" He further confided that "I work with somebody on what is called 'ancestral memory,' and I find it a source of spiritual strength," since the struggles of the past "are not something to be embarrassed by, but a resource to be valued and respected."

Took diverse film roles

In the meantime, an ambitious young director had been keeping an eye on Fishburne. One day in the mid-1980s, reported Mills in the *Washington Post,* Fishburne was watching a street performance when someone tapped him on the shoulder. "I don't know who this guy is. He says, 'You're Larry Fishburne.... You're a good actor.' So he introduced himself and said he was from Brooklyn and he was making movies." The Brooklyn filmmaker was Spike Lee, who wanted Fishburne to appear in a film called *Messenger.* The movie was never made, but Lee utilized Fishburne in *School Daze;* the actor played the campus activist Dap in that collegiate musical comedy.

Fishburne later passed up the role of Radio Raheem in Lee's 1989 smash *Do the Right Thing,* criticizing the film's plot for straying from reality. "I'm from Brooklyn too," he told Mills. "And I didn't grow up in that kind of Brooklyn." Though Fishburne experienced some friction with Lee, the actor's refusal of roles in subsequent Lee films has evidently had more to do with Fishburne's desire for a starring part than any lingering hard feelings.

While working on *School Daze,* Fishburne met Hajna Moss, a casting agent and producer. The two eventually married and had two children, settling in the Bedford-Stuyvesant section of Brooklyn. Fishburne accepted the role of an orderly in the 1987 horror film *A Nightmare on Elm Street 3* in order to make the down payment on a house. "My wife likes horror movies, we wanted to buy a house, and they offered me a gig," he explained to Ryan. "[The film's supernatural villain Freddy Krueger] and I never met." Fishburne also played a cop in the thriller *Red Heat,* and starting in the late 1980s had the continuing role of the lovable Cowboy Curtis on Pee-Wee Herman's Saturday morning television series *Pee-Wee's Playhouse.* Among his other television projects were the film *A Rumor of War* and guest appearances on episodes of *Hill Street Blues* and *Miami Vice.*

In 1990 Fishburne landed an important role playing "New Jack Gangster" Jimmy Jump in Abel Ferrara's *King of New York,* costarring Christopher Walken and Wesley Snipes. Though the part was originally written for an Italian American, Fishburne lobbied for it. "This cat was funny, enjoyed what he did," he said of the character in his interview with Gavin Smith for *Film Comment.* "He didn't deal drugs, he just killed people—the kind of lovable badman any actor would love to do. I talked to them for about four hours and I said, 'Look, young black people who saw *School Daze* in particular recognize me; there's at least two million of them living in New York, and if you put me in this role, a million of them will go see it, guaranteed, and they'll tell the other million.'" His extravagant performance was evidently as much fun for him to do as it was for his audience to watch. "I took some liberty," he admitted to Smith. "For some people it may seem exaggerated, overblown, like I'm going way over the top with it. But that's real stuff." Fishburne also began working with playwright Lanford Wilson in 1990 to develop the character of Sterling in Wilson's *Two Trains Running.*

True to his commitment to balance the cinematic "nuts" with responsible characters, Fishburne played an attorney working for activist lawyer Gene Hackman in Michael Apted's 1991 film *Class Action. People* correspondent Ralph Novak felt that Fishburne and the rest of the supporting cast were "first teamers." *Sight and Sound* praised "a perfectly formed performance from Larry Fishburne, a great black actor spoiling for a part in something really big." Fishburne also appeared in Martin Sheen's *Cadence,* a military drama costarring Sheen and his son Charlie. "Fishburne, as leader of the black stockade residents, has a sly Jack Nicholson-like way of ingratiating himself," wrote Novak.

Gained recognition with Boyz

Fishburne's next big project was *Boyz N The Hood,* a film directed by then-23-year-old John Singleton, who had been a production assistant on *Pee-Wee's Playhouse.* As Furious Styles, the entrepreneur-activist father who guides his son out of trouble and into responsibility, Fishburne earned rave reviews. *Sight and Sound* declared, "Larry Fishburne continues to be a matchless screen presence in the central role of Furious," while Stanley Kauffmann of the *New Republic* wrote that the actor "brings an even-tempered, unforced authority to the role."

Even critics who disliked the film's tone admired Fishburne's work. Novak noted that Fishburne "acts his way through most of Singleton's verbiage, conveying the determination of a father trying to give his son a chance." Edmond Grant of *Films In Review* lamented that "the finest actor in the film ... gets the corniest role." While admitting that Fishburne "does bring some depth to the role," Grant was disturbed that Furious functioned primarily as "an obvious mouthpiece for Singleton's concerns." Christine Dolen of the *Detroit Free Press* observed that with *Boyz* Fishburne "seemed to leap, like a major movie star at the height of his power, from the screen into our startled and appreciative consciousness." Yet Fishburne is quoted in the same piece as saying that "*Boyz N The Hood* did take my career to a different level. But I did what I've been doing for the last 20 years. I think it was the power of the whole film. I give the credit to the writing and the execution of that film."

Won awards for stage role

In his next role, in Lanford Wilson's stage play *Two Trains Running*, which opened on Broadway in 1992, Fishburne won a Tony Award for best featured actor in a play and also picked up Outer Critic's Circle, Drama Desk, and Theater World awards. As Sterling, an ex-convict espousing the black empowerment philosophy of civil rights activist Malcolm X, Fishburne once again stunned the critics. Frank Rich of the *New York Times* wrote that the actor "greets each of Sterling's defeats with pride and heroic optimism" and called Fishburne and his costar Roscoe Lee Browne "the jewels of the production."

Perew claimed that Fishburne's work in *Two Trains Running* "should convince any doubters that Larry Fishburne will forever play lead roles" and added, "Watching the play, you get black history the way Sterling has seen it. Fishburne is quirky, insightful, often humorous and, finally, a profound Sterling." Of the role, the actor himself stated in the *Los Angeles Times* interview with Pacheco that "Sterling's a man with an idea, and that's what makes him dangerous," and that the character has "just got out of jail, he's got no money and he's got no job. When a brother's got to get himself a hustle, that makes him dangerous." He told Dolen that working with Browne, Wilson and director Lloyd Richards was a bigger thrill than winning a Tony: "This is the longest time I've worked in the theater. It's the most exciting; it requires real discipline and develops your concentration to a level that I know when I come off this, no matter what the part is in what movie, I'll be able to do it. Because I feel like a bona fide actor now."

Playeд a дeep character in Deep Cover

Returning to film in 1992, Fishburne portrayed a genuinely challenging character in *Deep Cover:* Russell Stevens, Jr., an undercover cop who gets drawn into the world of drugdealing and begins to lose his moral bearings. Director Bill Duke found Fishburne's subtlety and range perfect for the part: "Larry can show a side of himself that will do whatever is necessary to get what he wants. He becomes as ferocious a bad guy as [he is] a cop. Looking in Larry's eyes, you don't see a lie, and that's what you want in an actor," Duke explained to Ryan, adding that he found Fishburne "confident but not egotistical." Commenting on Duke's improvisational, actor-centered approach, Fishburne observed in an *Entertainment Weekly* profile, "It's collaborative here. Everyone throws in his two cents." Duke contended in the same article that Fishburne was at first uneasy with the director's approach: "Larry hated working with me in the beginning. He's used to rehearsing a scene the way it's going to be shot. I said, 'Larry, that's not how I work.' It always made him nervous, but he started to trust me and we had a good collaboration."

In 1993 Fishburne starred in *What's Love Got to Do With It?* The film, based on singer Tina Turner's autobiography, *I, Tina,* details the years of abuse Tina suffered from her troubled husband Ike Turner. Wanting to show him as a real person and not as a caricature, Fishburne refused to play Ike until he was portrayed with more compassion. Critics praised his performance and Fishburne was nominated for an Academy Award. Fishburne followed *What's Love Got to Do With It?* with *Searching for Bobby Fisher,* in which he played a street chess master. Fishburne's next role will be to portray Jimi Hendrix, the legendary guitarist. Fishburne won an Emmy Award for Guest Actor in a Drama for Fox Television's *Tribeca* in 1993.

With an Academy Award nomination, an Emmy Award, and a Tony Award, Fishburne certainly moved to the first rank of American actors, retaining and strengthening his reputation for integrity and depth. Yet, he claimed in his discussion with Ryan that he has never been in a hurry to achieve fame. "I'm glad it took this long. I probably wouldn't have been able to deal with it when I was frustrated about it. I don't know what would have happened. It might have pushed my self-destruct button."

Sources

Black Elegance, June/July 1992.

Detroit Free Press, June 2, 1992.

Ebony, July 1993.

Entertainment Weekly, April 24, 1992.

Film Comment, July/August 1990.

Films In Review, February 1992.

Jet, July 15, 1991; October 4, 1993.

Los Angeles Times, January 12, 1992.

New Republic, September 2, 1991.

Newsweek, July 15, 1991; July 26, 1993.

New York, July 22, 1991.

New York Times, April 14, 1992.

Parade, June 28, 1992.

People, March 25, 1991; April 1, 1991; July 22, 1991.

Premiere, May 1992.

Sight and Sound, July 1991; August 1991; November 1991.

Time, May 11, 1992; December 27, 1993.

Video Review, March 1992.

Washington Post, July 1991.

Bridget Fonda

Born January 27, 1964

"I've just always gone in my own direction and done things in my own way for my own reasons. That's a healthy way of rebelling, because you don't destroy yourself."

ACTRESS

Bridget Fonda is emerging as one of the leading actresses of her generation. She has demonstrated her talent by skillfully playing a wide variety of roles in such films as *Scandal, Single White Female,* and *Point of No Return.* She also happens to be the latest in an impressive line of actors bearing the name Fonda. The Fonda dynasty began with Bridget's grandfather, the highly acclaimed actor Henry Fonda, and has continued with her aunt, Jane Fonda, and her father, Peter Fonda. When asked in *Cosmopolitan* about how it feels to bear the famous Fonda name, Bridget replied, "I'm not going to look a gift horse in the mouth. I know that's what got me in the door. But it doesn't bother me." Yet while she understood that the family name could provide opportunity, Bridget was also aware of its burden, as she struggled to establish her own accomplishments. She told *Cosmopolitan,* "I figured if I wanted to overcome my famous family, I'd have to dive right into doing that. But I was scared. "According to Bridget, it took her years to establish a name for herself based on her own merits.

Grew up in the free-spirited sixties

Bridget Jane Fonda was born in 1964 to Peter and Susan Fonda. The "Bridget" came from Bridget Hayward, an old flame of her father's who committed suicide, and the "Jane" came from her aunt, Jane Fonda. Her father was notorious for his freewheeling lifestyle, and Bridget's upbringing was unconventional and filled with the extremes of the 1960s counterculture movement. She was also exposed to the highly publicized turbulence in the Fonda family: divorces, suicides, feuds. In 1972 Bridget's parents divorced, and she and her brother, Justin, stayed with their mother in Los Angeles, California. When her mother moved to Montana to live with her new boyfriend, Bridget was forced to shuttle between her two parents' homes. She denies any resentment and remains close to them both.

When Bridget attended Westlake School for Girls in Los Angeles, she played the part of Nurse Kelly in the school production of the comedy *Harvey.* After that experience, she decided she wanted to become an actress. She applied, and was accepted to the prestigious Lee Strasberg Theatre Institute, at New York University. While there, she experienced some frustrations because she was a Fonda. Various teachers pulled her aside and told her that she would be treated no differently than any other student. Yet, Bridget recognized that she was already being treated differently by virtue of having been pulled aside. Bridget also encountered those that belittled her performances by implying that she never had to work at perfecting her craft because it was already "in her blood." Bridget told *Cosmopolitan,* "I *didn't* have it in my blood. I went to school for four years, and I was petrified—I had the *worst* stage fright. I never learned anything from my family. I didn't take classes with them."

Begins movie career

Fonda's first film was the 1988 *Aria,* in which she had a seven-minute sex scene but no dialogue. Her first speaking part was in the 1988 failure *You Can't Hurry Love,* which Fonda would just as soon forget. It was in 1989, in the film *Scandal,* that she found her breakthrough role. Based on a true story, the movie examined the "Profumo Affair," a notorious scandal that upset the British government in the early 1960s. Fonda played Mandy Rice-Davies, a London showgirl who served as an "escort" to important government officials along with her friend Christine Keeler. When the tabloids discovered that Keeler was involved with both John Profumo, the secretary of state for war, and Eugene Ivanov, a Soviet intelligence agent, a huge scandal arose. Because Britain and the Soviet Union had different political and economic philosophies, each country distrusted the other. When it was discovered that Keeler had had affairs with high officials from each government, it was perceived as a major security breach. It eventually led to the resignation of Profumo. The movie received mixed reviews, but Fonda gained notice for her provocative and comic performance.

Her next three films were generally considered box-office failures: in *Shag* (1989), Fonda played a mischievous preacher's daughter who enters a beauty pageant in order to gain the attention of a pop star; in *Strapless* (1989), her role was that of a party-loving younger sister to a female doctor; and in Roger Corman's *Frankenstein Unbound* (1990) she was Mary Godwin, the author of the original *Frankenstein* and wife of the poet Percy Bysshe Shelley. Despite the negative reviews, Fonda's performances were generally well received. For example, in a review of *Shag,* Hal Hinson of the *Washington Post* wrote, "This icy blond actress ... who earlier this year provided the best moments in the British film *Scandal,* has a startlingly confident camera presence. She takes over her scenes naturally—through sheer animal vigor, she makes it impossible to look at anyone else."

Fonda continued to work at an unrelenting pace. She won a small but notable role as a photojournalist in *The Godfather Part III* in 1990. Then, in 1991, Fonda appeared in six films: *Leatherjackets,* a movie about gangs and love; *Out of the Rain,* in which she played a victim of incest; *Iron Maze,* about a Japanese businessman who overruns a small midwestern town when he builds an amusement park; *Drop Dead Fred,* in which she appears as a cold-hearted bimbo; *Pie in the Sky*; and *Doc Hollywood,* the Michael J. Fox feature in which she plays the town sexpot. "I'm worried about burnout," Fonda told *Cosmopolitan* in the midst of her hectic schedule. "Now I've finally figured out why I never really knew where my dad was—he was always off filming."

In 1992 Fonda played in a clever comedy and a suspense thriller. In *Singles* Fonda was part of an ensemble cast of 20-something characters who are searching for love and meaning in contemporary Seattle. She played Janet Livermore, an architect who suffers from unreturned love and who waitresses because she can't find a job. Despite very positive reviews, the movie was only a minor box-office success. In *Single White Female* Fonda portrayed Allison Jones, a successful New York computer programmer whose new roommate turns out to be psychotic. Although some critics objected to the violence, most appreciated the film and Fonda's performance.

Fonda's first film in 1993, *Point of No Return,* was an American remake of the French thriller *La Femme Nikita.* Her role was that of a crass, young criminal who the government transforms into a sophisticated and lethal assassin. Reviews were generally unfavorable, with many finding the delicate Fonda too soft for the role of a tough killer. *Bodies, Rest and Motion* was similar to *Singles,* in that it explored the anxiety and depression of the X generation—that group of people who are coming of age in the 1990s. Fonda played a waitress in a small Arizona town who falls in love with a young house painter. The film was praised but received little attention at the theaters.

Fonda next tackled *It Could Happen to You,* which was released in the summer of 1994. Fonda is once again cast as a waitress. When a New York cop (Nicolas Cage) doesn't have enough money for a tip, he promises to split his lottery ticket with her if he should win. When he does win, he keeps his word and Fonda's life is transformed. The movie is a lighthearted comedy with a fairy-tale quality, and it performed well at the box-office. Fonda followed-up with 1994's *The Road to Wellville,* a period piece about upper-class visitors to a midwestern health spa that teamed her with Matthew Broderick and Oscar-winner Anthony Hopkins.

Sources

Cosmopolitan, August 1989; May 1991; April 1993.

Mademoiselle, April 1993.

Premiere, April 1993; June 1994.

Rolling Stone, April 20, 1989.

Washington Post, July 21, 1989.

Jodie Foster

Born in November 1962
Los Angeles, California

"Obsession is pain and a longing for something that does not exist. John Hinckley's greatest crime was the confusion of love and obsession. The trivialization is something I will never forgive him."

ACTRESS AND DIRECTOR

Jodie Foster, by her own admission, is unusual among Hollywood actresses. She is a self-taught, "instinctual" actress who has flourished as a product of the Hollywood system without becoming a part of it. She has successfully made the transition from child to adult actress, a rarity in Hollywood, because her mother-manager had a definite plan not to have Jodie perceived as a "child actor" who did "kiddie parts." But, even more unusual, Foster interrupted her career in 1980 to attend Yale University, where she majored in literature and excelled in a program with a rigorous curriculum. "Practical things didn't interest me. I really wanted to go into the ivory tower and study mind things," Foster told *Harper's Bazaar.*

Foster's freshman year at Yale was complicated when she learned that John Hinckley had attempted to assassinate President Ronald Reagan on March 30, 1981, as a symbol of his "love" for her. Hinckley had become obsessed with Foster after repeated viewings of Martin Scorsese's *Taxi Driver*, a 1976 film starring Robert De Niro as an urban psychopath and Foster as a young prostitute. Foster did not know Hinckley and has had to live with the confusion his actions have created in the public's mind.

Born in Los Angeles, California, in November 1962 and named Alicia Christian, Jodie Foster is the daughter of Lucius Foster III, a real estate executive, and Evelyn Almond Foster, known as Brandy. Jodie is the youngest child of four in a family that includes sisters Lucinda and Constance and brother Lucius IV. Her parents were divorced when Evelyn Foster was unknowingly three-months pregnant with Jodie, who has only met her father a few times. Evelyn Foster, a resourceful woman, worked as a publicist for producer Arthur Jacobs and then managed the career of Jodie's older brother, who appeared in commercials and on the CBS television series *Mayberry, R.F.D.*, and whose income first supported the family, eventually being supplanted by Jodie's.

Begins career as "Coppertone Girl"

Jodie's career was launched quite accidentally when she was discovered at the age of three at a Coppertone audition to which her mother had taken her brother. The advertising representatives spotted Jodie in the studio and then called Evelyn Foster with an offer. Jodie made 45 commercials while a child for products with national reputations, such as Crest toothpaste, before her mother decided that Jodie, at the age of eight, was ready for television and movies. She made her debut on an episode of *Mayberry*.

A precocious child, Jodie talked at nine months, spoke in complete sentences at one year, and could read and understand scripts by the time she was five. Besides being cute and photogenic, Jodie Foster was obviously an intelligent child who possessed an uncanny ability to act before a camera. As she explained to *Life* magazine: "I had tremendous responsibility, financial and otherwise, for my family. I never perceived myself as a kid. I saw myself as a small human being walking around."

Evelyn Foster regarded Jodie's education, and not the child's acting career, as the first priority. She took Jodie out of the public school system at the beginning of the third grade because school officials wanted Jodie to skip a grade and study science, a decision made on the basis of test scores determined by the state's gifted program. Evelyn Foster wanted her daughter to study a foreign language and enrolled Jodie in the bilingual Lycée Français, where she graduated class valedictorian in 1980.

TV Career

Following her acting start on *Mayberry, R.F.D.*, Foster's television career included a number of guest appearances on television shows such as *Bonanza*, *Gunsmoke*, and *My Three Sons*. A 1972 CBS pilot, *My Sister Hank*, did not make the fall lineup, and two ABC shows were short-lived. *Bob and Carol and Ted and Alice*, in which Foster played Elizabeth, the daughter of Bob and Carol Henderson (Robert Urich and Anne Archer), went off the air on November 7, 1973, after debuting on September 26. In the sitcom *Paper Moon*, based on the 1973 Peter Bogdanovich Depression-era film, Foster was cast as Addie Pray, the little urchin who believes the con artist Moze Pray (Chris Connelly) is her father. The series ran from September 12, 1974, until January 2, 1975. In the *ABC After-school Specials*, Jodie Foster starred in *Rookie of the Year*, which won an Emmy in 1973, and in *The Life of T.K. Dearing* in 1975.

Whenever young Jodie had to miss school because of acting commitments, her mother sought out the best teachers in California's educational program for child actors. "If there was stage-mothering, it was about her classes. If I couldn't get certain teachers for her, she didn't work," Evelyn Foster told Jesse Kornbluth of *Vanity Fair*. Jodie Foster is close to her mother and depends upon her guidance and companionship. The bond is so strong that Evelyn Foster often accompanies her daughter on location: "I need to be with someone who loves me and who I can come home to every night, and that might as well be Mom," Foster told Kornbluth, adding, "She's been through so much and has sacrificed so much for us, it's great to be able to give her what she loves and deserves."

The Disney years

Foster went through a Walt Disney period that included *Menace on the Mountains* and *Napoleon and Samantha* (1972), the latter starring Johnny Whitaker and Foster as Whitaker's "saucy chum" in the title roles, and costarring a pet lion. Off-camera the lion picked up the eight-year-old Jodie in his mouth, resulting in an injury that hospitalized the child. But she returned to the movie ten days later, even though her mother said she could quit if she wanted. In Disney's *One Little Indian* (1973), Foster had a small part, and she shared the lead with Barbara Harris in *Freaky Friday* (1977), playing daughter Annabel, who wishes she could change places with her mother, Ellen, who is wishing the same thing. The two get their wishes, but after one day of comic mishaps each is content to be herself. Foster's last Disney movie was *Candleshoe* (1977), in which she appeared as a Los Angeles street kid who is tricked by Leo McKern to pose as the heir of Helen Hayes in a comedy that has David Niven playing a smug British butler.

Other films of this period included British director Alan Parker's *Bugsy Malone* (1976), an original satire of American gangster movies of the 1920s, in which all the actors are children and gangland shootouts come equipped with machine guns that squirt Reddi-Whip, deadly custard pies, and hoodlums who race around in peddle-driven vintage automobiles.

Takes on controversial role in Taxi Driver

The role that changed Jodie Foster's career and would later have a larger, more personal meaning for her was that of Iris, the 12-year-old prostitute, in Martin Scorsese's *Taxi Driver* (1976), in which Robert De Niro delivered a dynamic performance as the psychotic Travis Bickle. The highly controversial film hit a cultural nerve at the time of its release. The reason, Canby in part explained, was that De Niro as Bickle "is a projection of all our nightmares of urban alienation, refined in a performance that is effective as much for what Mr. De Niro does as for how he does it." Foster at first did not want the part. "I was the Disney kid. I thought, 'What would my friends say?' I could just hear their little snickerings. So I didn't want to do it," she explained to Judy Klemesrud of the *New York Times*. But it was her mother who decided the opportunity to act with Robert De Niro in a Martin Scorsese film could not be passed up. Foster had appeared in Scorsese's *Alice Doesn't Live Here Anymore,* and the director had picked Foster for *Taxi Driver* on the strength of her *Alice* performance. The role won Foster best supporting actress awards from the New York Film Critics, National Film Critics, and Los Angeles Film Critics, as well as an all-important Academy Award nomination. She said no special research went into the role except being aware of the society in which she lives. However, the Los Angeles Welfare Board had Foster undergo psychological tests and an interview with a psychiatrist before approval would be granted for her to work on the film. A welfare worker was on the set each day, and Foster could not be present on the set when De Niro was doing a scene in which he used foul language. "Actually, I think the only thing that could have had a bad effect on me was the blood in the shooting scene. It was really neat, though. It was red sugary stuff. And they used Styrofoam for bones. And a pump to make the blood gush out of a man's arm after his hand was shot off," Foster explained to Klemesrud, with the typical enthusiasm of a 13-year-old.

Following *Taxi Driver* came *The Little Girl Who Lives Down the Lane* (1977), in which Foster, as the orphan Rynn, uses a vial of poison to keep the child-molesting Martin Sheen character away from her. Director Nicolas Gessner and screenwriter Laird Koenig depend more on atmosphere and a realistic performance from Jodie Foster than violence and gore to create the film's sense of terror and suspense. Jodie Foster refused to appear nude, saying the public does not want to see a 14-year-old naked on screen; Jodie's older sister Constance was used in her place.

Foxes and *Carny*, both released in 1980, are realistic slice-of-life films that demanded different kinds of performance skills from Foster, which she deftly provided. *Foxes* portrays the lives of four high school girls in the San Fernando Valley. In *Carny* Foster plays a restless, unhappy small-town girl named Donna who is transformed into a hard-nosed carnival worker. *Carny* captures the atmosphere of carnival life while telling the story of Donna's loss of innocence.

Hinckley's effect on her life

Foster dislikes talking about John Hinckley, and she recognizes that any public statement she may make gives the incident a kind of permanent life that she clearly does not want to perpetuate, although reporters feel compelled to continue to question her. In 1981, in the aftermath of the assassination attempt, the media attention took on a life of its own that was difficult to handle, even for a young woman as poised and full of self-control as Foster. The Hinckley publicity unfortunately brought death threats from other disturbed individuals. Foster had hoped that her social experience at Yale would be such that she would not draw attention purely for her celebrity status. She had wanted to be accepted as a typical Yale student. The media and public attention shattered her illusion; she realized that from the first day on campus she had been the object of constant public observation.

In 1984's *Hotel New Hampshire* Foster meshed her interest in serious literature with filmmaking. British director Tony Richardson, who previously brought Henry Fielding's *Tom Jones* to the screen, adapted John Irving's novel about the eccentric Barry family and their odd assortment of guests. Foster is Franny, the oldest of five children, "who talks tough but is true blue underneath." Her brother, John (Rob Lowe), the film's narrator, is in love with her, and the relationship between the two provides the film with much of its dramatic tension.

Wins respect with **The Accused**

Between 1986 and 1988 Foster appeared in five films. But it is clearly *The Accused* that brought her the most critical praise and renewed respect as an actress delivering a top-rate performance in an important role of social significance. Foster plays Sarah Tobias, a lower-class young woman who is brutally raped one night in the back room of a seedy bar on a pinball machine by three men while a crowd of male onlookers cheers the rapists on. (The film takes its premise from a real incident in which a group of men raped a woman in a tavern in New Bedford, Massachusetts, an event described by one critic as "one of America's ugliest public moments.")

Sarah, a foul-mouthed, hard-living woman, is initially part of the mostly male crowd's revelry, having smoked marijuana and danced provocatively with one of the rapists prior to the attack, even letting him kiss her. The assistant district attorney, Katheryn Murphy (Kelly McGillis), decides to settle for a plea-bargained lesser charge, reckless endangerment, given Sarah's unreliability as a witness, which enrages Sarah because she was not consulted. Sarah wants to redeem her self-esteem by having her day in court. The case does end up in court with McGillis charging three men who cheered the rapists on with criminal solicitation in a tricky and difficult legal move.

The Accused was Foster's first movie in which she plays an adult whose presence dominates the screen. Described as "a model of no-nonsense, tightlipped movie making" by Janet Maslin in the *New York Times*, *The Accused* succeeds because of Foster's command of the character, culminating in the movie's brutal rape scene, which sets a new film standard for realism. David Ansen in *Newsweek* stated: "Always good, even in less than great films, Jodie Foster is one of Hollywood's more undervalued assets. In *The Accused*, she unleashes a performance of blunt but marvelously controlled fury: one from the gut." Foster won her first Academy Award for her portrayal of Sarah Tobias.

In Tony Bill's *Five Corners* Foster plays another victim, this time of an attempted rape by Heinz (John Turturro), a violent psychopath. Foster as Linda, a young woman who works in a pet shop, is in need of protection when Heinz is released from prison. Set in the Bronx in the fall of 1964, *Five Corners* is a period piece of urban violence and terror. Foster first saw the script as an update of the King Kong myth, but Turturro's interpretation of Heinz changed the film into something much more menacing and disturbing. Asked by Nina Darnton of the *New York Post* why she would make a movie that parallels her own personal experience with John Hinckley, Foster replied: "It's odd, I never even thought of the script in terms of Hinckley until about three weeks into the shooting. I don't know why. Maybe I was blocking it. But even my mom didn't think of it. When I read the script it seemed funnier. I laughed at some of the scenes.... There's another thing. I can't stop playing a victim just because of Hinckley. Being a victim is unfortunately a big part of women's lives."

In this busy two-year period, Foster also appeared in Mary Lambert's *Siesta,* an artsy experimental film set in Spain starring Ellen Barkin, and in Steven Kampmann and Will Aldis's *Stealing Home,* a coming-of-age story starring Mark Harmon as a washed-up baseball player who first learned about life and love from Foster's Katie Chandler character.

Wins Second Academy Award for Silence of the Lambs

Perhaps Foster's most acclaimed performance to date is that of Clarice Starling in the 1991 production of *Silence of the Lambs*. The psychological thriller focuses on the relationship between Starling, an eager young FBI agent, and Hannibal Lecter, a psychopathic killer who eats his victims. The FBI sends in Starling to interview Lecter in prison and gain information about another serial killer the agency is tracking. Lecter offers cryptic clues about the killer's identity, but only after Starling recalls some painful and revealing memories. According to Terrance Rafferty of the *New Yorker*, "Foster, with amazing delicacy, shows us the constant tension between the character's emotions and her actions—the omnipresent self-consciousness of inexperience." Foster won a second Academy Award for best actress for her work in this film.

Foster also debuted as a director in 1991 with *Little Man Tate*. This movie looks at a young boy with exceptional abilities, and details his need for creative and intellectual stimulation and the resulting conflict with his single, working-class mother's need to protect him and give him a "normal childhood." Foster played the role of the mother, and some felt that by directing herself she was unable to use the full range of her dramatic talents. The film won modest reviews, with many critics expressing a desire to see her direct more in the future.

Jodie Foster is 5'4", weighs 110 pounds, has long straight blond hair, deep blue eyes, and a unique voice that has been a distinctive personal trademark since childhood. She stays in shape by kick boxing four times a week with a trainer. Foster has kept her success in perspective and has lived modestly for someone at her level of the acting profession. She has a reputation of being polite and thoughtful with the press despite the rough treatment she received at the time of the Hinckley incident. She admits to being outspoken with a definite point of view concerning films and her ideas in general, but her own self-awareness takes the sting out of her brashness. She reads constantly but has decided not to pursue graduate school because the academic study of literature did not appeal to her. Foster's next project is producing *Nell*, a film about a small-town doctor who treats a woman who was raised in rural isolation and has developed her own language. Foster will star as the woman and Liam Neeson will play the doctor.

Sources

American Film, October 1988.

Chicago Tribune, February 14, 1988.

Dayton Daily News, October 14, 1988.

Esquire, December 1982.

Film Journal, September-October 1988.

Harper's Bazaar, July 1987; November 1991.

Life, September 1987.

Mademoiselle, September 1987.

Newsweek, October 24, 1988.

New York, October 31, 1988.

New Yorker, April 7, 1973; February 21, 1991.

New York Post, January 19, 1988.

New York Times, July 20, 1972; August 26, 1972; January 30, 1975, February 9, 1976; March 7, 1976; May 15, 1976; September 16, 1976; September 26, 1976; January 29, 1977; February 29, 1980; March 19, 1980; March 9, 1984; January 23, 1988; August 26, 1988; October 14, 1988; October 16, 1988.

Phoenix Gazette, March 18, 1988.

Rocky Mountain News, May 8, 1988.

Time, April 2, 1973; February 14, 1994.

Vanity Fair, September 1988.

Variety, August 10, 1988.

Washington Post, October 14, 1988.

Michael J. Fox

Born June 9, 1961
Edmonton, Alberta, Canada

"When I came home and said I wanted to be an actor [my parents] weren't angry. There was a bit of concern that it was a difficult way to make a living and that I might get hurt, but there was never a feeling that I couldn't accomplish anything I wanted to accomplish."

ACTOR

A familiar face to movie and television audiences alike, Michael J. Fox became one of the country's best-known entertainers before reaching age 25. His credits include *Family Ties,* for some time the second-most-popular series on television, and several top-grossing feature films, including the *Back to the Future* series. The 5'4" Canadian native exudes a mixture of energy and vulnerability; most of his roles have stressed his youthful appearance and small-town good looks. In an April 1987 *Ladies' Home Journal* profile, Susan Granger suggested that Fox's appeal "cuts across the generations"—that to young girls he is a sex symbol, to men he is something of a kid brother, and to women of all ages he is simply adorable.

Fox is equally popular with producers and directors, both for his ability to wring profits out of somewhat marginal films and for what director Robert Zemeckis called his "incredible comic sensibility" in a *Maclean's* cover story. Both offstage and on, Fox has espoused such basic values as hard work, family togetherness, and a drug-free lifestyle; he has also expressed his obligation to fans. Accessible and humble despite his fame, Fox has, in Zemeckis's words, "that twinkle that all great movie stars need to have."

Fox is a veteran actor, having begun working as a professional at the age of 15. He was born in Edmonton, Alberta, Canada, on June 9, 1961, the fourth of five children. His father spent 25 years as a career officer in the Canadian army, followed by another 15 years as a policeman, and the Fox family moved often. "I learned to adapt to new environments quickly," Fox told *Us*. "The attitude I took was, 'I might be getting negative attention right now, but I'll figure out how to turn it into positive attention. Right now, I'm the New Short Kid, but in a couple of weeks I can be Funny Mike or Smart Mike.'" Fox also remembers his childhood years with his family as a positive experience, and one that gave him valuable training as a budding comedian. "The oldest form of theater is the [family] dinner table," he told *Rolling Stone*. "It's got five or six people, new show every night, new script, same players. Good ensemble; the people have worked together a lot." Fox also claims that his family, still living in Vancouver, Canada, helps him to keep a proper perspective on his success. As he told the *Washington Post:* "If I was a brat, I'd get shot down up there pretty quick. If it gets out of proportion, there are five or six people in Canada who can put it back in proportion."

At the age of 15, Fox discovered acting through his high school drama classes in suburban Vancouver. On a tip from his drama teacher, Fox auditioned for the role of a ten-year-old in a Canadian Broadcasting Company (CBC) situation comedy series called *Leo and Me*. "Being fifteen, I figured I'd be the brightest ten-year-old they'd ever seen," Fox recalled in *Us*. "I went down to the audition, and they thought I was a prodigy." Fox won the role, and began his professional career.

Drops out of school to pursue acting

The television series consumed a great deal of Fox's time over the following year, and his school teachers began pressuring him to quit acting. "One teacher said, 'You're not going to be cute forever,'" Fox recalled in *Us*. "'If you want to be a cute dummy, it's up to you.' That was the stupidest thing I'd ever heard, so I left." With one year remaining in his education, Fox quit school to pursue performing full time. *Rolling Stone* quoted Fox on his decision: "I don't care about not finishing [school]. They did nothing there but hold me back.... But I think I would like to go to college

Roughing It While Unemployed

Although deeply in debt, Fox refused to return to Canada and instead sold a sectional couch piece by piece and subsisted on macaroni and cheese. He had lost 20 pounds by the time he was asked to audition for *Family Ties*.

some day, I've always felt I had a writer's mentality, but between my brain and my hand are routes that haven't been completely charted yet. I'd like to go to school to begin developing those paths."

Soon after turning 18, Fox left Canada for Los Angeles, where he hoped for more acting opportunities. In the process of joining Actors' Equity, he discovered that the organization already had a Michael Fox on its rolls, so he added a middle initial to his professional name. Though his middle name is actually Andrew, Fox chose J as a middle initial because of his admiration for Michael J. Pollard, one of the stars of the film *Bonnie and Clyde*. Fox's diminutive stature and youthful appearance helped him to land guest appearances on a number of television shows, including *Trapper John, M.D., Lou Grant,* and author Alex Haley's unsuccessful series, *Palmerstown, U.S.A.* He also starred in the Disney comedy *Midnight Madness*.

From 1980 until 1982, however, Fox was unemployed, due in part to a Screen Actors Guild strike. "My phone suddenly stopped ringing," Fox told *People*. "I'm sure it happens to every actor, but I'd never planned for it." The *New York Times* also quoted Fox on this period of his life: "I didn't have a phone, a couch, or any money.... When NBC called me in to say I had a part [in *Family Ties*], I called my agent from a phone booth in front of the Pioneer Chicken to negotiate the contract." Fox told *People*: "I was on the phone with my agent, saying it had to be so many thousand per week, wishing I just had $1.99 to go in and buy chicken and biscuits."

Becomes a star through Family Ties

The part that boosted Fox's career was that of Alex Keaton on the NBC situation comedy *Family Ties*. In the series, Fox played the ultra-conservative, would–be–yuppie son of ex-hippy parents Meredith Baxter-Birney and Michael Gross. First aired in 1982, the show gained popularity steadily and then jumped to the top of the Nielsen ratings when it began to run immediately after the popular *Cosby Show*. After several seasons, *Us* magazine reported, Fox had become "the star of the 'Family Ties' ensemble." Fox enhanced his own viability in the role by suggesting that the script writers use his height as a vehicle for jokes. Having learned not to be sensitive about his stature, Fox told his producer, "If you can use it to get some laughs, go ahead." The series ended in May 1989, still one of the top-rated shows in television.

Fox's role in *Family Ties* brought him to the attention of producer Steven Spielberg, who was searching for an actor to star in the Robert Zemeckis production *Back to the Future*. Zemeckis and Spielberg approached Fox to read for the role of Marty McFly, an exuberant teenager of the 1980s who is transported through time to the 1950s, but Fox's *Family Ties* producer would not grant the young star leave from his television responsibilities. Instead, Spielberg cast Eric Stoltz, only to find, after five weeks of filming, that Stoltz was not right for the part. Again the film producers approached Fox, and this time he was given permission to take the role.

Thus began what Fox calls his "year of living dangerously." From mid-January 1985 until mid-March of the same year, he worked on *Family Ties* and *Back to the Future* simultaneously. The schedule was extremely grueling. Fox described a typical day for *Us* magazine: "A driver would come and pick me up around nine a.m., and I'd go and work on 'Family Ties' from around ten to six. Then a driver would take me to Universal, and I'd work [on *Back to the Future*] till about two in the morning. Then they'd drive me home and I'd go to sleep. And then they'd come pick me up in the morning. I got in the habit of sleeping in sweat pants and a T-shirt so I could just get up in the morning and go." Fox admits that the demands became so tough that his personal life suffered, but he maintained a cool head throughout. "If I did drugs to get through that time," he told *People*, "I wouldn't have a nose left."

Makes successful transition to wide screen with Back to the Future

Back to the Future was released in the summer of 1985, and immediately became a box-office hit as well as a critical success. "It's probably the wittiest and most heartfelt dumb movie ever made," wrote David Denby in *New York* magazine. As Marty McFly, Fox is transported 30 years into the past, where he meets his parents as teenagers and sees his hometown as it appeared in the 1950s. Critics praised Fox's performance, noting especially his uncanny sense of comic timing. "Fox's performance is remarkably controlled," noted Ira Hellman in *People*. "He has a natural comic ability that adds a little flair to every situation." Producer Robert Zemeckis was also been enthusiastic about Fox's portrayal of McFly. "He's got the perfect blend of traditional leading man qualities. He's vulnerable, but he's calm," the director told the *New York Times*. *Us* also quoted Zemeckis on Fox: "It's a wonderfully designed performance. You've got to want to go on the adventure with him—that's how much the film is on Michael's shoulders. It's a real breakthrough for him." *Back to the Future* was a breakthrough for Universal Studios as well, earning $180 million in 1985 for an easy victory as the most popular motion picture of the year.

Shortly after the film debuted, a second feature starring Fox was also released, entitled *Teen Wolf.* It earned $32 million, as *People* magazine suggested, "on the strength of [Fox's] name." A comedy, *Teen Wolf* follows the character Scott Howard (Fox) as he discovers that he is a werewolf. This new-style werewolf finds he can use his powers to star in basketball games and win the best prom dates. According to Vincent Canby in the *New York Times,* the film is "overacted by everybody except Mr. Fox, who is seen to far better advantage in *Back to the Future.*" Though Canby wrote, "No silver bullet is needed to dispatch this movie, it dies a natural death as one looks on," the film was a modest summer hit in a year when several more promising teen movies failed.

On the heels of this early success, Fox made the transition to adult roles with the 1987 releases *The Secret of My Success* and *The Light of Day.* While the former performed quite well, Fox has called the latter "a movie with great intentions that just wasn't very good." His next two films were dramas in which Fox attempted to stretch himself as an actor. *Bright Lights, Big City* (1988) focused on the emotional troubles of a cocaine-addicted magazine researcher who was struggling to survive in New York City's fast lane. The 1989 film *Casualties of War* detailed an atrocity committed by Americans during the Vietnam war. While both films received some good reviews, neither met with much box-office success. In a *TV Guide* interview Fox commented on his experience with dramas: "I know that, in dramas, I haven't gotten much more than a deafening silence from people. But I've had to try them for me. Dramas challenge me. I guess you could say I did these films because I didn't want to get pigeonholed in comedies."

Yet it is with comedies that Fox appears to bring in the dollars. With *Back to the Future Part II* and *Back to the Future Part III*, Fox regained his status as a top box-office draw. Fox's subsequent films, then, have continued to be comedies: *The Hard Way* (1991), which is essentially a "buddy movie" that plays off the comic tension between a street-wise cop and a matinee idol; *Doc Hollywood* (1991), which focuses on an arrogant and money-hungry young doctor who gets waylaid in a sleepy southern town; *Life With Mikey* (1993), where Fox plays a washed-up ex-child star whose shot at success now lies in being an agent for a street-smart kid with star potential; *For Love or Money* (1993), a tale in which Fox must choose between his career aspirations and his love for a young department-store clerk; and *Greedy* (1994), a wicked comedy about members of a money-grubbing family that try to ingratiate themselves with an elderly millionaire uncle. Fox also provided the voice of the young pup in the heartwarming 1993 animated feature *Homeward Bound: The Incredible Journey.*

Fox currently makes his home in a large New York City apartment with a view of Central Park. He married actress Tracy Pollan in 1988 after the two met while working together on *Family Ties.* Their son, Sam, was born in 1989. When the family needs a break from the hectic pace of the city they make a trip to their farm in Vermont, where they keep sheep, chickens, horses, and cows. In a *Ladies' Home Journal* piece Fox commented on his family: "I love being married, being a Dad. It gets better all the time.... You know, until my father passed away [in 1990], my parents were married almost forty years. And Tracy's parents have been married thirty-five, forty years. So when we got married we both had the same attitude about what that commitment is."

In late 1993 Fox started his own production company, Snowback Productions, and plans to direct his own films. The first will be *Thirty Wishes,* a film about a disillusioned young man on his thirtieth birthday. So his career surges ahead. As he told *Ladies' Home Journal,* "Look, I'm here to tell you, I was turning up on 'Who's Out' lists back in 1984. Now it's 1993, and I'm still here."

Sources

Chicago Tribune, June 8, 1986.

Ladies' Home Journal, April 1987; July 1993.

Los Angeles Times, September 22, 1986.

Los Angeles Times Calendar, August 3, 1986.

Maclean's, July 15, 1985; January 13, 1986; February 9, 1987.

Newsweek, July 8, 1985; October 21, 1985.

New York, July 15, 1985.

New York Times, September 22, 1982; July 3, 1985; July 21, 1985; July 26, 1985; August 23, 1985.

People, February 11, 1985; July 15, 1985; August 12, 1985; September 23, 1985; December 23, 1985; February 24, 1986; March 10, 1986; May 15, 1989; November 1, 1993.

Rolling Stone, August 29, 1985; December 19, 1985.

Time, July 1, 1985.

TV Guide, March 5, 1983; April 20, 1984; June 22, 1991.

Us, July 29, 1985.

Variety, October 6, 1982.

Washington Post, July 21, 1985.

Morgan Freeman

Born June 1, 1937
Memphis, Tennessee

"I don't ask myself what's down the road. Sometime between now and never there'll be another role ... I'm a firm believer that you get what you want. I make a distinction between what you want and what you'd like to have. You'd like to have everything. If you can narrow that list down, that's what you get."

ACTOR

Morgan Freeman is a versatile actor who has performed in numerous roles from children's television to Shakespearean drama. He is best known, however, for his appearances in a string of well-regarded motion pictures, including *Driving Miss Daisy, Lean on Me,* and *Glory.* Praise has been bestowed upon Freeman in the form of several awards and award nominations. *Time* correspondent Janice C. Simpson noted that his performances "are so finely calibrated that [the] characters emerge as men of true heft and substance." A private man who says acting "comes easy" for him, Freeman does not care for the movie star label and all that it implies. The actor observed in *Ebony* that "once you become a movie star, people come to see you. You don't have to act anymore. And, to me, that's a danger."

The big screen has brought Freeman to a wider audience, but he has long been a figure in New York City theater, appearing only in Broadway and off-Broadway plays that suit his very particular tastes. As early as 1967 he held a part in the Broadway cast of *Hello, Dolly,* which starred Pearl Bailey, but the bulk of his work has come in nonmusical, intensely serious dramas that relate various aspects of the African American experience. "I have a special affinity for seeing to it that our history is told," Freeman declared in *Ebony.* "The Black legacy is as noble, is as heroic, is as filled with adventure and conquest and discovery as anybody else's. It's just that nobody knows it."

Named best actor in junior high

Freeman endured a tumultuous childhood, and he prefers not to reveal much in interviews about his early years. The fourth child in the family, he was born in Memphis, Tennessee, in 1937. While still an infant, he was sent to live with his maternal grandmother in Charleston, Mississippi. She died when Freeman was six years old, and he spent the next several years traveling with his mother from Chicago to Nashville, Tennessee, and finally to Greenwood, Mississippi, where they settled down.

Like most youngsters of his generation, Freeman loved the movies. "When I was a kid, it cost 12 cents to go to the movies," he related in a *People* interview with Susan Toepfer. "If you could find a milk bottle, you could sell it for a nickel. Soda and beer bottles were worth 2 cents. If you were diligent, you could come up with movie money every day." The World War II-era films Freeman saw inspired him to be a fighter pilot. At first, drama served mainly as a pastime until he could enter the armed services.

Freeman recalled in *New York* that his acting hobby began in junior high school. "It all started with a girl named Barbara," he said, "the class princess, as nice as you please. I wanted to get her attention, so one day I pulled a chair out from under her. Sure enough, I got attention. The teacher grabbed me by the nape of the neck, lifted me onto my toes, and marched me down the hall. I thought for sure I was gonna be expelled.

"But he opens this door and flings me into this room, and there's this English teacher and he asks me, 'You ever done any actin'?' Well, under the circumstances, I'm quick to say yes. Turns out there's these dramatic tournaments—every school does a play—and the winner goes to the state finals. Well, we do this play 'bout a family with a wounded son just home from the war—I play his kid brother. We win the district championship, we win the state championship, and dadgummit, I'm chosen as best actor. All 'cause I pull this chair out from under Barbara."

Freeman's tale shows that he exhibited talent early but did not take acting seriously, even when others recognized his skill. After graduating from high school in Greenwood he entered the U.S. Air Force, hoping to become a pilot. Aptitude tests showed that he had the ability, but he was instead assigned duties as a mechanic and a radar technician. "I was aced out," he explained in *Esquire.* "Racism, the southern old-boy network."

Goodbye Air Force, hello Hollywood

Freeman spent his spare time while in the air force contemplating other careers, and he ultimately decided to become an actor. He left the service in 1959 and headed straight for Hollywood. Once there, he looked up the address of Paramount Studios in the telephone book and went over to apply for a job. Only when he noticed that the questions on the application concerned familiarity with office machinery and typing did it dawn upon him that he would not be hired as an actor on the spot. He opted to follow a more conventional route, taking acting classes at Los Angeles City College while supporting himself as a clerk. He also took tap dancing lessons, becoming good enough to land a part-time job performing at the 1964 World's Fair.

By his own admission, Freeman did not gain much insight from his acting classes. "I'm not much for talking about acting," he noted in *New York.* "I've been called an intuitive actor, and I guess that's right. I go with what I feel. It doesn't do me any good to intellectualize about it." Freeman moved to New York City in the early 1960s and supported himself with a series of day jobs while auditioning for theatrical roles. At one point he even served as a counter man in a Penn Station doughnut stand. His first important part came in an off-Broadway play called *The Nigger-Lovers,* which opened and closed quickly in 1967.

From The Electric Company *to Shakespeare*

Freeman's brief experience in *The Nigger-Lovers* was valuable, however, because it helped him land a role in the all-black cast of *Hello, Dolly,* which opened on Broadway in 1967. When the show closed, he moved on to a series of off-Broadway and repertory plays in New York City and elsewhere. In 1971 he was cast in a television series produced by the Public Broadcasting System, *The Electric Company.* On the air for five years, the educational show was aimed at school-aged children, and Freeman played a hip character called Easy Reader. The actor commented in *People* that he is still remembered for his role. "It's like being known as Captain

Kangaroo," he said. "It irks me when I meet people who are parents now who talk about how they grew up with me."

Freeman earned his first major awards for his role in the play *The Mighty Gents,* produced at New York City's Ambassador Theatre in 1978. Even though he won the Clarence Derwent Award, Drama Desk Award, and earned a Tony Award nomination, the play closed in nine days and Freeman was out of work. For a while he found himself scuffling for jobs. This experience taught him that awards do not guarantee future success, and he has been decidedly indifferent about them ever since.

The New York Shakespeare Festival ultimately proved fertile ground for Freeman. There he appeared as the lead in *Coriolanus* in 1979 and had principal roles in *Julius Caesar* and *Mother Courage and Her Children.* His work in *Coriolanus* and *Mother Courage* earned him yet more awards, this time Obies. The breakthrough play for Freeman was *The Gospel at Colonus,* first performed in 1983. The musical, based on the ancient Greek drama about Oedipus—a fictional character who kills his father and marries his mother—is set in a modern Pentecostal church. *The Gospel at Colonus* featured Freeman as the preacher, a charismatic Oedipus figure around which the frenzied action revolves. Freeman won yet another Obie Award as best actor in a drama, and the play eventually moved to Broadway in 1988 with Freeman still in the lead.

Two Academy Award nominations

Freeman's success with the New York Shakespeare Festival helped him to land a starring role in the stage play *Driving Miss Daisy,* for which he won an additional Obie Award. The drama examines the close friendship that develops between a wealthy Jewish widow and her black chauffeur, Hoke, in the post-Civil War South. By the time he appeared in *Driving Miss Daisy* onstage, Freeman had also earned several film roles, most notably in the Robert Redford movie *Brubaker* and *Harry and Son,* starring Paul Newman. And because of *Driving Miss Daisy*'s success in the theater, Freeman was eager to portray Hoke in a film version of the play.

The actor almost missed his chance. In 1987 he took the part of a near-psychotic pimp in the movie *Street Smart.* Although the film was a box-office flop, Freeman's powerful performance earned him an Academy Award nomination. "*Street Smart* essentially serves as a backdrop for Freeman's tour de force performance," wrote Anthony DeCurtis in *Rolling Stone.* "As the Yoo-Hoo-swilling Fast Black, he alternates fierceness with irresistible charm, engaging intelligence with a bone-chilling capacity for

Success has allowed Freeman to indulge himself at length in his favorite hobby, sailing. One of his acquisitions is a 38-foot sailboat that he has piloted through the Caribbean and the North Atlantic. "When you live in the world of make-believe, you need something real," he remarked in *Time*. "I go sailing, I'm in the real world." Freeman is often accompanied on his trips by his second wife, costume designer Myrna Colley-Lee, and one of his seven grandchildren, E'Dena Hines.

evil. He is the epitome of knowingness." The stage director of *Driving Miss Daisy* admitted that he never would have hired Freeman to play Hoke if he had seen the actor as the menacing Fast Black first.

Freeman's portrayal in the violent *Street Smart*, however, did not deter the makers of the critically acclaimed 1989 film version of *Driving Miss Daisy* from casting him in his original role of the kind-hearted Hoke. Once again Freeman was nominated for an Academy Award for best actor. That same year he took another important role, this time as a grave digger-turned-soldier in the Civil War epic *Glory*. The film, a poignant drama about an all-black regiment that was chosen to lead an assault on a southern fort, received much praise and provided Freeman with just the sort of work he relishes. "I've been offered Black quasi-heroes who get hanged at the end," he pointed out in *Essence*. "I won't do a part like that. If I do a hero, he's going to live to the end of the movie." Freeman's character in *Glory*—eventually promoted and decorated—is indeed one of the last fighters to perish as his battalion storms the fort.

Because Freeman is highly critical of negative representations of African Americans onstage and in films, Freeman is very careful about choosing roles. After ending the 1980s with a hectic spate of film and stage work, he took a brief breather before accepting work on a new project. Cast as Petruchio in the New York Shakespeare Festival's production of *The Taming of the Shrew* in 1990, Freeman garnered lavish reviews, and he subsequently appeared as Azeem, a Moor, in the 1991 film *Robin Hood: Prince of Thieves*. In 1992 Freeman appeared in Clint Eastwood's blockbuster western *Unforgiven*. He played a run-down gunslinger who reluctantly accompanies his old partner to the town of Big Whiskey where, for a handsome reward, they will be hired to kill.

Most recently Freeman has worked in two films that revolve around South Africa—*The Power of One* (1992) and *Bopha* (1993). In the former, Freeman plays a prisoner in a camp for political detainees who befriends a young English boy and then witnesses the boy's gradual initiation into ideas of racial equality. In the latter, Freeman directs the first anti-apartheid movie without a white person as the hero.

Sources

Ebony, April 1990.

Esquire, June 1988.

Essence, December 1988.

Jet, March 6, 1989.

Los Angeles Magazine, October 1993.

New Leader, June 14, 1993.

New Republic, April 27, 1992.

New York, March 14, 1988.

People, April 4, 1988.

Rolling Stone, May 5, 1988.

Time, January 8, 1990.

Village Voice, July 24, 1990.

Photo Credits

The photographs appearing in *Performing Artists: From Alvin Ailey to Julia Roberts* were received from the following sources:

AP/Wide World Photos: cover photographs (Robert Townsend, Julia Roberts, Andy García), pages 1, 4, 10, 15, 24, 30, 49, 67, 71, 77, 93, 106, 113, 120, 126, 138, 152, 157, 159, 166, 175, 178, 190, 208, 212, 220, 226, 249, 258, 264, 271, 275, 284, 289, 295, 299, 302, 306, 309, 314, 319, 323, 347, 350, 355, 357, 363, 371, 374, 380, 384, 400, 404, 407, 417, 425, 432, 435, 446, 458, 464, 492, 502, 512, 516, 519, 523, 533, 537, 547, 552, 556, 567, 571, 575, 585, 593, 599, 606, 610, 620, 623, 628, 656, 662, 666, 668, 675, 681, 693; UPI/Bettmann: pages 22, 53, 185, 255, 544, 596, 635, 650; The Bettmann Archive: pages 35, 38; UPI/Bettmann Newsphotos: pages 40, 55; Reuters/Bettmann: pages 61, 101, 104, 131, 182, 280, 393; Archive Photos/Fotos International: pages 81, 168, 172, 335, 641; Patrick Harbron/Sygma: page 87; Archive Photos/Saga: page 97; Courtesy of A&M Records: page 146; Archive Photos/Popperfoto: page 162; Copyright © 1985 Columbia Pictures Industries, Inc.: page 195; Archive Photos/Saga/P. Iovino: page 201; Archive Photos: pages 252, 282; Courtesy of Arista: page 330; Photograph by Harrison Funk, © 1991 Sire Records Company: page 341; Archive Photos/American Stock: page 369; Archive Photos/Express News: page 413; Courtesy of ICM Artists, Ltd.: page 442; Photograph by Chris Cuffaro, © 1991 The David Geffen Company: page 487; Courtesy of Priority Records: page 498; Photograph by Lance Mercer, © 1993, Sony Music, courtesy of Epic Records: page 527; Photograph by Ernie Panicioli, © 1991 Sony Music: page 561; Photograph by Chris Cuffaro/Visages, © 1991 Warner Bros. Records: page 580; Archive Photos/Darlene Hammond: pages 615, 624; Springer/Bettmann Film Archive: page 638.

Index

Bold denotes profiles and volume numbers.

R

Rabbit Test **1:** 148
A Rage in Harlem **2:** 317
Ragtime **1:** 13
Rain Man **1:** 143, **2:** 319, 322
Raising Arizona **1:** 83
A Raisin in the Sun **3:** 545, 547
Rambo **3:** 639
Rambo: First Blood, Part II **3:** 639
Rambo III **3:** 639
Rapid Fire **2:** 382
Rashad, Phylicia **1:** 10, 129
Rastaman Vibration **2:** 419
Raw **3:** 660
Raw Deal **3:** 612
Rawhide **1:** 184-185
Rebecca **3:** 509
Redford, Robert 3: 571-579
The Red Hot Chili Peppers **3:** 527, 530, **580-584**
The Red Hot Chili Peppers **3:** 581
Red Rock West **1:** 85
The Remains of the Day **2:** 327
Renacer **1:** 191
Repo Man **1:** 195-197
Resource Center for Nonviolence **1:** 43
Revelations **1:** 5, 8, 10
Revolver **1:** 56
Rhinestone **3:** 521, 639
Rhyme Pays **2:** 342
Rhythm Nation 1814 **2:** 347, 349
Rich and Famous **1:** 65
Richardson, Patricia **1:** 19
Richard III **3:** 510
Ricochet **2:** 344
The Right Stuff **3:** 685
Ringo **1:** 59
Rising Sun **1:** 125, **3:** 633
Risky Business **1:** 141-142
The Ritz **2:** 451, 455

A River Runs Through It **3:** 571, 577-578
The Road to Wellville **1:** 105, **2:** 328
Roberts, Julia 3: 585-591, 667
Robin Hood: Prince of Thieves **1:** 136, 230
The Rockford Files **2:** 451, 455
Rock the House **3:** 625
Rocky **3:** 637, 639
Rocky II **3:** 637
Rocky III **3:** 637
Rocky IV **3:** 637
Rocky V **3:** 637
Roddenberry, Gene **3:** 643
Rogers, Ginger **1:** 37
Rogers, Mimi **1:** 143
The Rolling Stones 3: 592-598
Romero **2:** 362
A Room With a View **1:** 168-169
Ropin' the Wind **1:** 71, 74
The Rose **2:** 438
Roseanne 3: 606-609
Roseanne **1:** 18, **3:** 606-607
Roseanne: My Life as a Woman **3:** 609
Rose, Axl 3: 599-605
Rose, Leonard **2:** 405
"Round Midnight" **2:** 433
Roxanne **2:** 425-426, 430
Royal Wedding **1:** 38
Rubber Soul **1:** 56
Running Man **1:** 31
Running Scared **1:** 150, **2:** 317
Russia House **3:** 542
Ruthless People **2:** 439

S

Sarafina: The Movie **2:** 269
Saturday Night Live **1:** 89-90, 101-102, 104-105, 146, 149-150, **2:** 428, 464, 466468, **3:** 504-505, 677
Scandal **1:** 208-209